LEGENDARY LOCALS

OF

FORT PIERCE

FLORIDA

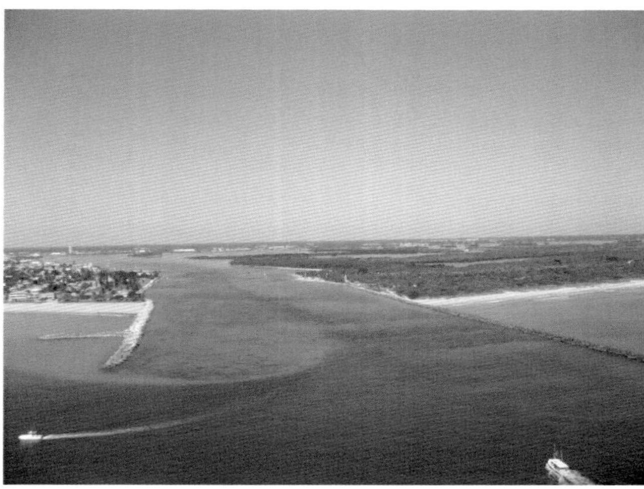

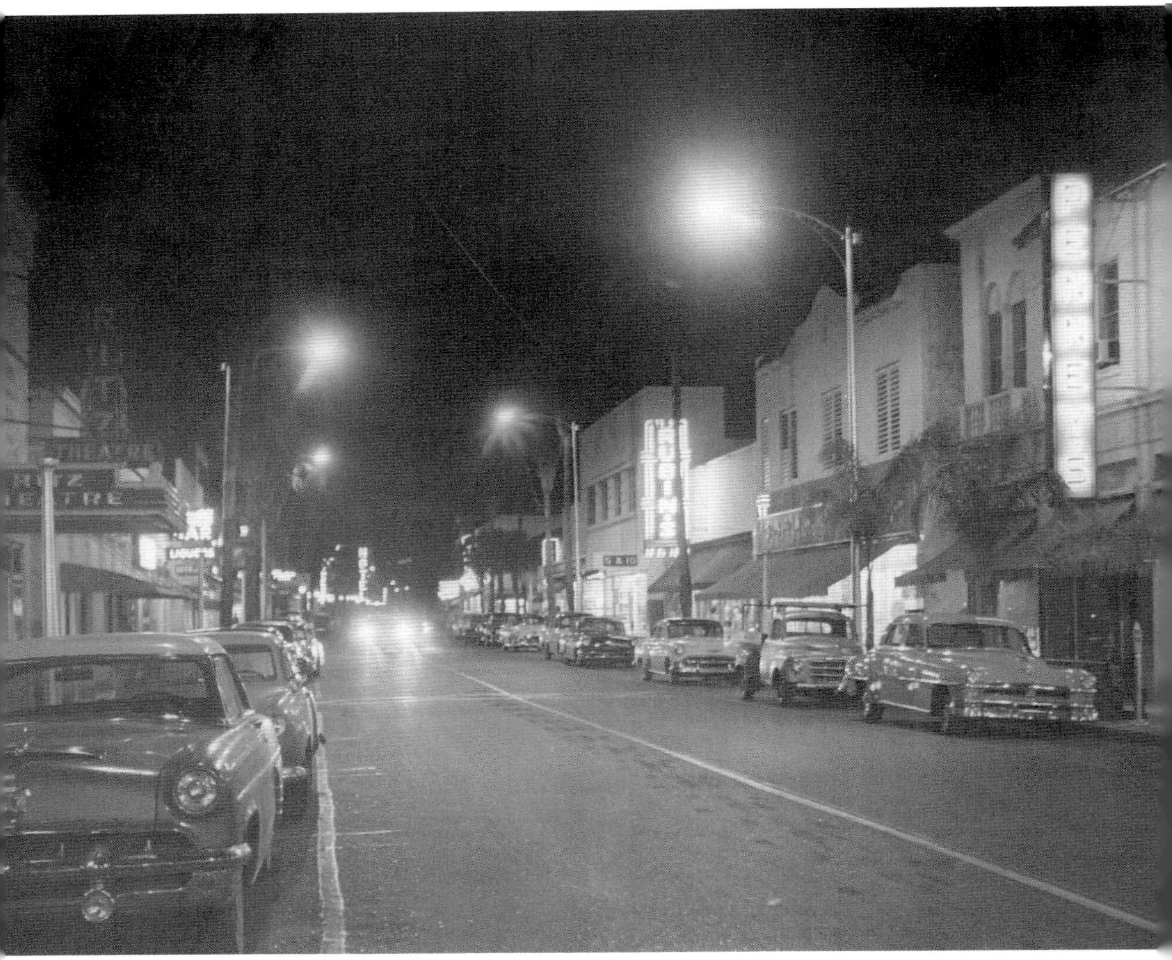

Main Street Fort Pierce
Second Street, originally named Pine Street, has always been the main street of downtown Fort Pierce. The state of its health, vibrancy, and relevancy continues to gauge the vitality of the community. A town has to have a center that connects all the streets and all the neighborhoods to its core. A downtown is a symbol of a community's heart that allows people the emotional experience of calling a place "my hometown." Second Street in Fort Pierce is Main Street, USA. (Courtesy of St. Lucie County Regional History Center.)

Page 1: **Indian River Inlet**
The Indian River Inlet profoundly influenced the course of Fort Pierce history—from shipwrecks to settlement. Early explorers called the old naturally flowing inlet north of present day Pepper Park "the mouth of the Indian River," yet shoaling created dangerously unpredictable ocean access. The manmade Fort Pierce Inlet, dredged in 1920, has for decades provided the safest passage of any inlet between Daytona and Palm Beach. Today, every kind of water transport, from cruising yachts to fishing trawlers, ocean research vessels, pleasure craft, Coast Guard vessels, treasure salvagers, and small cargo ships utilize the inlet. (Courtesy of Buzz Smyth.)

LEGENDARY LOCALS

OF

FORT PIERCE

FLORIDA

JEAN ELLEN WILSON

LEGENDARY LOCALS

ISBN 978-1-4671-0127-1

Legendary Locals is an imprint of Arcadia Publishing
Charleston, South Carolina

Printed in the United States of America

Library of Congress Control Number: 2013946445

For all general information, please contact Arcadia Publishing:
Telephone 843-853-2070
Fax 843-853-0044
E-mail sales@arcadiapublishing.com
For customer service and orders:
Toll-Free 1-888-313-2665

Visit us on the Internet at www.arcadiapublishing.com

Dedication
To the volunteers of the St. Lucie Regional History Center, who share Fort Pierce heritage with curious adults and busloads of school children.

On the Front Cover: Clockwise from top left:
Crew of the first C-54 to fly war wounded over the Crescent Caravan route from France to headquarters of the 2nd Ferrying Group near New Castle, Delaware, in 1945, with Osmond C. Peterson at far left (courtesy O.C. Peterson; see page 59); Frances Ross, attorney (left) and Joyce Jackson, historian (photograph by the author; see pages 81 and 116); Billy Bowlegs III, Seminole leader (Florida Memory; see page 14); John Brandon, sunken treasure hunter (courtesy of John Brandon; see page 10); Keith Anderson, proprietor of Roy's Liquors and Fine Wines (photograph by Tom Baumker; see page 93); Elizabeth McCarty, pioneer educator (St. Lucie County Regional History Center; see page 30); Lisa Fasnacht, kayaker (courtesy of Lisa's Kayaks; see page 71); Lucia Zora Card Alispaw, Bravest Woman in the World, with Old Snyder (St. Lucie County Regional History Center; see page 86); and Patty Magee, proprietor of Archie's (photograph by Tom Baumker; see page 101).

On the Back Cover: Left: The Adams family of Adams Ranch is pictured around 1960. From left to right are Mike, Dot, Lee, Robbie, and Bud. (Courtesy of the Adams family.) Right: Yacht *Dohema* enters the old inlet around 1911, bringing Edwin Binney and his family to his beloved Fort Pierce. (Courtesy of Sally Putnam Chapman.)

CONTENTS

ACKNOWLEDGMENTS

Collecting the images and information for *Legendary Locals of Fort Pierce* has allowed me to meet interesting folks I had only heard about and to discover new depths of talent and experience in people I knew. Any project approached wholeheartedly scares up unexpected allies and in the quest for legends, I have made new friends and cemented old relationships. Tom Baumker, apparently born to hold a camera, has patiently accompanied me through days of back-to-back appointments in which he drew out, with his lens, the best in our legendary subjects. My dear friend O.C. "Pete" Peterson has opened doors for me through the trust and admiration in which he is held by the best people of Fort Pierce. Not the richest, mind you, but the best. Susan Enns Stans, with her serenity and quiet wit, kept me focused. And how good it is to know that Anne Sinnott is always there to ask, "How can I help?" And help me she did; she read, edited, suggested, corrected. Nancy Bennett, president of the St. Lucie Historical Society, met every request with gracious alacrity. And then there is Lucille Rights, who was active in the St. Lucie Historical Society as early as 1960, the author of *A Portrait of St. Lucie County,* and recognized as the area's premier historian. I have been privileged to call her a friend, and she has acted as mentor and guide through the main thoroughfares and back alleys of local history. Among those who kindly supplied numerous family photographs from which to choose selections for this book are Robbie Adams, Sally Putnam Chapman, Barbara McCarty Cofer, Sam Gaines, Margaret Holmes Carlton, Polly Ann Summerlin Moore, and Harold Holtsberg. The main source for historical photographs in this book was the St. Lucie County Regional History Center (SLCRHC).

INTRODUCTION

God's Protecting Providence, Jonathan Dickinson's narrative of the ordeal of shipwreck survivors stranded on the Florida coast during the hurricane season of 1696, provides vivid historical accounts of some of the first locals of Fort Pierce—the Ais Indians. These early peoples were displaced by Seminoles, Native Americans who had split off from the Creek tribe.

There are hints of Spanish contact with Indians on the Lower River during the years of Spain's sovereignty over Florida, from discovery to transfer to the English in 1763, and a few references are recorded of British attempts at colonizing the area. There remains evidence of the Spaniards in sunken treasure under the sea off the coast of Fort Pierce; there is, as yet, no evidence discovered of English presence.

The presence of Seminole Indians predicated the several false starts by Americans at the settlement of the Lower Indian River and Fort Pierce, as detailed in the following paragraphs.

False start one: The US Navy, in the form of an expedition composed of an integrated force of black and white seamen under Lt. Levin Mynn Powell, located the site for a fort on the last day of December 1837. Then, as the fort's physician Jacob Rhette Motte wrote in *Journey Into Wilderness,*

> On the morning of the 2nd Janry 1838 we moved over to the west side of Indian river; to a spot four miles south of the Inlet, designated as "the bluff," par excellence; being the highest point of land on the whole river though only about ten or fifteen feet above the water. We there established ourselves; first by pitching our tents on a narrow esplanade between the river and the bluff, which rises perpendicularly behind us; next by erecting a block-house upon the top of the bluff. Being pretty much like all other block-houses in Florida, except that this one was built of palmetto logs, we deemed it worthy the title of fort, and the distinction of a name; it was therefore dubbed Fort Pierce, after our worthy commander (Colonel Benjamin K. Pierce).

Fort Pierce was established as a supply post and staging area in the US government's campaign to remove the Seminoles west of the Mississippi. The fort was abandoned in 1842, after a majority of the Seminole enemy had been shipped to Arkansas and Oklahoma.

False start two: With the remaining Seminoles relegated to the interior, the Armed Occupation Act of 1842 encouraged settlement by offering 160 acres along the coast to anyone willing to make improvements and defend the land against the "savages." Land-hungry pioneers claimed what is now Fort Pierce north to St. Lucie and south to the Jupiter Narrows. This narrow, riverside "village" was decimated when a few Indians killed four men—one of them at St. Lucie—and the frightened whites fled in 1849.

False start three: US troops were sent to reassure the settlers and a few civilians returned under the protection of Fort Capron, established at St. Lucie. It was a standoff between soldier and Indian until December 1856, when ever-encroaching surveyors resulted in an "outbreak." Fort Capron, because of the shipping access provided by the Indian River Inlet at that place, became the supply post and staging area for US troops and Florida militia to kill or capture and relocate the Seminoles who insisted upon clinging to their land. With overwhelming force, the Army and Navy succeeded in decimating the tribe but finally gave up without discovering every last Indian hiding in the swamps and hammocks. Their descendants are now the thriving Seminole tribe of Florida.

On July 23, 1858, Capt. Abner Doubleday, the last commander of Fort Capron, wrote: "I have the honor to report that Company 'E' 1st Arty. constituting the regular garrison of Fort Capron Fla. left that post for Fort Moultrie S.C. on the 14th of June 1858 on the steamer 'Gordon' pursuant to S.O. No.

37 Head Qrs. Dept. Fla. The Post itself together with the mules carts and other public property which could not be transported were left behind under charge of Mr. W. E. Ransom, Quar. Mas. Agent. A Sergt & nine men of Capt. McNeil's Company of Fla. Volunteers remained as a guard."

Many of the officers who served at Capron had to choose sides after Sumter; some would fire upon their old comrades in the War Between the States. The aforementioned Doubleday kept his blue uniform; A.P. Hill became a Confederate general. John Schofield stayed with the flag and his name would eventually grace Schofield Barracks, famous in the Pearl Harbor saga. Truman Seymour commanded the Union troops at Olustee, Florida, and Rufus Saxton became military governor of Florida after the Confederate defeat. William Tecumseh Sherman, Union general, and Joseph Johnston, of Confederate fame, had both served at Fort Pierce.

False start four: A few families continued to live at St. Lucie, but sometime after the outbreak of the Civil War, they were forced to abandon the place due to the uncertainty caused by the blockade runners and the US gunboats that chased them into the refuge of the river through that all-important Indian River Inlet.

It was not until after Appomattox that settlement of Fort Pierce began in earnest. Cattlemen, farmers, and fishermen homesteaded land. Northern immigrants planted pineapple plantations and citrus groves. Docks and fish houses sprang up along the waterfront. The railroad came in 1894, and by 1915, Fort Pierce was a settled division point and passenger trains stopped here for engine and crew changes of conductors, trainmen, engineers, and firemen. Shops and roundhouses employed a large force and the families of railroad workers accounted for another wave of settlers.

As Florida became the nation's playground when World War I kept the affluent from their European excursions, well-heeled tourists filled the hotels in season and some liked the place enough to build winter homes. The automobile proliferated, and "tin can tourists" came. The boom of the 1920s saw the number of realtors in Fort Pierce increase 10 times as land frantically changed hands. Then came the bust in 1928 preceding the Depression, and only the stout-hearted remained to found family dynasties.

World War II affected Fort Pierce more than most other locales where bases sprang up in the emergency because it was a small town and its population was far outnumbered by the young men who trained at the naval amphibious base established there in 1943. After the war came the halcyon times when everyone had work. Fort Pierce was the center of the Indian River fruit industry, wide fields of tomatoes and vegetables produced fresh produce for Northern winter tables, and the fishing industry flourished. Older generations look back on that Fort Pierce as a great place to grow up. One could ride a bike anywhere, swim in the ocean, fish in the river, ride a horse into a bar, and go downtown on Saturday afternoon to see Gene Autry with friends at the Sunrise Theatre. Edgartown was occupied by fishing families. The Lincoln Park area with its churches, juke joints, entertainment venues, and beloved Lincoln Park Academy burst with black culture. But the town was firmly segregated; the black population was expected to come in by the back door and be on the other side of the canal after dark.

Today, Fort Pierce is the center of an amalgamation of descendants of old families and new blood with fresh ideas, seasonal snowbirds and year-round salt life devotees, cowboys and cowgirls, grapefruit pickers and bird watchers, hyphenated Americans and Native Americans. Our town is an exciting mixture of legendary locals living among cosmopolitans, crackers, and characters with tectonic layers of interests that produce continuous rumblings of cultural conflict, compromise, and chatter.

CHAPTER ONE

Forts and the Military

In 1943, the US Navy occupied North and South Hutchinson Island, the barrier islands across the Indian River Lagoon from Fort Pierce. The beaches were closed to civilians for the duration of World War II and—famously—frogmen, underwater demolition teams, and amphibious landing forces were trained on those beaches.

But it was not the first time the Navy was part of Fort Pierce's history.

On December 29, 1837, the Everglades Expedition of the US Navy scouted the southern Florida coast for a likely place for a military post and chose a bluff a few miles south of the Indian River Inlet. On this site Fort Pierce was built and served as a staging ground and supply depot for the remaining years of the Second Seminole War.

In 1849, a settler was killed at Old St. Lucie and though his neighbors had received their land free in return for bearing arms and protecting the frontier, they, not being made of the sterner stuff of Western movies, fled. The alarm was sounded and the artillery rather than the cavalry arrived at St. Lucie to establish Fort Capron, active for the duration of the Third Seminole War. Some of the settlers returned to live under the fort's protection and remained until the outbreak of the Civil War.

The shock of Pearl Harbor was hardly realized when World War II came bloodily to Fort Pierce in the form of burned survivors of a ship sunk offshore by a German submarine. Then, on January 26, 1943, the United States Naval Amphibious Training Base was established at Fort Pierce. Here, thousands of combat troops were trained in amphibious warfare, leaving Hutchinson Island with the skills needed to face the enemy in the Atlantic and Pacific. Fort Pierce old-timers remember when their windows shook and their fireplace bricks were dislodged as bombs exploded in training exercises. Young men in white uniforms periodically flooded downtown Fort Pierce, invading the bars, whistling at the girls, dancing at the USO, and attending local churches.

An unsuccessful attempt in the 17th century to establish a Spanish outpost somewhere along our coast was motivated by the desire to monitor the shipping lanes used by the annual Spanish fleet of galleons that transported the gold and silver of Mexico and South America to Spain. In 1715, the fleet was struck by a particularly savage hurricane and a number of vessels sank, scattering treasure along the ocean floor. The hunt to recover those sunken riches has given our locale the name "Treasure Coast."

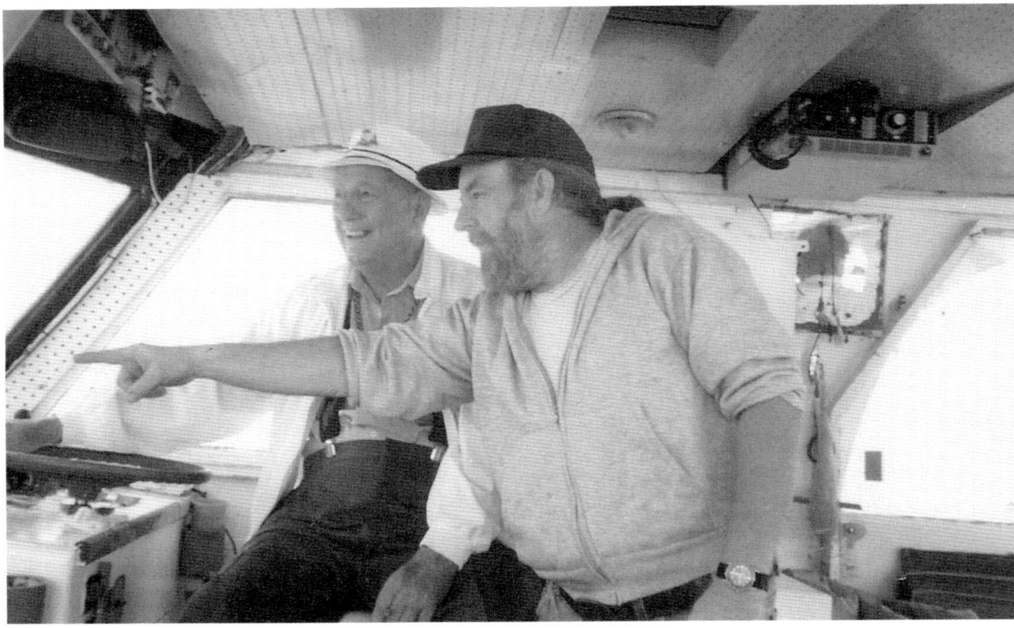

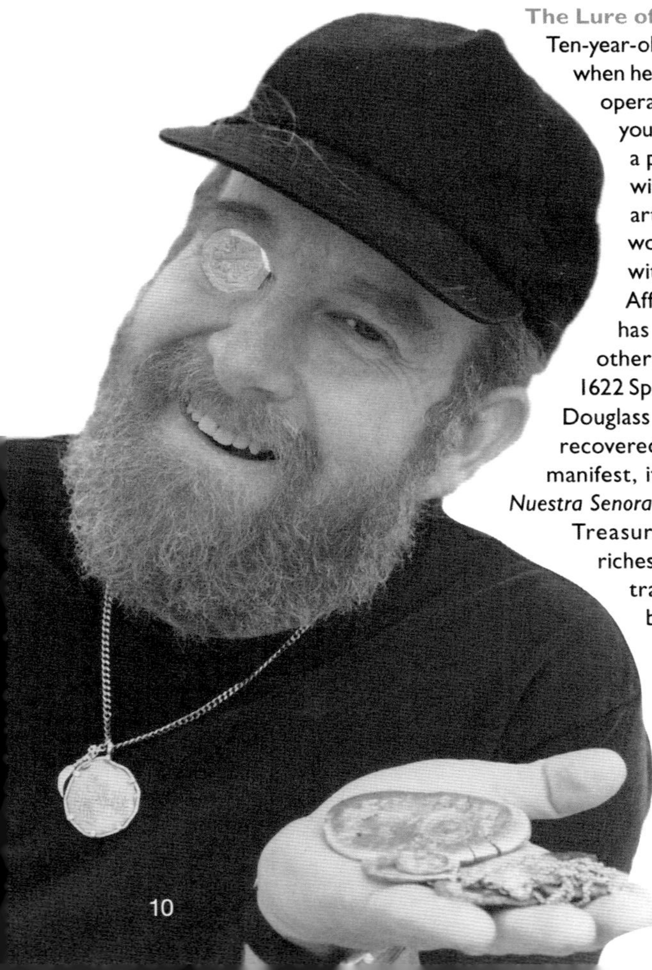

The Lure of Sunken Treasure

Ten-year-old John Brandon was already interested in discovery when he began to hang out around Mel Fisher's (above, left) operations on the Treasure Coast. At 19, he became the youngest boat captain of Fisher's salvage fleet and later a partner. In his boat *Endeavor*, Brandon is credited with finding millions of dollars worth of treasures and artifacts, finds which include an eight-foot gold chain worth $350,000 and 23 links of gold belt embedded with rubies, diamonds, and pearls worth $1.2 million. Affable and modest, with a sense of history, Brandon has many stories about the crew that found, among others, the richest trove in Florida off Key West, the 1622 Spanish galleon *Atocha*. At the wreck site off Fredrick Douglass Beach at Fort Pierce, Brandon and his crews have recovered hundreds of gold coins not listed on the ship's manifest, if the shipwreck remains are indeed that of the *Nuestra Senora de las Nieves* as currently believed.

Treasure hunting is more than adventurers out for riches—success depends on meteorologists, historians, translators, electronic experts, turbidity experts, boat handlers, and, of course, divers. The quest is not a smooth one, but rather a series of extreme highs and extreme lows. Brandon's lows have included disappointment, death, legal challenges, and loss. The highs include exhilaration, celebration, breaking the water with both hands filled with gold coins, and a profound sense of a job well learned and well done. (Both, courtesy of John Brandon.)

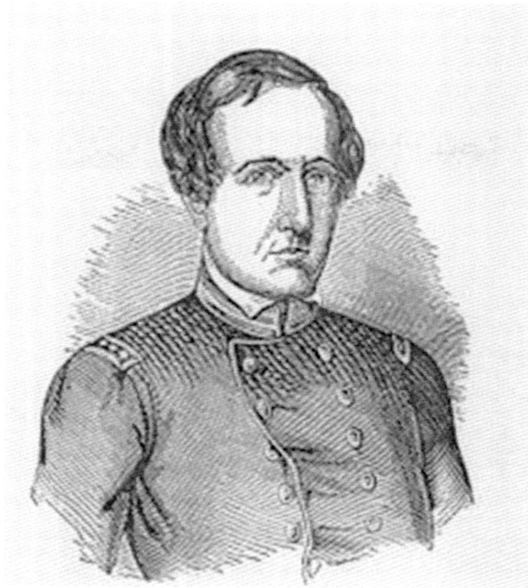

The Artillery Arrive

Maj. Thomas Childs wrote in March 1838: "My command was constantly engaged in erecting quarters & defenses until my position was secure. These qrs. and defenses consist of four buildings, 30 ft. by 15 ft. covered by Tarpaulins for the accommodation of the troops. Officers qrs. 124 x 18 ft. covered with boards, and a Hospital 28 by 16 ft. In consequence of this timely shelter, the troops have remained healthy. I have thus been enabled, from time to time, to scout within 8 to 10 miles round the Ft. having about 12–13 horses for that purpose." On the ancient Ais Indian mound, just south of the fort buildings, a guard of the garrison manned a lookout post. This was Fort Pierce in the Second Seminole War. (Above, courtesy of Library of Congress; below, courtesy of SLCRHC.)

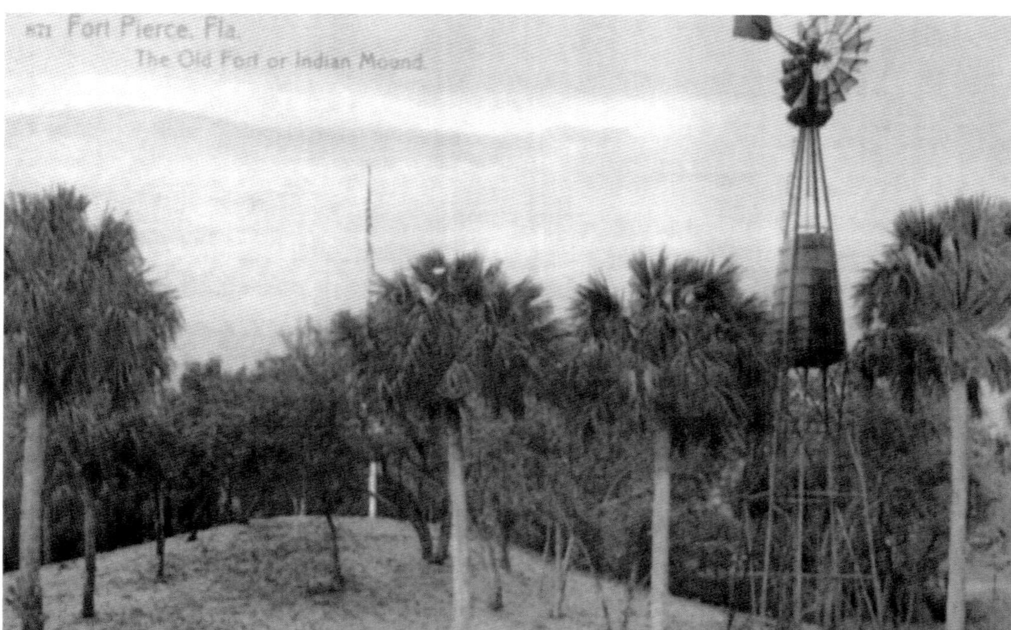

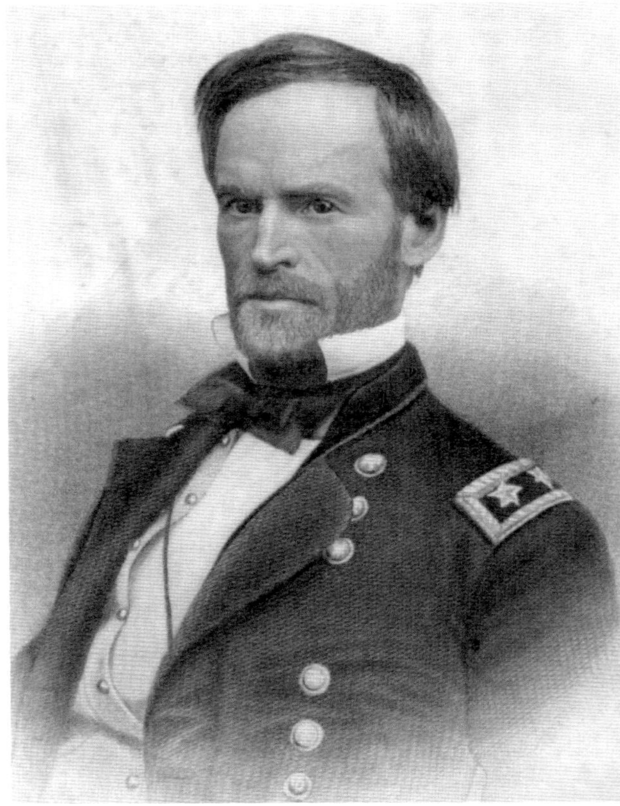

William Tecumseh Sherman and Coacoochee

In 1841, while stationed at Fort Pierce, the future Union general met the Seminole leader in a hammock some six miles west of Fort Pierce. Coacoochee, known as "Wild Cat," accompanied Lieutenant Sherman back to Fort Pierce where he opened negotiations with Major Childs about surrendering his people for emigration. "I can live like a wolf or a dog," he said, after years of resistance. But the women and children could not. The whites were too many, too well-armed. Coacoochee and his band arrived at Fort Gibson from Fort Pierce on November 12, 1841. (Both, courtesy of SLCRHC.)

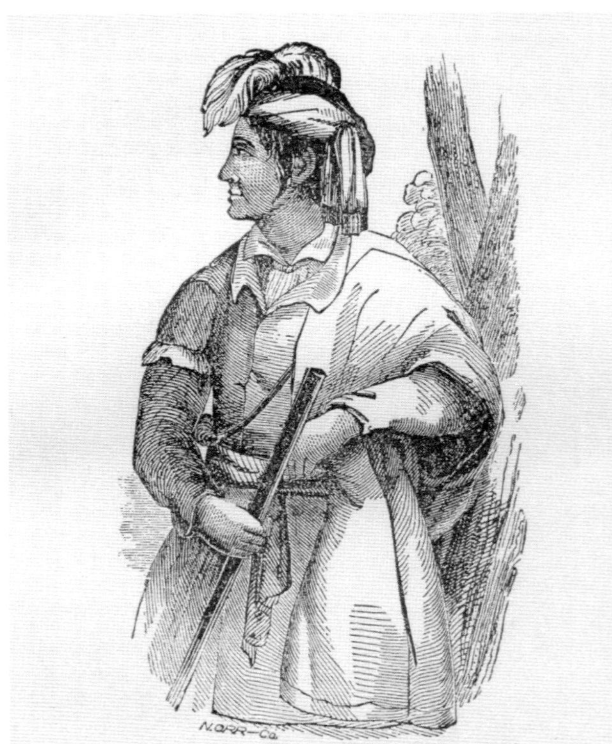

Coacoochee, (Wild Cat.)

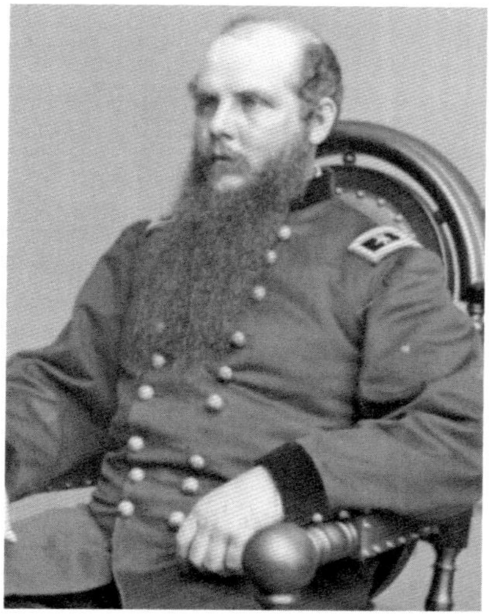

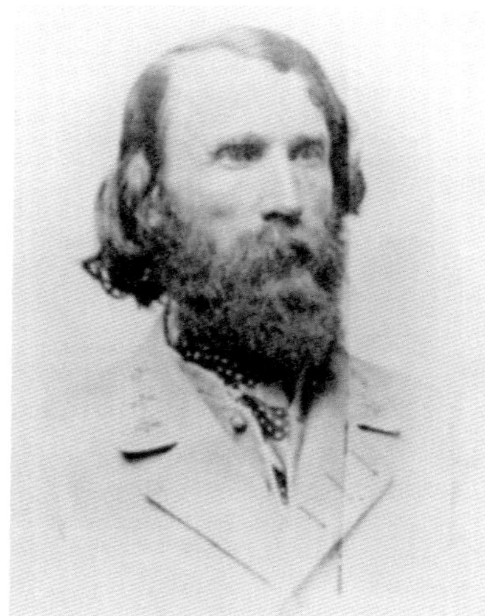

Schofield Barracks, Hawaii

Lt. John Schofield (top left) described arriving at New Smyrna, Florida, in 1853 as follows: "At length old Captain Davis took the mail and my baggage and me on board his sloop, bound for Fort Capron, opposite the mouth of Indian River. He divided his time fairly between carrying the United States mail and drinking whisky, but he never attempted to do both at the same time." Schofield said life at Fort Capron was "not by any means monotonous. It was varied by sailing, fishing, and shooting." Serving with Schofield at Capron was Lt. A.P. Hill (top right); the two would choose opposite sides in the War Between the States. Hill was killed, but Schofield went on to command the US Army from 1886 to 1895. Because of his recommendation to establish a base at Pearl Harbor, his name was attached to the barracks there made famous on December 7, 1941. Below, these "Heroes of Fort Sumter" appeared on the cover of the March 23, 1861, issue of *Harper's Weekly*. Of those in the photograph, the following had served at Fort Capron: Capt. Truman Seymour, back row, far left; Lt. J.C. Davis, back row, center; Lt. Theodroe Talbot, back row, far right; and Capt. Abner Doubleday, front row, far left. (Top left, courtesy of the National Archives; top right and below, courtesy of SLCRHC.)

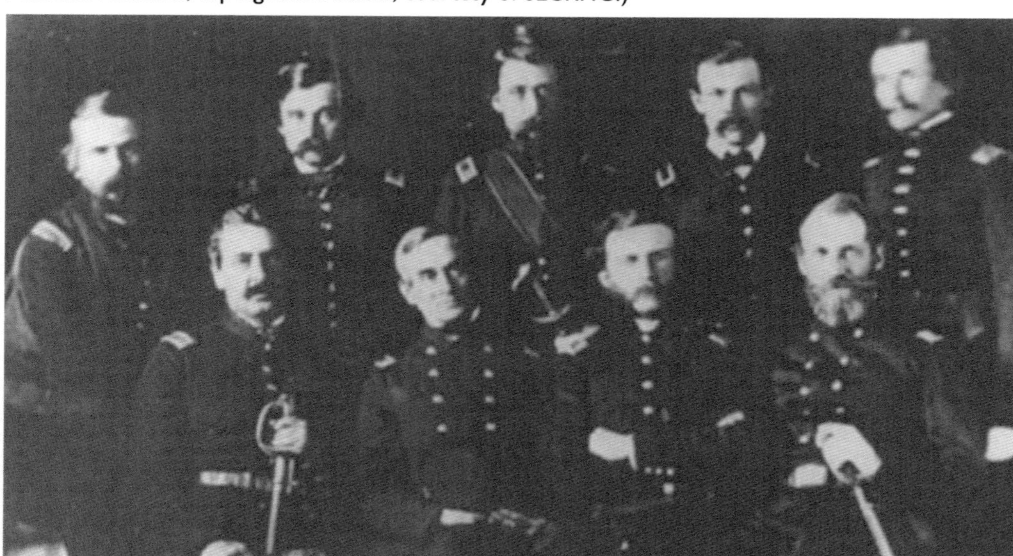

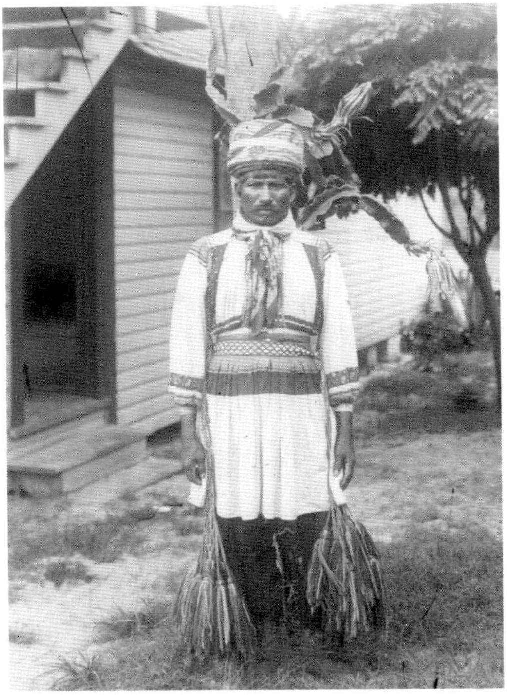

The Billy Bowlegs War

This hunt for stray Seminoles left in Florida was provisioned through the Indian River Inlet. The leader of the hunted was Billy Bowlegs II. Neither he nor Billy Bowlegs III, pictured here in a photograph by Harry Hill, was bowlegged—the name was a garbled translation of "Boleck." By way of a whimsical footnote, the warrior leader of the 1850s, on a trip to visit the Great White Father in Washington, registered at a hotel as "Mr. B. Legs." Born while the Civil War raged, Bowlegs III died in a chickee just days short of 103. He was a renowned hunter and guide and an always courteous source for historians. He willingly participated in parades and folklore gatherings. He roamed all over south Florida but spent a great deal of time in Fort Pierce and was often photographed by Hill. A columnist for the *Miami Herald* stated, "You were always impressed by the regal dignity, the proud bearing with which he carried himself. He possessed a natural, easy courtesy and honesty which captured the respect of all who knew him." (Courtesy of SLCRHC.)

A Seminole Evangeline

The Third Seminole War, as it was called, was little more than a roundup of stray Indians to be relocated west of the Mississippi. Among those was Polly Parker. Her service as a guide to the swamp sailors hunting down Seminoles in the Glades did not save her from forced emigration. She was put on a ship bound from the west coast of Florida for New Orleans. When the ship anchored en route, she professed to go ashore for medicinal plants but instead, struck out for home and walked all the way back to her Cow Creek kin west of Fort Pierce. She was a familiar sight to the early settlers, pledging friendship to some of the white families, including the family of Minor Jones, whose descendant lives at St. Lucie. She lived to be over 100, and probably died on Adams Ranch where some of her camp items were found in Polly Parker Hammock. (Courtesy of SLCRHC.)

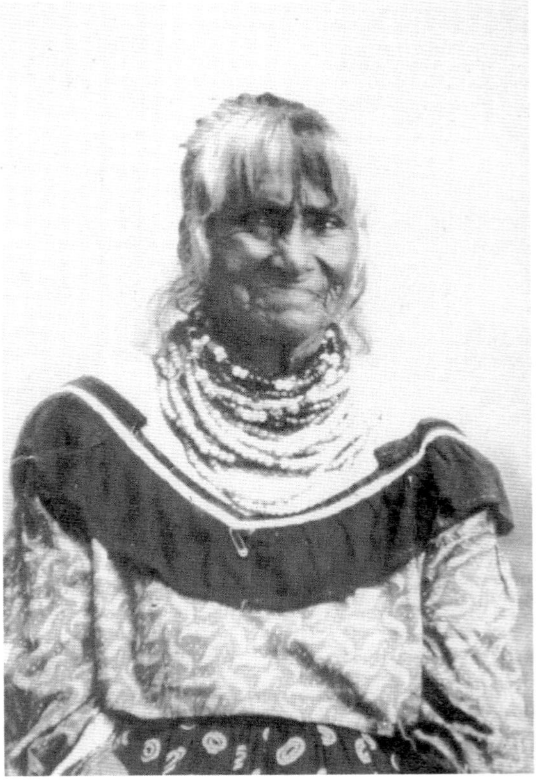

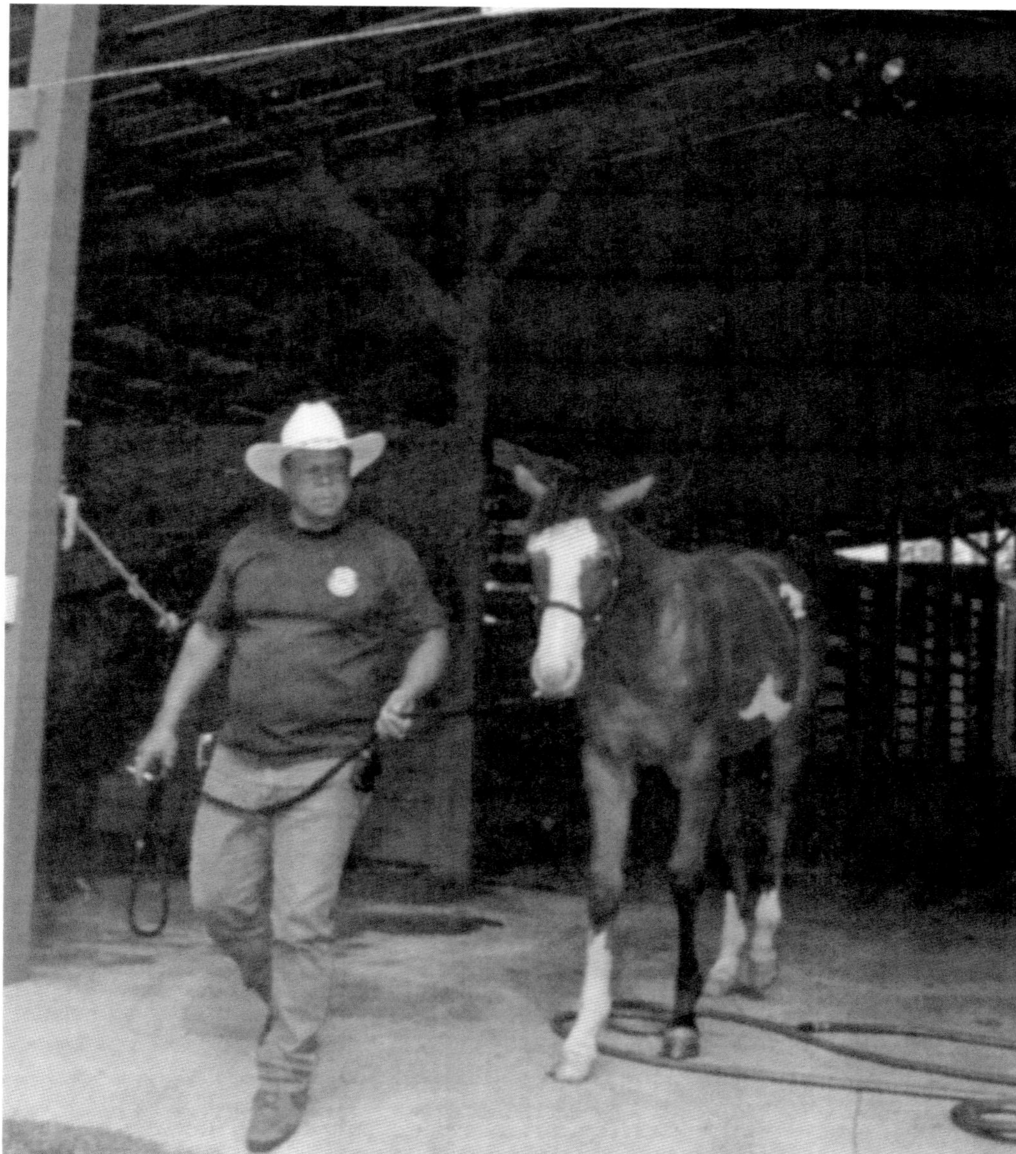

Horseman

Shamy Tommie, a great-great-grandson of Polly Parker, grew up in a chickee on Midway Road. Shamy had a working childhood, taking on cheerfully the responsibility to help Minnie Tommie, his full-blooded Seminole mother, provide for his younger siblings. He hunted for game, he picked tomatoes, and, on Easter, he made money selling palm fronds to area churches. Of course, help also came from the extended Tommie family living in the camp. However, civilization encroached and in the 1960s, the ownership of the land changed hands and the Seminoles were, rather ruthlessly, evicted. Tribal members scattered, most moving to the Brighton reservation. Later, the Seminole Tribe obtained acreage on Okeechobee Road that had been part of its original home territory. Chupco's Landing, built in 2005, is a gated community exclusively for Seminoles. Shamy, pictured with colt Chupco, is the director of Chupco Youth Camp next door. (Courtesy of Shamy Tommie.)

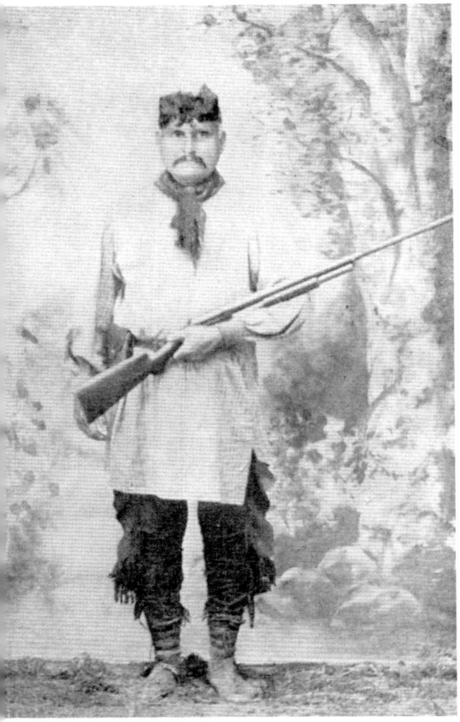

Seminole Tiger

Capt. Tom Tiger died in 1906, struck by lightning while hewing out a canoe. He came from a good family—his brother had been the chief of the Cow Creek band and Chief Tallahassee was his brother-in-law. His appearance was remarked by several observers including Frederick Ober, the explorer and writer, who met him while on an expedition to find Lake Okeechobee in 1875: "He was over six feet in height, large and muscular. His eyes were black and fierce; his mouth, firm, but not cruel, was shaded by a small black mustache. We soon made friends with him, and found him gentle and pleasant voiced." He was the first Seminole to bring charges against a white man in court, charging, in 1898, one Harmon Hull with horse theft. Among the witnesses who vouched for the character of Mr. Tiger were P.P. Cobb, James T. Gray, and R.A. Swearingen of Fort Pierce. Tom's reaction to the not guilty verdict was reported by the local newspaper thus: "White man tell heap lies, and lawyer talkee, talkee too much—all time." Upon his death, Tom was "buried" in Seminole manner by being enclosed in wood above ground but his bones were taken up by one Flourny, proprietor of an amusement park in Johnstown, Pennsylvania, who attempted to sell Tom's remains to the Smithsonian. Through the good offices of Sheriff Dan Carlton, the bones were retrieved and reburied in a secret place. (Courtesy of Florida Memory.)

Girl of the Panther Clan

Born Louise Jones in Fort Pierce, Louise Gopher recalls that when her family went to town, she had to stay in the car because her grandparents feared the stories of family members being kidnapped by soldiers in the Seminole War. "There were a lot of families in one camp," Louise recalls. "There was always a pot of sofkee on the fire in case you got hungry. Sofkee is coarse grits that is boiled in a big pot. We had coffee. We either boiled our food or fried it, like bacon and fry bread. We had hogs so we ate pork." Louise was the first Seminole woman to graduate from college, attending Indian River Community College in Fort Pierce and finishing at Florida Atlantic University. She has dedicated years to cultural education for the Seminoles at Brighton Reservation. She was the driving force in establishing a magnet school at Brighton for Seminole students where they learn their Creek language and their tribal history along with the prescribed curriculum. She was married to Charlie Steel Gopher, a hero and casualty of the Vietnam War. Tom Tiger was Louise's great-grandfather. Her maternal grandfather, DeSoto Tiger, was murdered by John Ashley, the notorious outlaw of Prohibition. Pictured from left to right are daughter Rita, Louise, and daughter Carla. (Courtesy of Louise Gopher.)

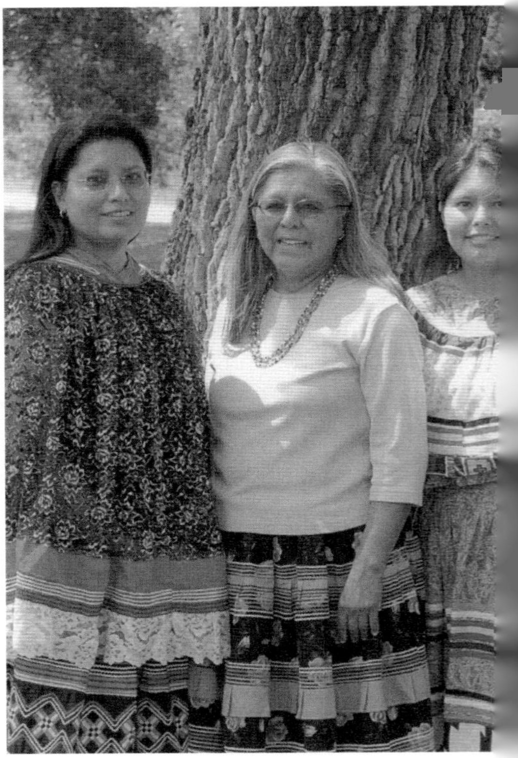

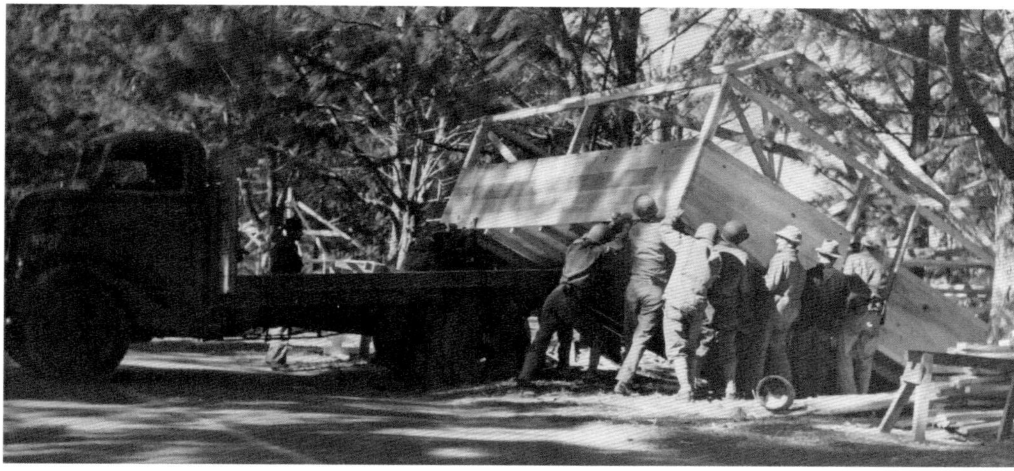

US Naval Amphibious Training Base
These Army engineers are setting up housekeeping, literally, on Hutchinson Island, Fort Pierce in February 1943. Fort Pierce was a major training base in World War II for landing forces on enemy beaches and for the training of Underwater Demolition Teams. (Courtesy of SLCRHC.)

Andy Brady and the Navy SEAL Museum
The history of the SEALs and their forerunners, the Underwater Demolition Teams and the Frogmen, is told in exhibits and artifacts at the Navy SEAL Museum in Fort Pierce. On the grounds are vessels and other large equipment that tell the story of this elite service, including the lifeboat used in the famous 2009 rescue of American Captain Phillips held hostage by Somali pirates. Andy Brady is pictured here in front of the marble arc around the sculpture of a Navy SEAL. The names of SEALs who died in combat or combat training are carved in the marble. Brady does community outreach for the museum and is active in organizations with goals compatible with his lifelong love of the salt life. He is president of Conservation Alliance of St. Lucie County and the local Surfriders Association and is active in the Sealife Habitat Improvement Project, which puts on an annual oyster fest. (Photograph by Tom Baumker.)

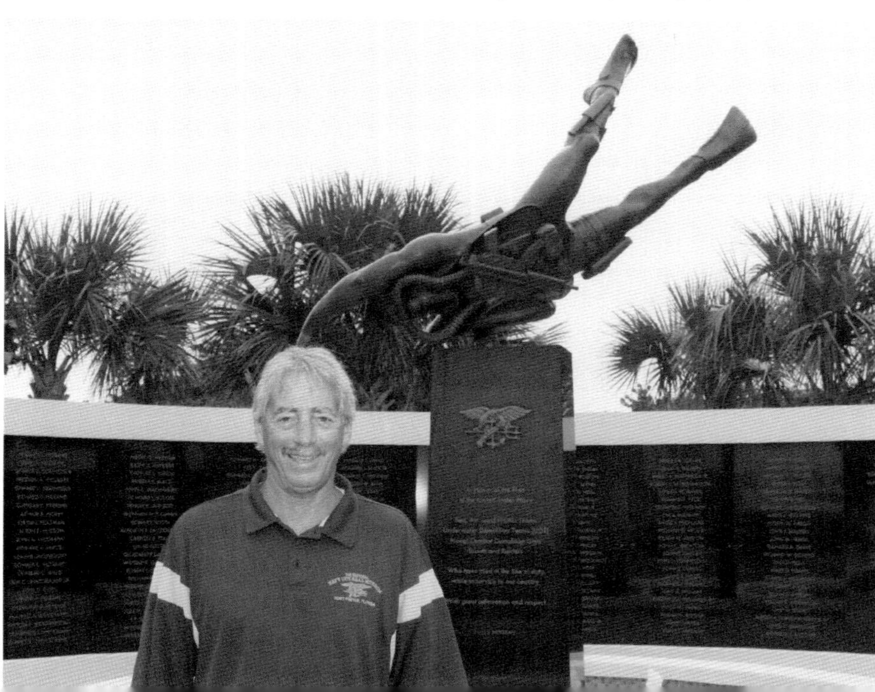

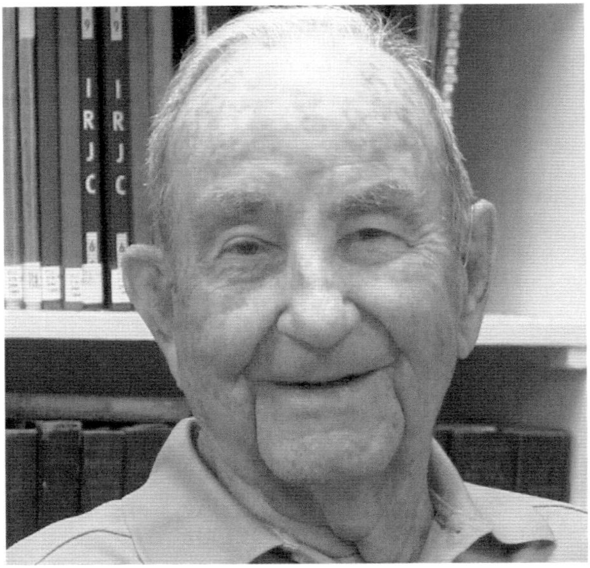

Trained at Fort Pierce
Veteran Jim Weeks, who trained at Fort Pierce and went on to a Navy career, remembered that before daylight trainees were on the beach doing strength exercises and running. There were obstacle courses to negotiate under fire; in the afternoon and evening, classes; at night, boat training included being taken out to sea, going overboard, and swimming back to a dark shore. Weeks opined that training at this base was intensive and well designed to enable men to survive the inevitable engagement with the enemy. (Photograph by the author.)

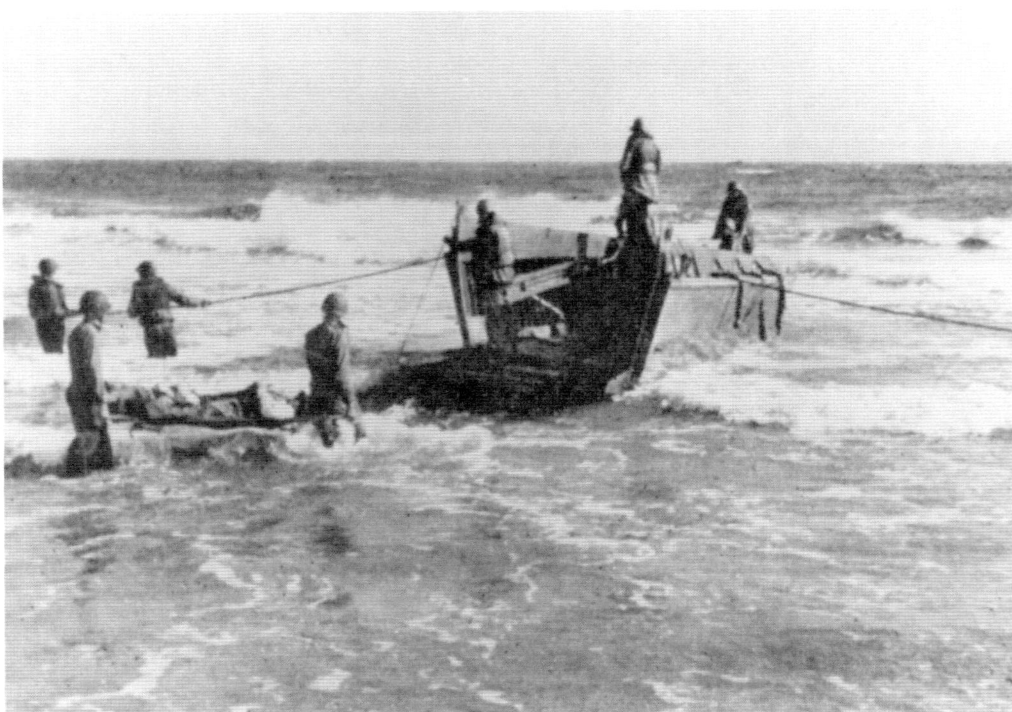

Rehearsal for D-Day
On the beach at Fort Pierce, young men learned to handle ammunition, overrun barricades, pilot landing craft, pick up wounded, and a hundred other skills in preparation for Operation Overlord on June 6, 1944. The first Underwater Demolition Teams whose job it would be to destroy the obstacles on Normandy beach had begun their training at Fort Pierce a year before. Training for taking Japanese-held islands in the Pacific was informed by the experiences in Europe. (Courtesy of SLCRHC.)

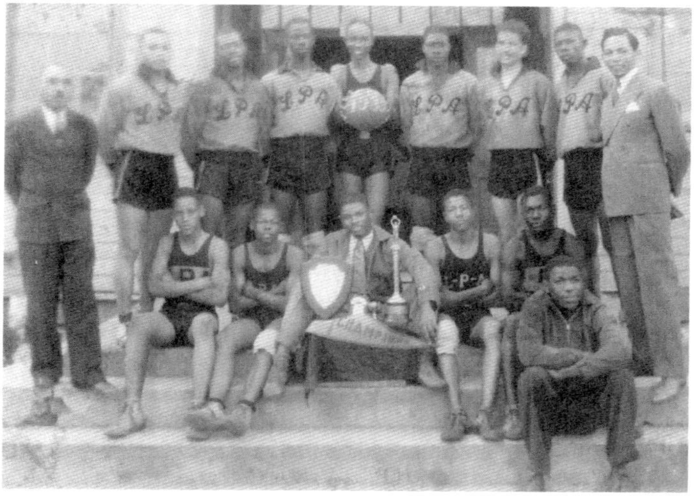

James Hair and the Golden Thirteen

African Americans served in the Navy from the time of the Revolution—as deckhands, cooks, stewards, sail makers, and ordinary seamen—but, until World War II, never had there been a black naval officer. With Hitler's obsession with racial purity, the segregated US military was viewed more and more as an obscenity. Under great pressure, in 1943, the Navy chose a group of black officer-training candidates. These men, who broke the Navy color ceiling, received their commissions in 1944 and came to be known as "The Golden Thirteen." One of these was James Hair, of Fort Pierce, who is pictured above (back row, second player from the right) with the Lincoln Park Academy basketball team, class of 1937.

These first black US naval officers told their stories in the book *The Golden Thirteen*. James Hair (pictured below in the first row at far left) related his experience of growing up in Fort Pierce. He greatly admired his brother-in-law Estes Wright, a proud man who did not bend easily to the rules of segregation. Estes was beaten by a white man, jailed, and carried home to die. The KKK threatened Estes's widow, James's sister, Margaret, to the point that she never allowed family or friends to speak of the deceased, never revealing to the children where their father was buried. The location of his grave is a secret to this day. (Above, courtesy of Samuel Gaines; below, courtesy of SLCRHC.)

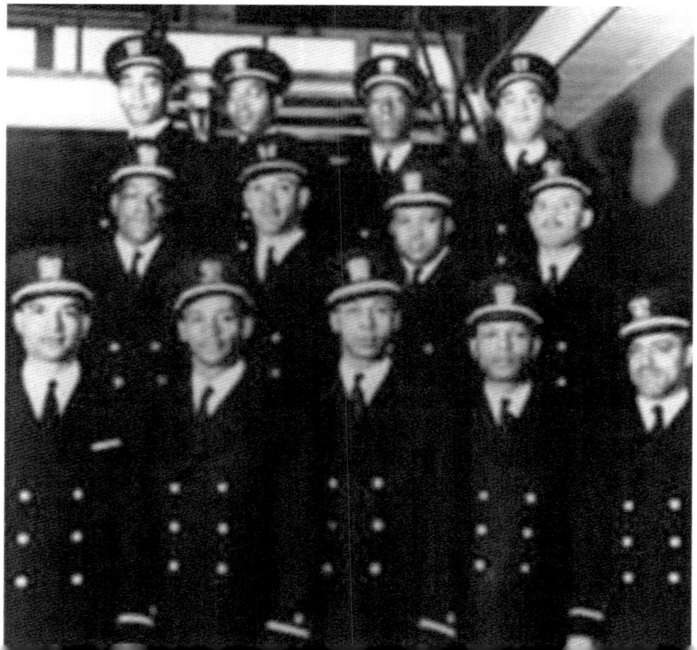

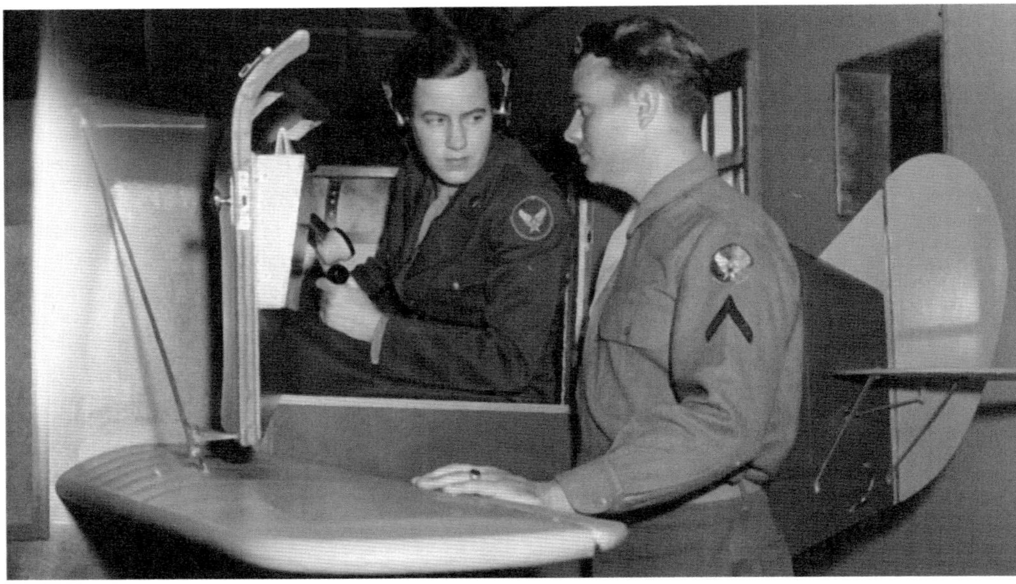

The Link Trainer

Edwin Albert Link, inventor of the flight simulator that trained some 500,000 men as pilots during World War II, turned from air to sea in peacetime. Link and J. Seward Johnson founded Harbor Branch and created the Johnson Sea Link submersible. Link is pictured below with his wife, Marion, atop the submersible in 1971. Today, the old Link Port, its laboratories, fisheries, plankton-gathering equipment, and some of its exploration vessels are part of Florida Atlantic University. Link submersibles have been used to great purpose in recovering rockets and failed mission wreckage (Space Shuttle *Challenger*), in underwater archeology (Civil War USS *Monitor*), and rescue missions. Edwin Albert Link, born in 1904, was the holder of over 27 patents and was inducted into the National Aviation Hall of Fame in 1976. He died in 1981, but there are those who still remember running into him ferreting for some special nut or bolt at Putnam Mercantile or Sewell's Hardware in Fort Pierce. (Above, courtesy of SLCRHC; below, courtesy of Harbor Branch Oceanographic Institute.)

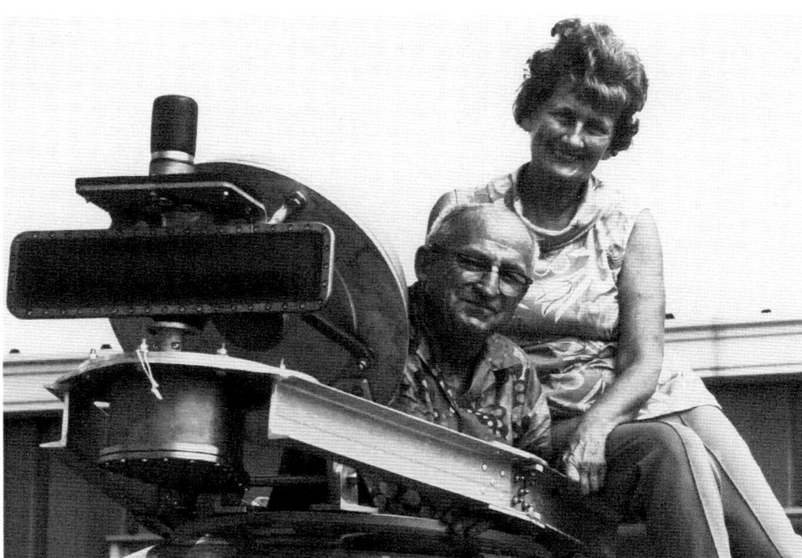

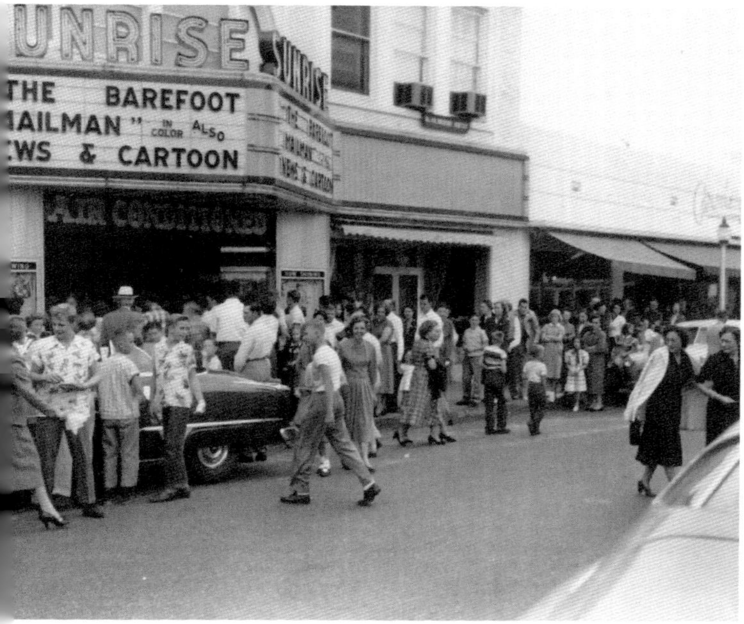

Sunrise Theatre
Peace came and Fort Pierce settled back into its slow-paced routine. Shops and offices closed on Wednesday afternoon so clerks could go fishing. The light plant blew its whistle every day at noon so residents could check their clocks. On Saturday afternoon, children went to the Sunrise Theatre to see a cowboy movie, and grownups shopped and visited with their friends on the benches that lined Second Street. (Courtesy of the Koblegard family.)

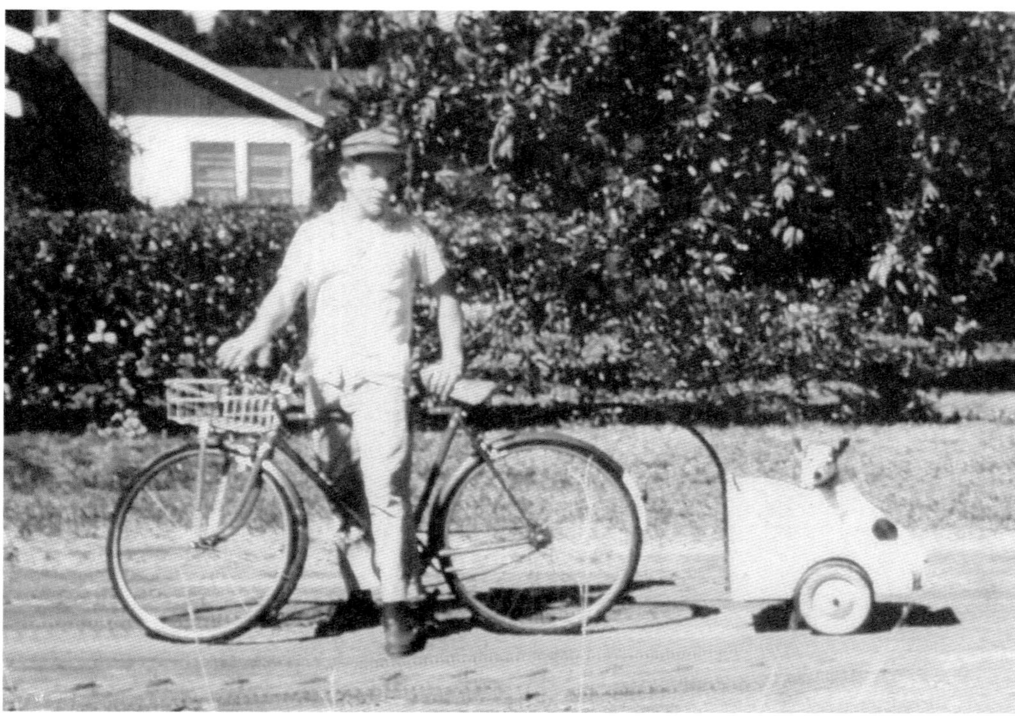

Postwar Halcyon Days
"You could ride your bicycle from your house to the river where you could put your feet in the water or fish if you were lucky enough to have a pole. There seemed to be no threats to children and, anyhow, everyone knew who you belonged to." So remembered Jack Favorite, pictured here with Molly, his dog, in the cart behind. (Courtesy of Jack Favorite.)

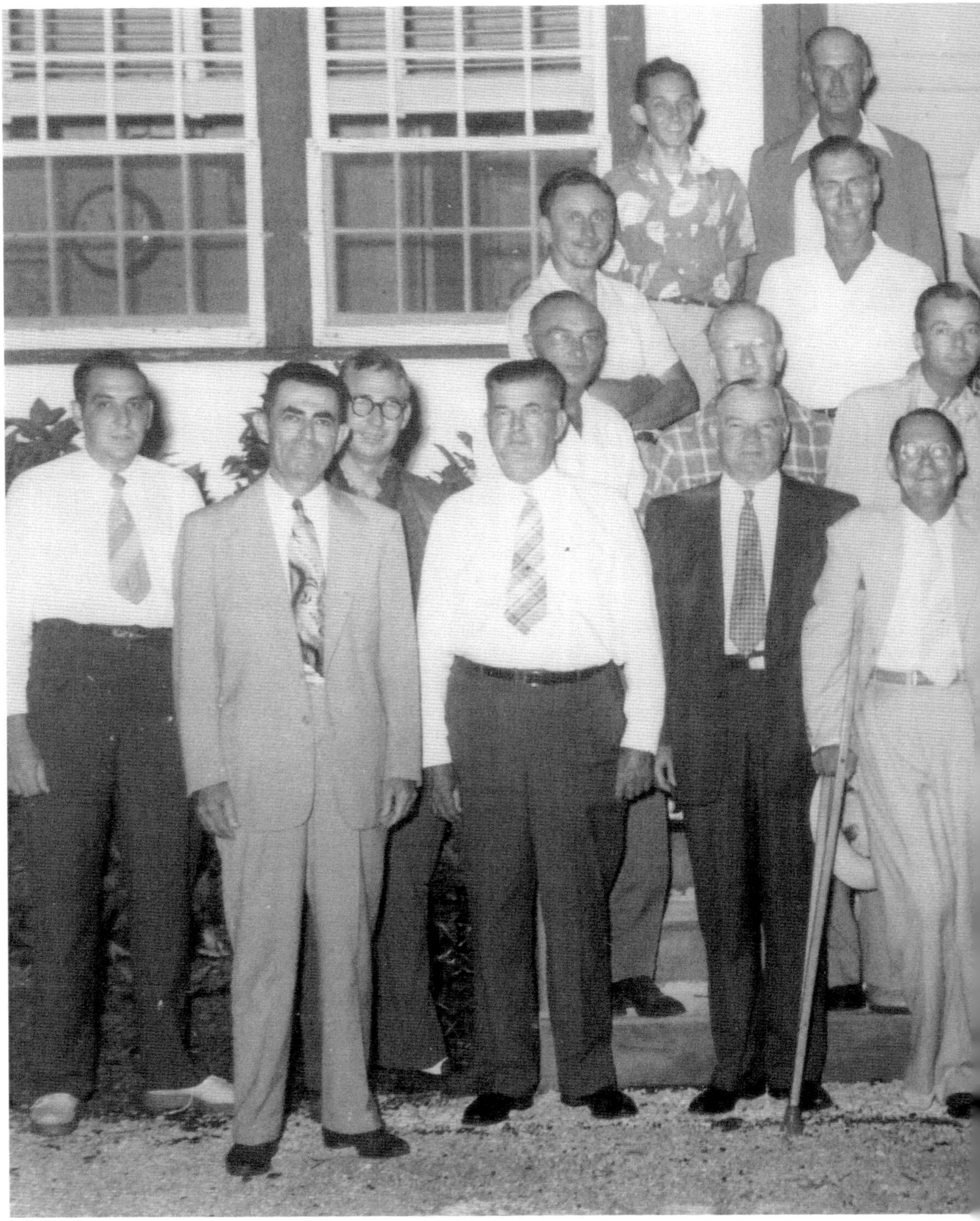

Bounty of the Outback

Fort Pierce was once rated as one of the 10 top counties in the country when measured by producing acreage. Here is a group of players at the state farmers market when it was doing a booming seasonal business. From left to right are (first row) R.B. Alvarez; M.E. Williams; Alto Adams, Florida Supreme Court; J. Meadows; D.H. "Banty" Saunders, Florida state representative; Verna Switzer; Lou English; and Dan McCarty; (second row) Evans Crary; Henry Richardson; Douglas Silver, president, radio station WIRA;

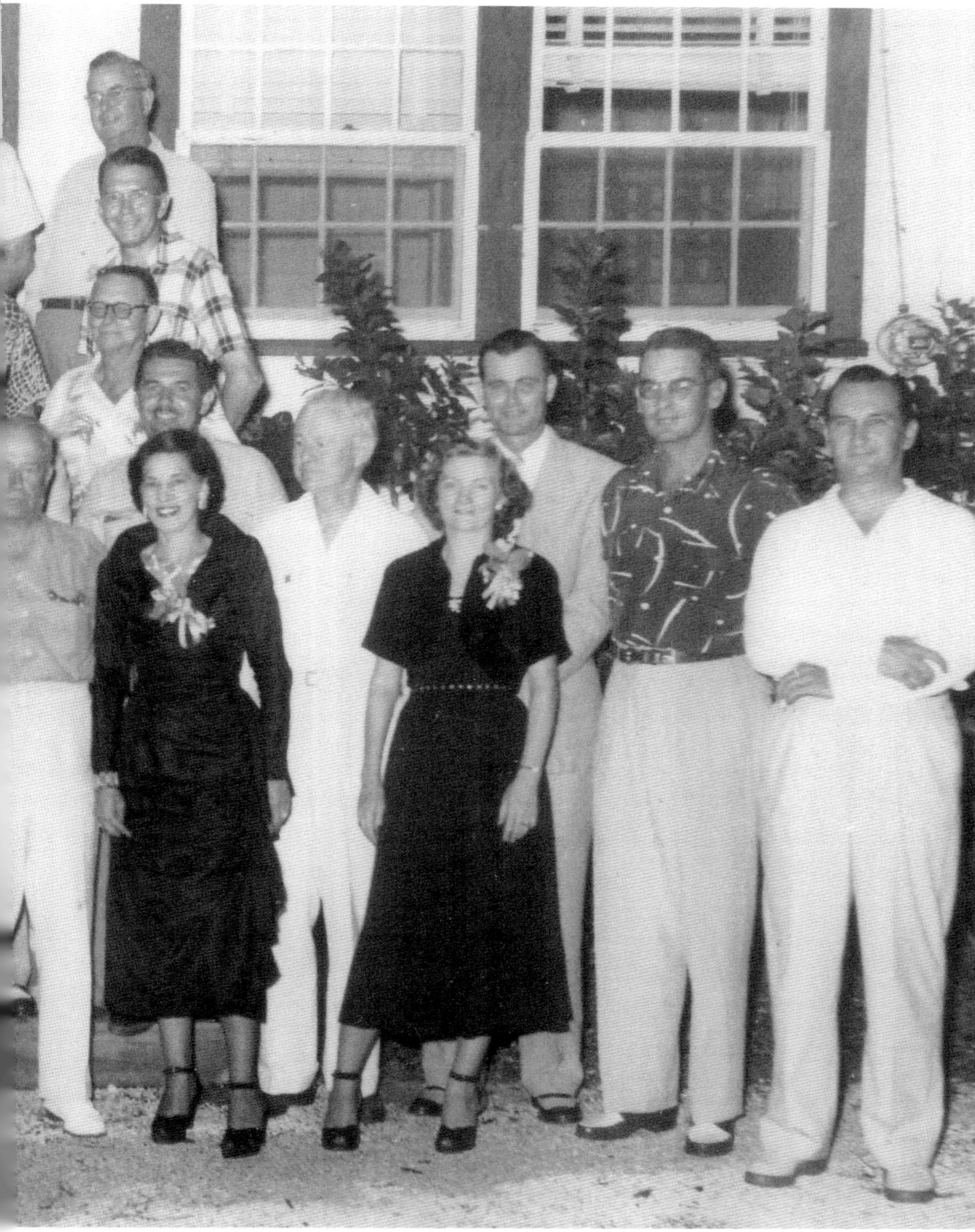

Cornelius van der Lugt; Heine Enns, editor of the *Fort Pierce News Tribune*; Kingley Butt; Ernest Tyner, mayor of Stuart; George Mather; Marcil Boudet, Vero Beach county agent; Charles Kim, St. Lucie county agent; and Lee Thompson; (third row) Bob Terry, St. Lucie County Bank; Rudolph Matteson, grower; Tollie Bass; and Ed Colean, (fourth row) Warren Blackmon, manager, chamber of commerce; R.L. Leonard, St. Lucie County Commissioner; D.C. Mustaine, freight agent, F.E.C.; and C.C. Bush. (Courtesy of SLCRHC.)

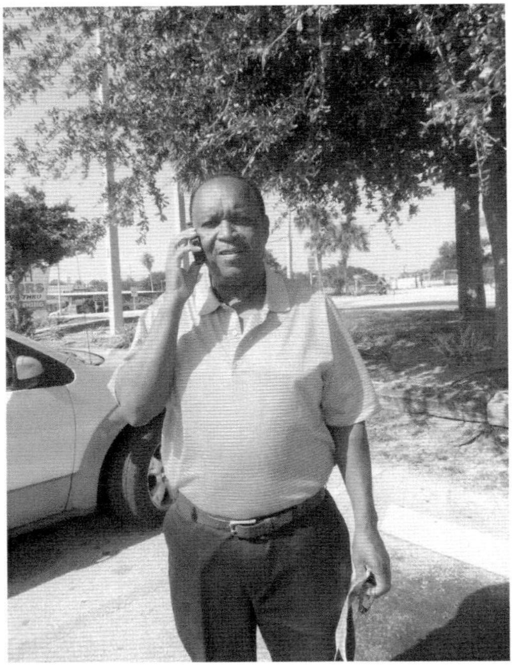

Agribusiness
In the old days, those wanting work waited under a tree on Thirteenth Street to board a bus or truck going west to the fields. Vernon Dixon, pictured here doing business on his cell phone, is a labor contractor who has improved on that old system of recruiting workers. He also operates a fleet of trucks that hauls citrus to the packinghouses. In his younger days, Dixon managed the Flamingo Club, which was the Cotton Club of the central Florida coast. Dixon supports Lincoln Park Main Street and other local community causes. (Photograph by the author.)

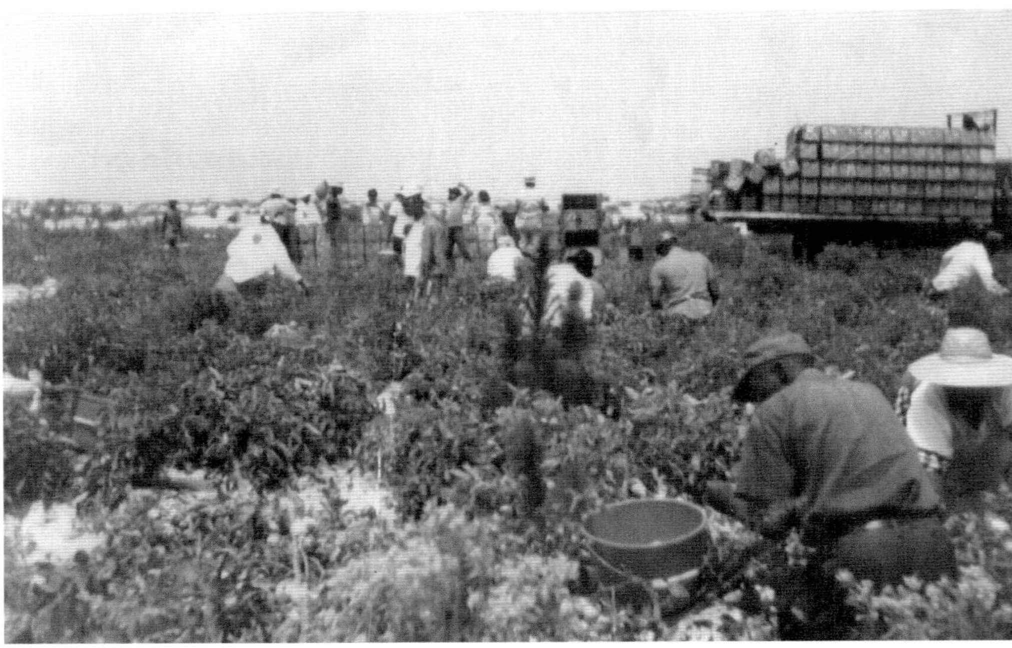

Pickers
Fort Pierce was the center of the winter tomato crops in the 1950s when this photograph was taken. It was hard work and whole families worked side by side through the season. Paid by the box, the legendary fast-pickers could make a fairly good living. In this photograph, the man in the back of the truck with his back turned is Walter Brunson and the woman to his left is his mother, Mary Brunson. (Courtesy of Josephine Titus.)

CHAPTER TWO

A Frontier Town

Coming to Florida in the 1870s to hunt or fish was an adventure akin to tramping through darkest Africa. Frederick Ober led two expeditions from Old St. Lucie to the interior to "discover" the fabled Lake Okeechobee and wrote about his adventures for *Forest and Stream*, the predecessor to *Field and Stream*. The extensive reports made by the Army and Navy when they were chasing Seminoles around the lake had been temporarily forgotten. Prof. John Whipple Jenks of Brown University joined Ober on his second adventure. He amassed a collection of specimens of flying and creeping things. Amos Cummings stayed at Paine's in Old St. Lucie, writing for the *New York Sun*. L. French Townshend, an Englishman, came through the old inlet to stay a few days on his voyage around Florida and to the Bahamas. He was followed by Lord Parker, the Earl of Dunraven, who reportedly shot a "score of deer." James Henshall, writing about the voyage of the *Blue Wing* in 1878, reported what he found at the site of Old Fort Capron: "The only vestiges of the old military post are a fallen chimney and the debris of a brick bake-oven; but the parade-ground and a moat or ditch can still be distinctly traced. There are evidences of a good state of cultivation at some remote period in the favorable ground, the groves of sour and bitter-sweet oranges, limes, lemons, and guavas; in the hedges of oleander, Spanish bayonet, and Cherokee rose, and in the ornamental group of date palms, century plants, cacti and sisal hemp." Other sportsmen followed to fish and to hunt.

The cattle barons, many of whom had fought in the Civil War, began to come in the 1870s, bringing their herds to graze the open range west of Fort Pierce. Descendants of these families, Carlton, Hendry, Alderman, and Holmes, continue to live in and around Fort Pierce. Alto Adams, a young attorney, arrived in 1924 to represent unpopular clients like the Ashley widows and even African Americans. He had the foresight to see that there would not always be free range; he acquired land, fenced it, and established the famous Adams Ranch.

The carpetbaggers also began to arrive in the 1870s, but if there was any initial animosity, it did not "take." Alongside the "crackers," northern investors began to settle down and thrive. The Ankenys and McCartys came from Iowa. P.P. Cobb and Milton Card came from Cazenovia, New York. A group of Connecticut Yankees acquired the old Indian trading post where they established a store and oyster cannery. Led by Julius Tyler, whose family remained in the area, the group laid out Cantown in 1881, and the Tylers built the first Fort Pierce Hotel. The Fee family came in 1888 via Melbourne, from Kansas. The Archambaults led a minor French Canadian invasion. The George Backus family came accompanied by Mrs. Backus's brother Reginald Goodwin in 1898 from New York and New Jersey.

For a long time, the chief money crop was pineapples, but when foreign competition overtook the plantation owners, citrus became the principal crop. Indian River Citrus became internationally famous. Later, cattlemen leased fallow land to tomato growers. Workers cleared the fields, the owners cleared a crop or two, and then the land went back, enriched, to pasturage.

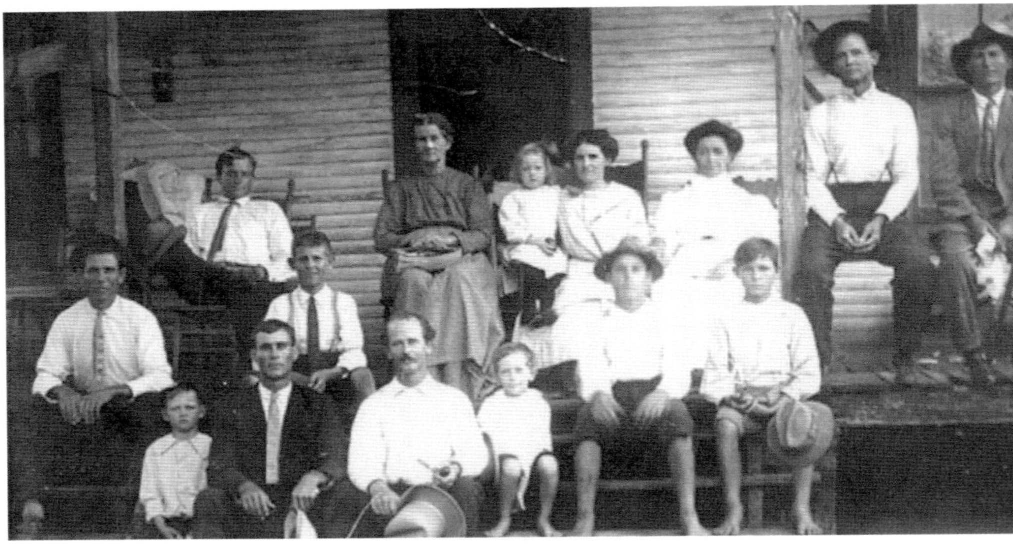

Open Range

Elizabeth Crews Carlton (1844–1918) and her first four children followed her husband, Reuben, across Florida and into the Kissimmee Valley, seeking grazing land for their cattle. The cattle arrived around 1875, and by 1878, the family was settled at Ten-Mile in St. Lucie County along with the tutor they brought with them, as Elizabeth was determined to have her children educated. A founding member of the first church in Fort Pierce, First Baptist Church, Elizabeth was also a nurse and midwife who answered calls for help in her horse and buggy. The land that is now downtown Fort Pierce was homesteaded by Elizabeth and Reuben. Four more children were born to the couple after settling in Fort Pierce, and their progeny hold giant legendary sway in local history. (Courtesy of SLCRHC.)

Second-generation Carltons

Daniel and Reuben, sons of Elizabeth and Reuben Sr., ride the Ten-Mile range. Daniel served as the first sheriff of St. Lucie County. He retrieved the bones of Tom Tiger from a grave robber, appeasing disgruntled Seminoles. He was killed by a man named Disney in a shootout in a Fort Pierce alley in 1915. (Courtesy of SLCRHC.)

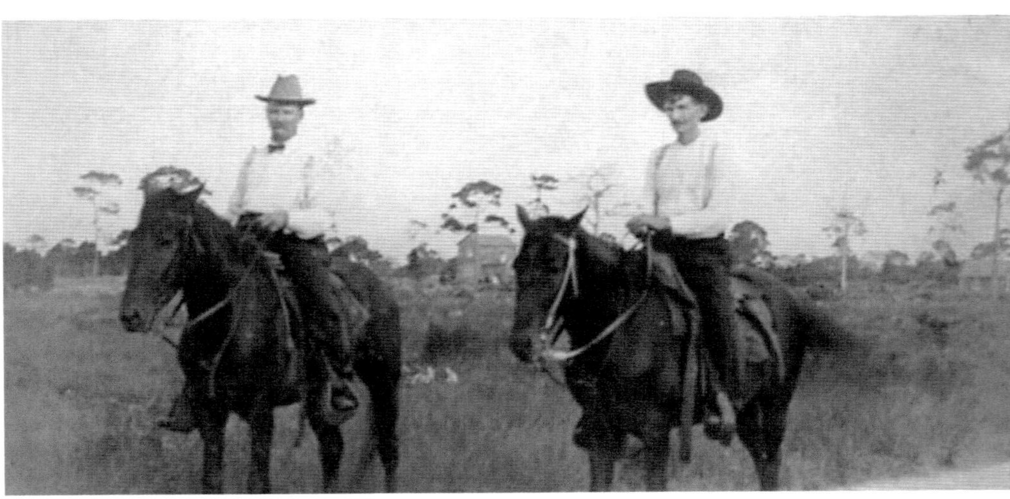

Third-generation Carltons

The clan gathered for Aunt Sallie's 81st birthday. Present are, from left to right, (kneeling) Carl "Big Boy" Carlton and Dan "Squeeks" Carlton; (standing) Louise Carlton Whitice, Margaret "Maggie" Carlton, Ruby Carlton Teague, Sid Carlton, Sallie Carlton Boykin, Wright Carlton, and Thad Carlton. (Courtesy of SLCRHC.)

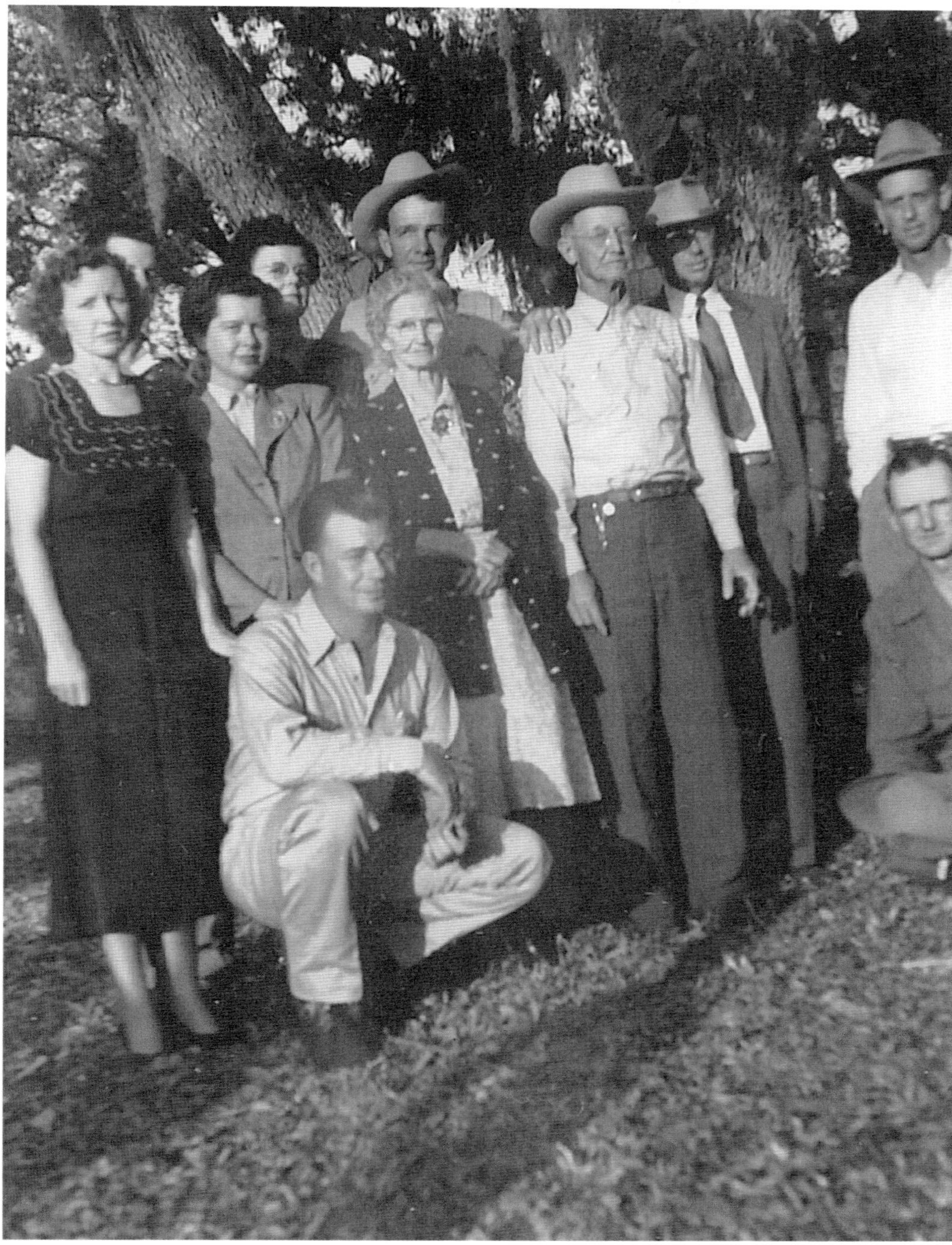

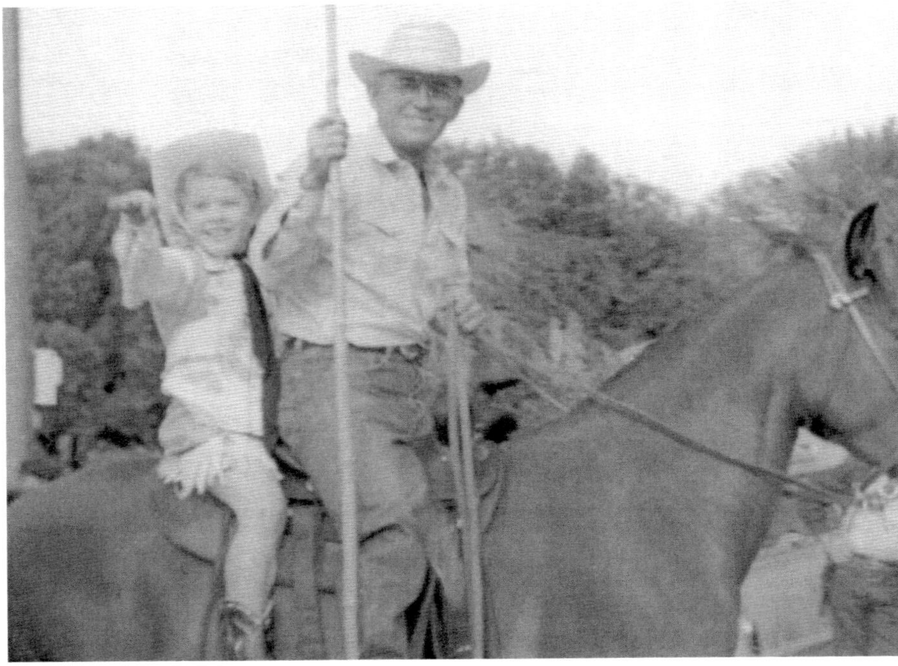

Ten-Mile Pioneers on Eleven-Mile Road

Ten-Mile Creek is a very old name on the maps. The soldiers, scouting from Fort Pierce for hostiles, named Five-Mile Creek and Ten-Mile Creek on their maps for their distance from Fort Pierce. Ten-Mile is the name given to the community settled by the Carltons. Joanne Carlton Humphries, whose address is Eleven-Mile Road, talked about her family history at a St. Lucie Historical Society program in 2013. Her granddaughter Kayla Rigel came dressed in the cowgirl outfit Joanne wore, riding behind second-cousin R.D. Bass, in the 1957 Cattlemen's Parade (above) while Joanne wore her mother's (Jacqueline Carlton) duplicate creation. (Both, courtesy of Joanne Humphries.)

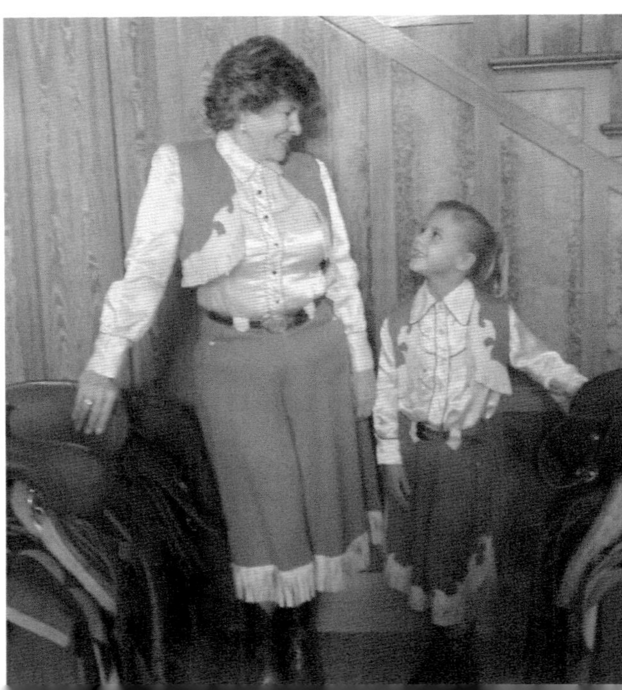

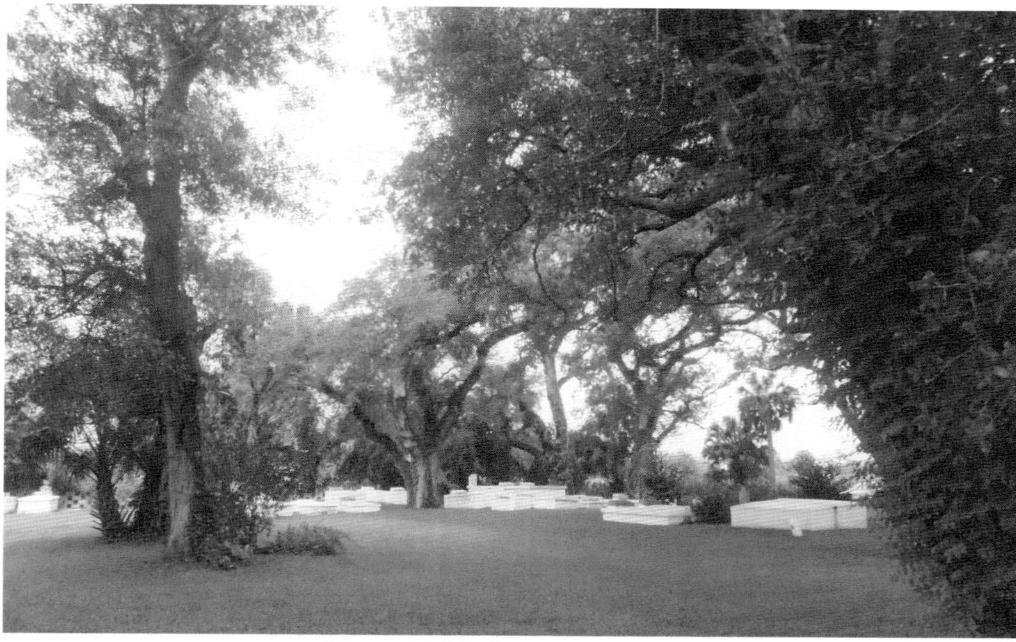

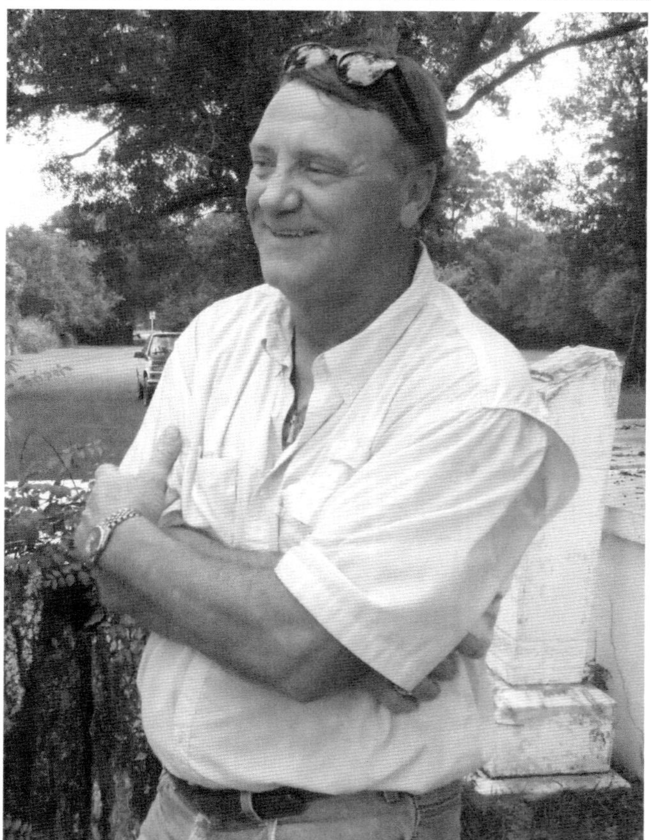

Historic Carlton Cemetery
Rick Modine, a great-grandson of Elizabeth Crews Carlton, is gathering the biographies of all the people laid to rest here. All headstones, save that of two friends of the family, sit at the head of a member of the Carlton family. (Photograph by Tom Baumker.)

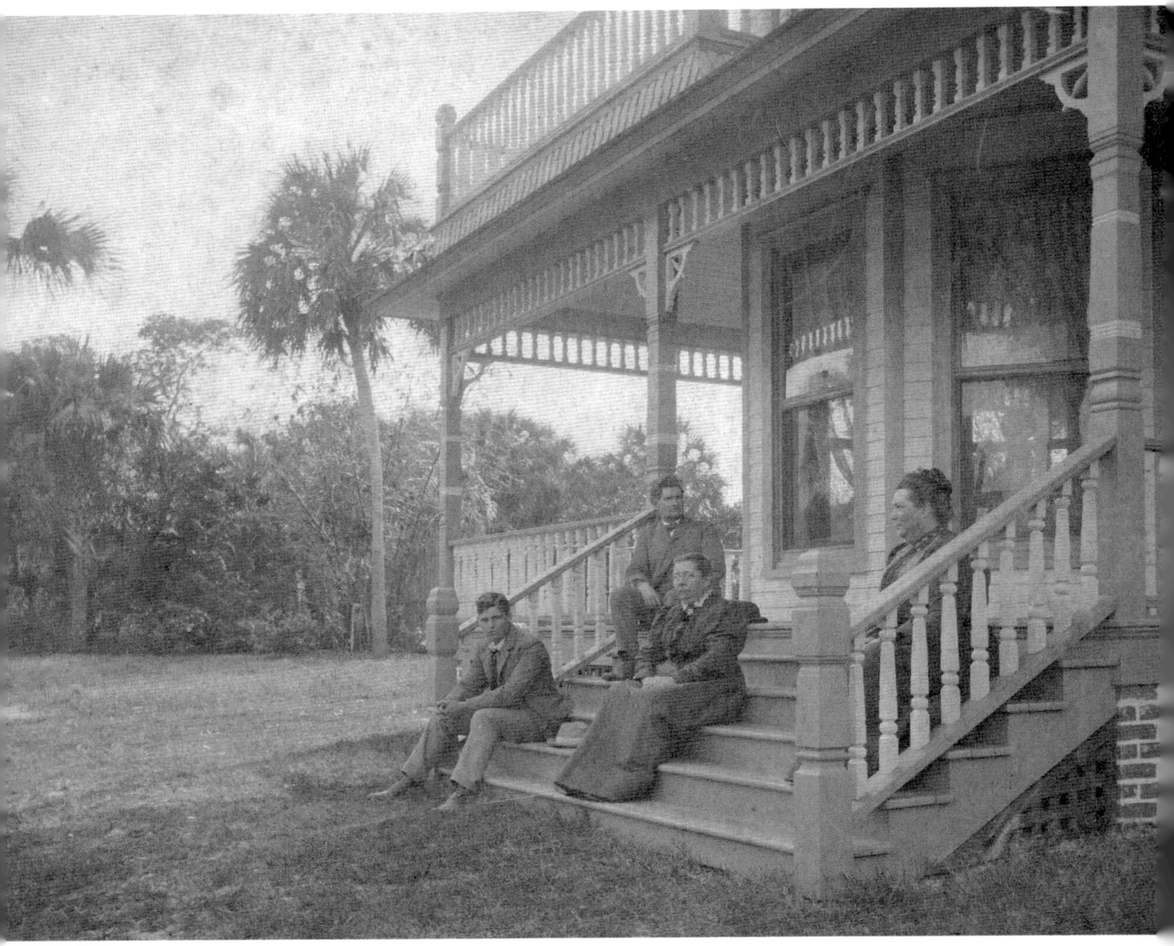

Carpetbaggers Welcomed

Elizabeth McCarty (top right), on the steps of the McCarty home at Ankona, followed her husband, Charles Tobin McCarty (top left), to the area in 1889. They both had taught at Tilford Academy in Vinton, Iowa, and "Lizzie" almost immediately began to teach in the local pioneer school. She was instrumental in founding the local women's club, raised money for the Episcopal church, performed in community entertainments, and continued to buy and sell real estate and to contribute time and money to civic progress over many years of widowhood after C.T., a successful attorney, realtor, horticulturist, and pineapple grower, was murdered in an alley off Pine Street by a neighbor angered by a real estate deal. (Courtesy of SLCRHC.)

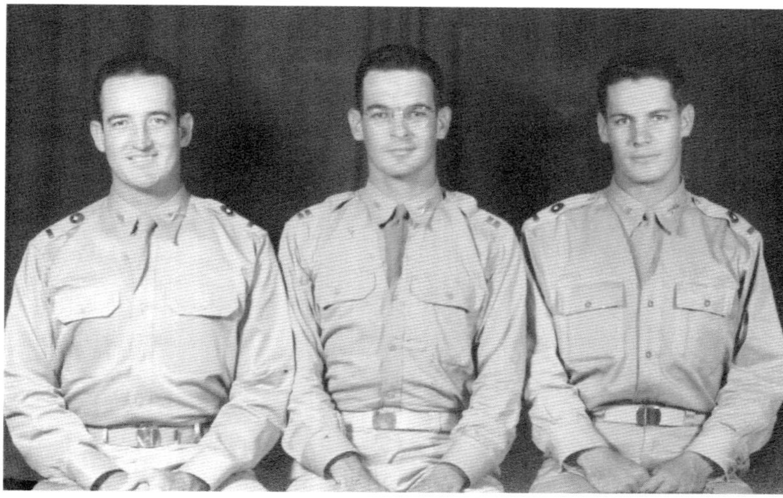

Third-generation McCartys

Dan (center) won a Purple Heart flying in Europe in World War II and came home to become Florida's 31st governor in 1952. John (right) received a Bronze Star fighting with the 292nd Joint Assault Company in the Pacific and came home to serve as municipal judge, judge of the Ninth Judicial Circuit, and state senator in the 1960s. Brian (left) tended the cattle and citrus and was a leader in water management. All three were staunch members of the Episcopal church on Indian River Drive where their grandmother Elizabeth had been a founding member. (Courtesy of SLCRHC.)

The Fourth Generation

The family of Margaret McCarty Boudrias Monahan is pictured on the occasion of the wedding of son Chester Joseph Boudrias and Caroline Collins in 2010. Her daughter Lillian Boudrias Ewen stands next to her husband, Nicholas H. Ewen (far left), and Peggy stands next to her husband, Michael O. Monahan (far right). The father of Peggy's two children, Joseph Anthony Boudrias, was killed in an automobile accident in 1985. Mike Monahan, whom she married in 1988, retired as a major in 2012 after 37 years with the St. Lucie County sheriff's department. Peggy and her family continue to follow longtime McCarty interests—citrus and cattle. Lillian, an attorney, was president of the St. Lucie Bar Association in 2013 as was her grandfather John McCarty before her. (Courtesy of Peggy McCarty Monahan.)

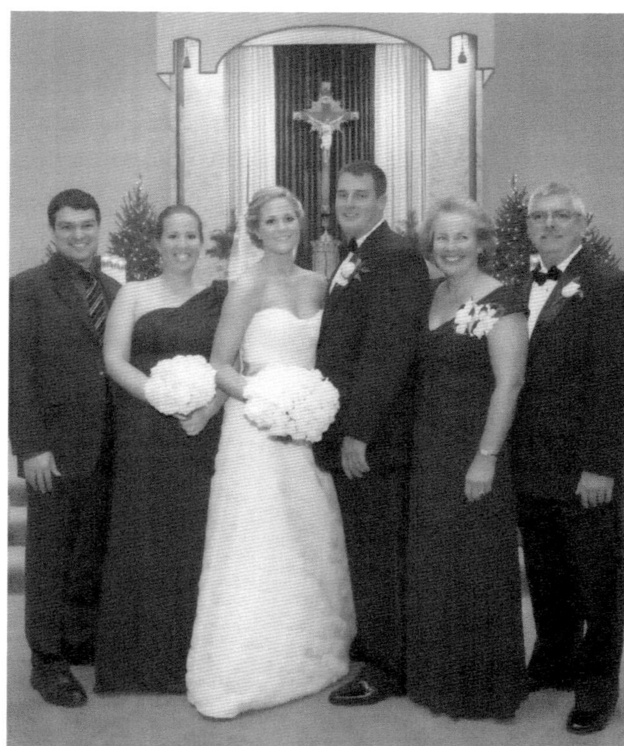

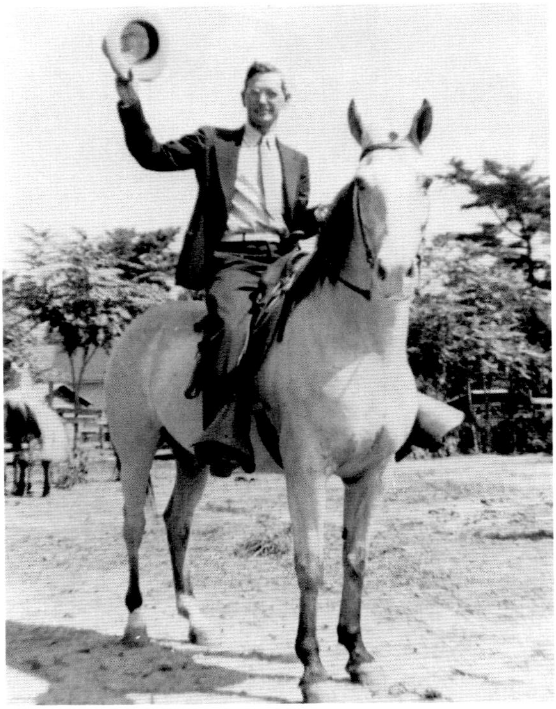

Cattleman and Gentleman

Nathan "Teet" Holmes always rode a white horse. He ascribed to the honor code that existed among the early cattlemen—he did business on a handshake. His father, Henry Allen Holmes, raised 12 children at Fort Drum, then he and Teet's stepmother, Caroline, moved to Fort Pierce in 1908 where they built an octagon house on Seventh Street and behind it, a casino with a dance hall and a 100-foot pool. (Courtesy of Margaret Holmes Carlton.)

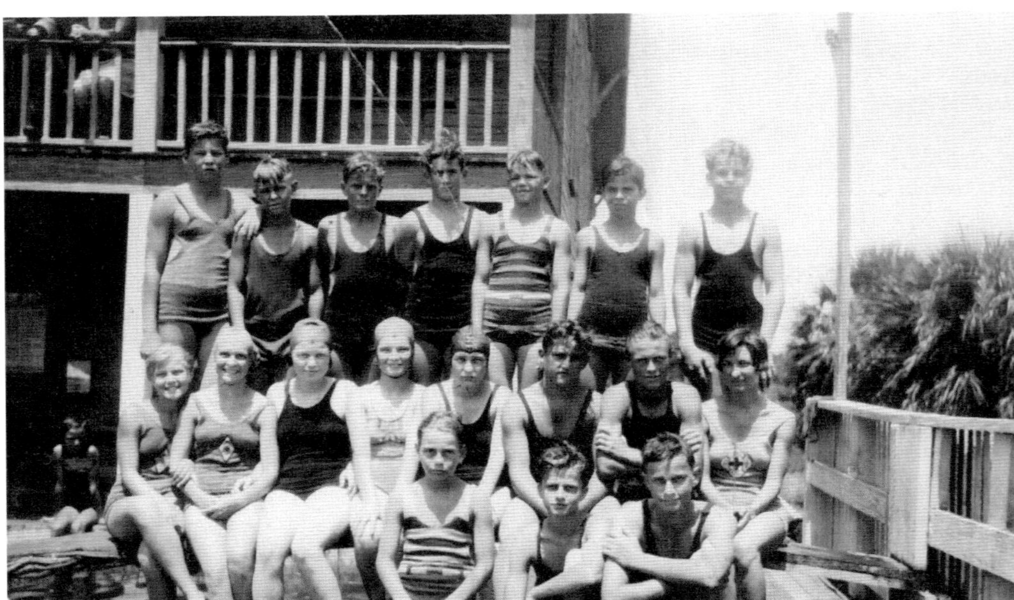

The First Swimming Pool in Fort Pierce

The first Holmes in Fort Pierce built the first swimming pool. There were dances at the casino—the Roseland Orchestra from Los Angeles was advertised in 1922 and the Sundodgers in 1927. Boxing matches were popular and the American Legion hosted parties there. Once a week, a pair of lucky boys got to swim free in return for cleaning the pool. (Courtesy of Margaret Holmes Carlton.)

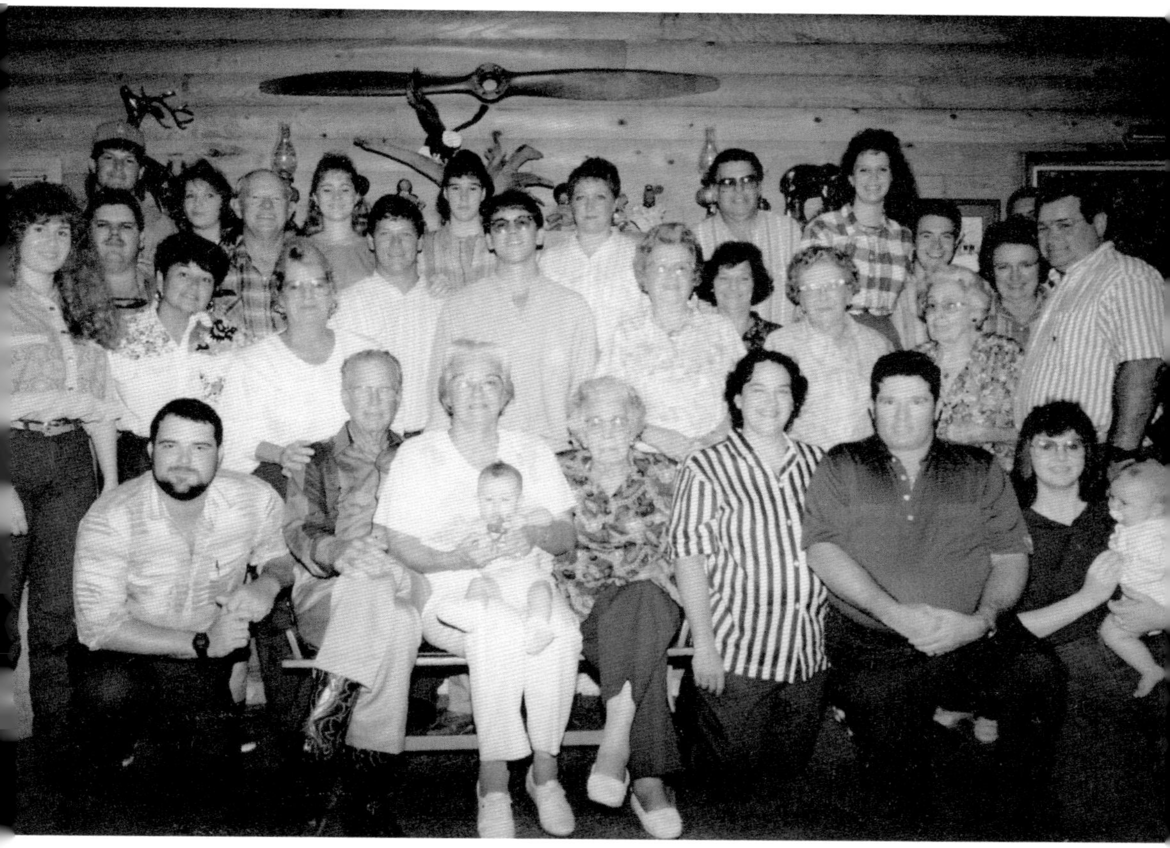

Two Cattle Families Unite
This photograph was taken at the Bluefield family place. Margaret Holmes, daughter of Teet Holmes, married a third-generation Carlton, Reuben. Grandmother Margaret is pictured front and center holding the baby. Descendants of Vieva Holmes Hardie are evident in this photograph: Conrad Hardie, Vieva's son, is in the middle row, far right, next to his wife, Pommy Van Tilborg Hardie. (Courtesy Margaret Holmes Carlton.)

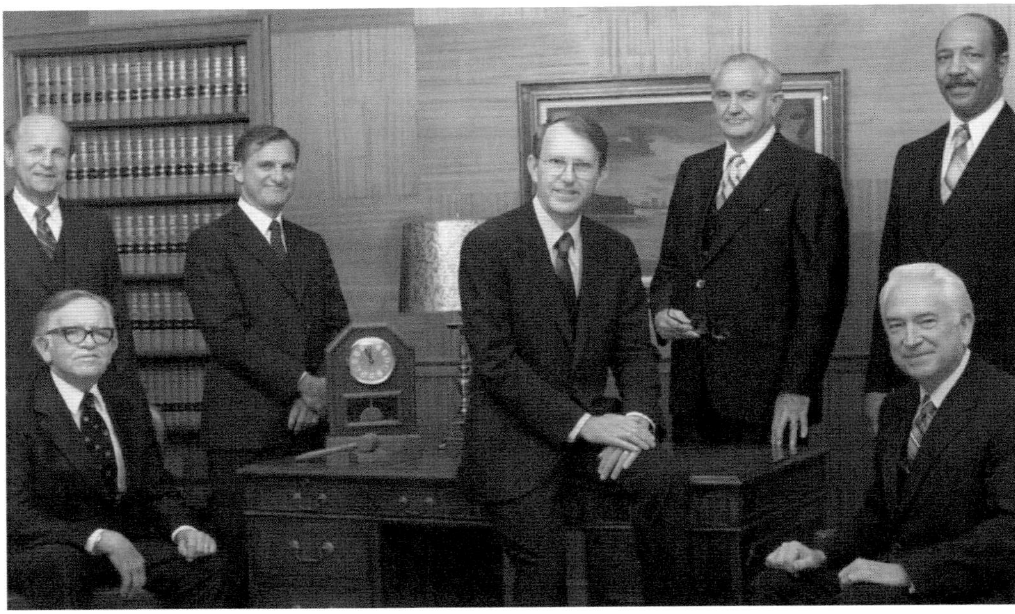

Duty Calls

Supreme Court Justice James Alderman (above center) was happy in Tallahassee, enjoying the challenge of hearing groundbreaking cases and the intellectual process of reasoned decisions on the merits of opposing legal arguments. But, when his father's health faltered, Jim Alderman resigned his seat and came home to manage the family ranch. He left the comfort of a judge's bench to herd, brand, and doctor cattle, coming home to do the grueling daily work required of a cowboy. Jim's cowboy heritage goes back to before Florida was a state. A fourth-generation Florida cattleman, Judge Alderman is the great-great-grandson of the renowned Streaty Parker of Florida's Civil War cattle battalion. (Both, courtesy of Hon. James Alderman.)

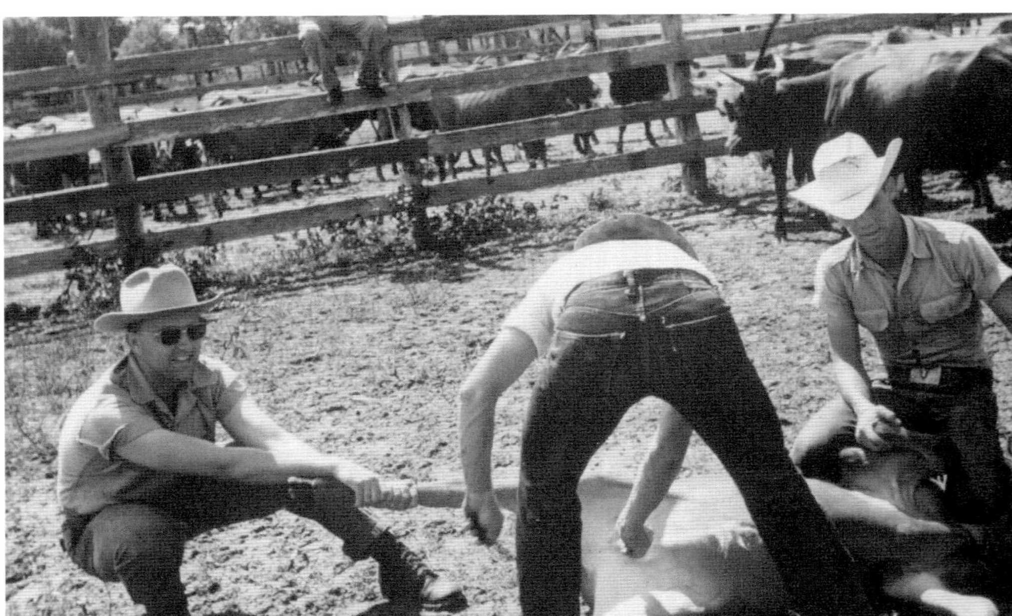

Sandy Shoes Parade
The cattlemen were always a big part of annual festivals. Charles Wilson is at the wheel of a Sunrise Ford tractor as a c. 1970 parade passes between the Arcade Building (the part visible on the right burned to the ground) and the 1937 post office on the left (now abandoned). (Courtesy of the author.)

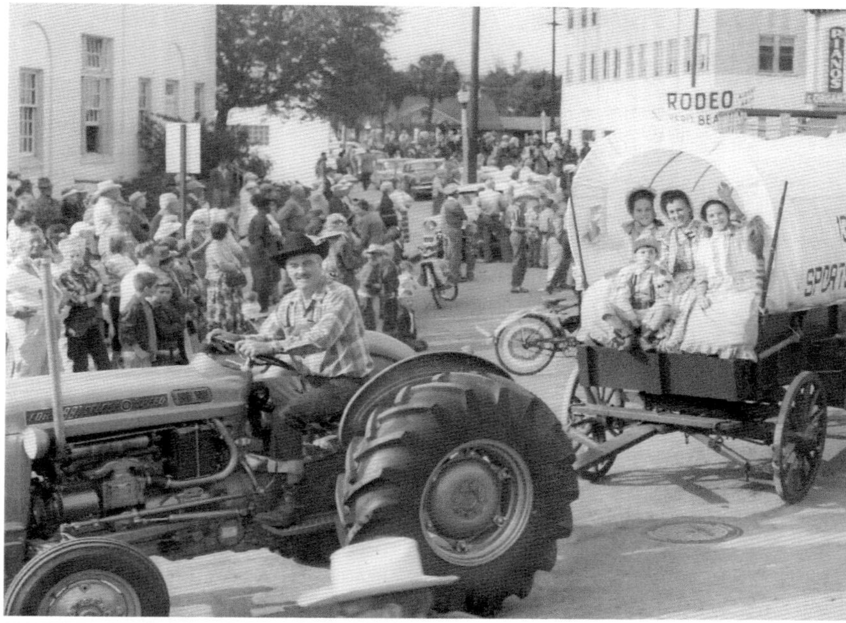

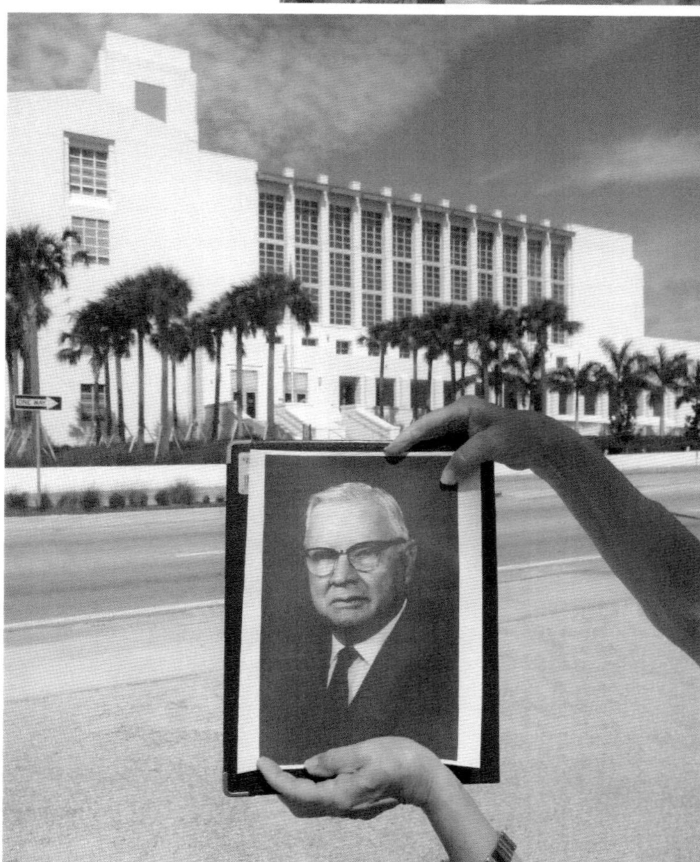

The Honorable Judge Adams, Rancher
The new Alto Lee Adams Sr. Federal Court House in Fort Pierce was dedicated in 2012. Judge Adams was a rancher, chief justice of the Florida Supreme Court, and respected jurist, historian, scholar, author, and bibliophile. (Photograph by Tom Baumker.)

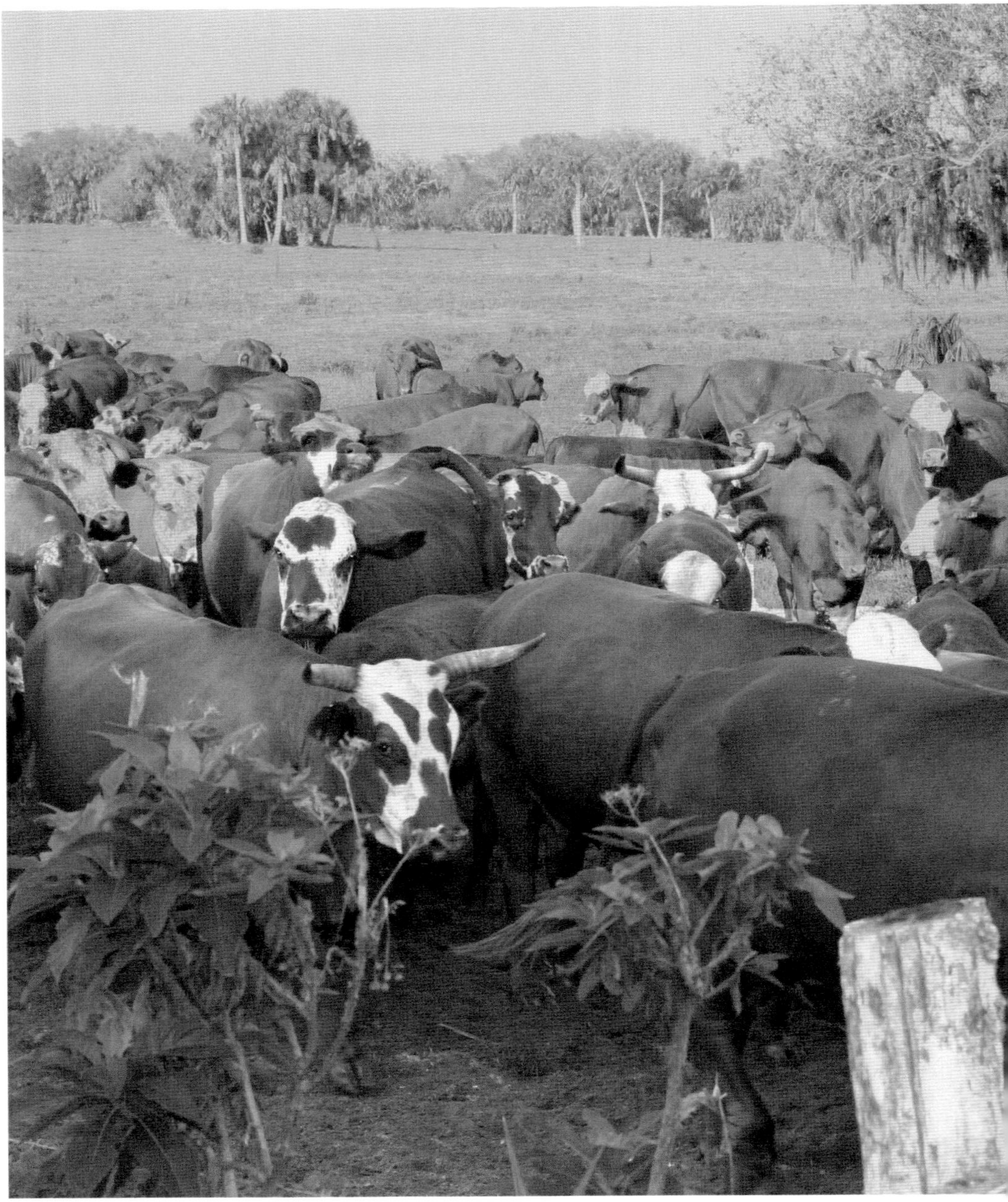

A New Breed by Adams

Pictured is a herd of Brafords, a superior breed of beef cattle, bred by Alto Lee "Bud" Adams Jr. Adams Ranch, which is the 12th-largest cattle ranch in the United States and has herds in three Florida counties, has its headquarters west of Fort Pierce on the original site of the enterprise founded by the senior Adams. Bud Adams manages the ranch productively with advanced environmental practices, no pesticides, and skillful water management. The cattle live entirely on ranch grass—no commercial feed. There are also citrus groves on the ranch property. Bud's sons, Lee, Mike, and Robbie, and some of the grandchildren also work on the ranch. (Courtesy of Adams Ranch.)

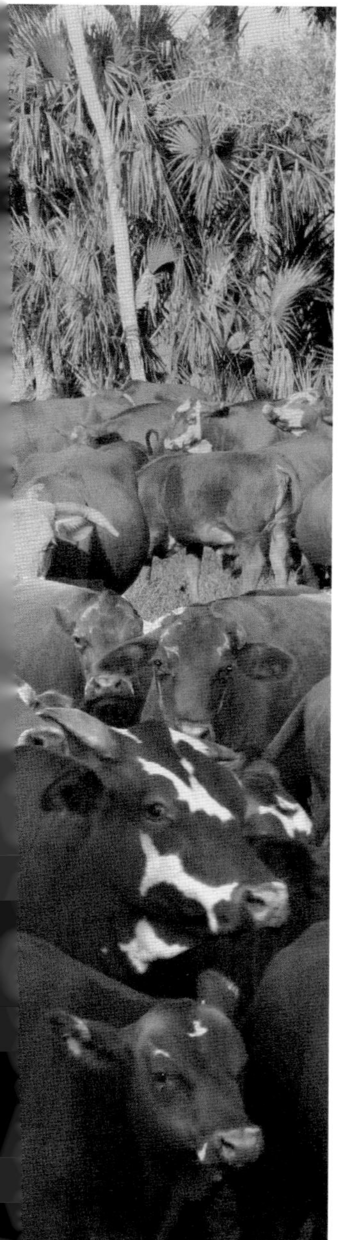

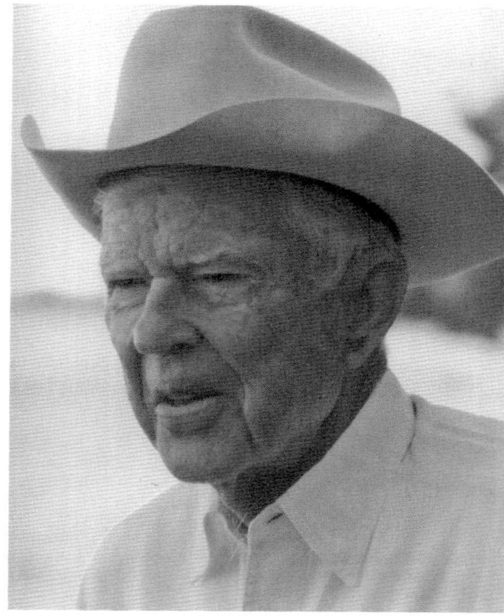

The Patriarch

In addition to tending to the business of the ranch, Bud is a talented photographer who has recorded on film the wildlife in the backcountry and the cowboy lifestyle. He heads a family noted for its continuous community support and philanthropic largess. Because of his sense of history, Bud purchased the P.P. Cobb building, the oldest in the town of Fort Pierce, in the interest of preservation. His life's goal is to preserve the unique landscape that is Adams Ranch so future generations can experience what Florida was like pristine. When one is with Bud Adams, one listens; his quiet voice of authority is served by wisdom. (Courtesy of Adams Ranch.)

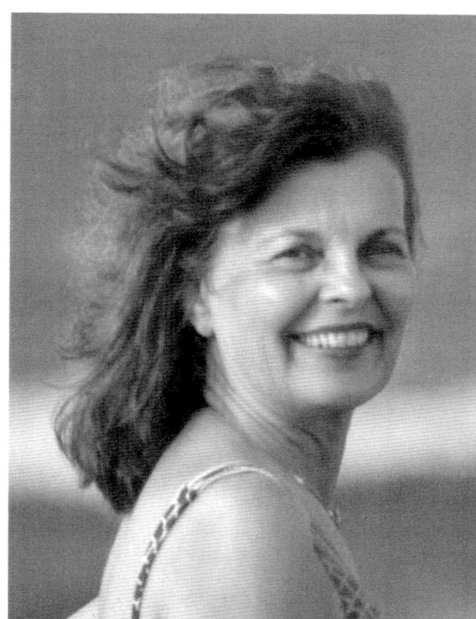

The Matriarch

Dorothy Snively Adams won beauty contests before she became a rancher's wife. She was able to shoot a rattlesnake or play hostess to visiting dignitaries who wanted to view Adams Ranch, the only place of its kind in the world. (Courtesy of Adams Ranch.)

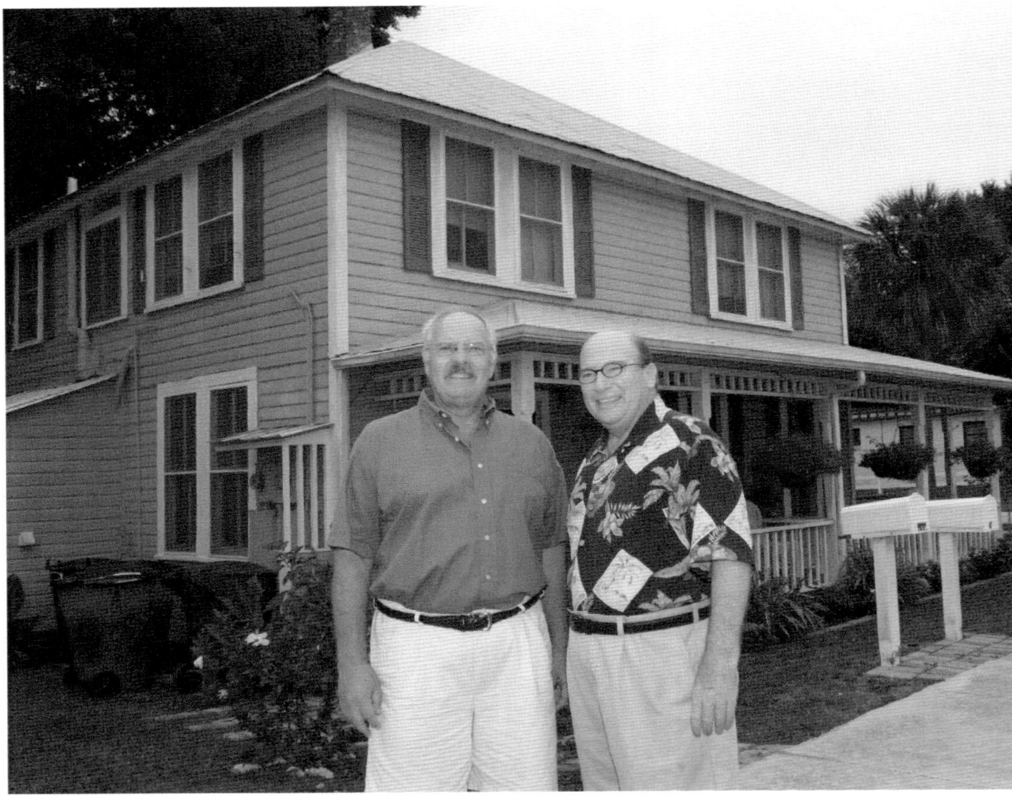

Matt Hurley and Keith Lustig

The oldest residential section of Fort Pierce, Edgartown, was platted as a town in 1889 by the LaGows. Lucinda LaGow asked her daughter, Emily, who was about to marry a Floridian, "Does he know you are a Yankee?" They named the main roadway along the river Union Street.

Partners Matt Hurley (right) and Keith Lustig (left), Chicago-area transplants, have critically strengthened fledgling efforts to restore Edgartown to a sit-on-the-front-porch, walk-around-visiting neighborhood. They are shown here in front of the 1910 boardinghouse for fishermen and railroad workers that they restored. This project gave them so much satisfaction that they purchased and restored the 1906 fishing cottage next door. In the meantime, they discovered that many original families of Fort Pierce had lived in Edgartown. Located here were the first church, first school, and first doctor in the area. Lustig's efforts to encourage and assist in regenerating the settlement included becoming an active member of the Fort Pierce Historic Preservation Board and the Edgartown Working Group and helping route a biking and walking path down its main street. Hurley became the block captain of the new neighborhood watch program. He worked tirelessly to bring the residents together on both a business and social level. He regularly attends city meetings to track and anticipate developments that could affect their enclave, and he volunteers every Saturday at the downtown farmers market.

With their efforts—voila! Edgartown has become the place to live. Lustig and Hurley have been wholeheartedly welcomed by "Old Fort Pierce" as well as the "artsy crowd." The hardy fishermen who once lived in these mostly small houses when the river lapped their back steps (now a block from shore due to fill) would wonder at the rising worth of their property. (Photograph by Tom Baumker.)

St. Lucie Village

Pioneer Edward Cabell Summerlin and his wife, Polly, arrived in Old St. Lucie in 1888. They purchased land from homesteader Judge James Paine in 1904, and in 1911 they built a small house (their second) that withstood hurricanes for more than 100 years, though it burned in 2012. Polly gave birth to 14 children, raising all who survived in two rooms without inside plumbing. (Son Richard and his wife, Claudia, bought the house in 1921 and raised nine children there.) Son Ned sold chickens, eggs, and oysters to the snowbirds who began to come south in the late 19th century. Son Astor cut wood for the steamboats. Clarence fished, and Aden often served as a fishing guide. Marion Pryde Quay wrote an article published in a national sports magazine about an alligator hunt she went on, wearing a fashionable hat and white gloves, guided by the Summerlin boys.

Today, hundreds of Summerlins and related family descendants do everything in Fort Pierce from building bulkheads and docks to cutting hair, selling fire equipment, and mixing drinks. Over the years, Summerlins, who sometimes called themselves "the Mullet Mafia," have made their living largely from the sea. A handsome family, of many who have made their mark, a few stand out. Clarence Summerlin was the proprietor of Honeydew Ranch. Archie Summerlin was the longtime proprietor of Archie's Seabreeze and an entire book could be written about him, his escapades, and his sayings. Dennis Summerlin was mayor of Fort Pierce. Wesley Davis Island in the Indian River is named for a Summerlin descendant. Current patriarch Herman Summerlin operates a maritime construction company. This photograph was taken in 1903. (Courtesy of the Summerlin family.)

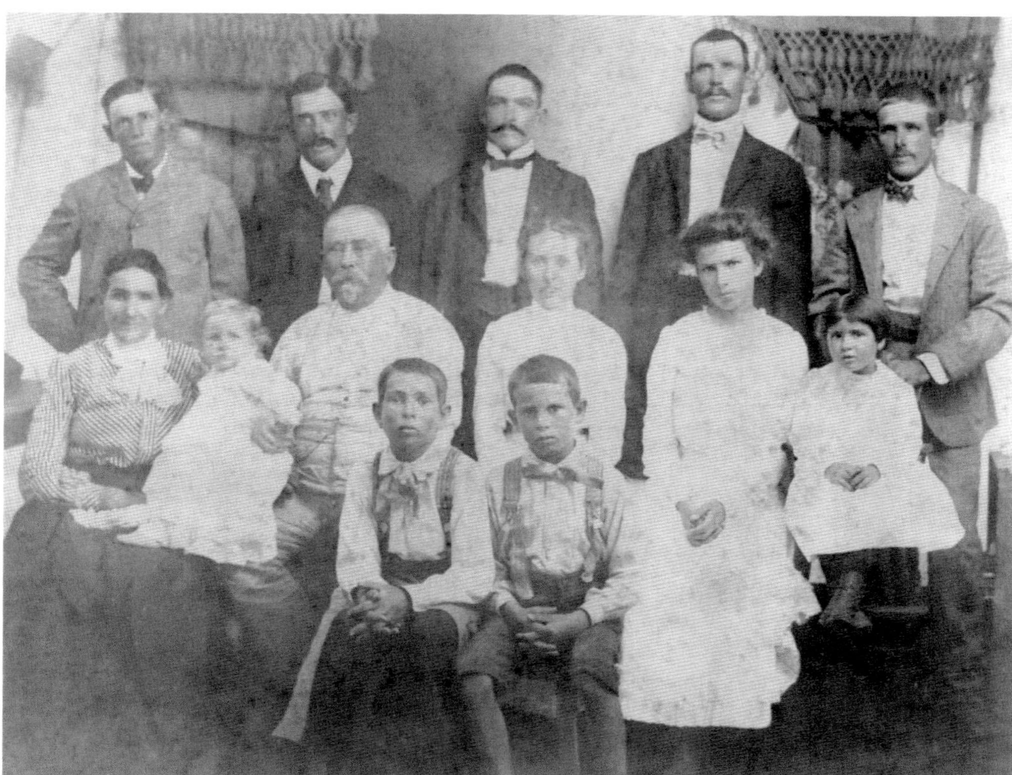

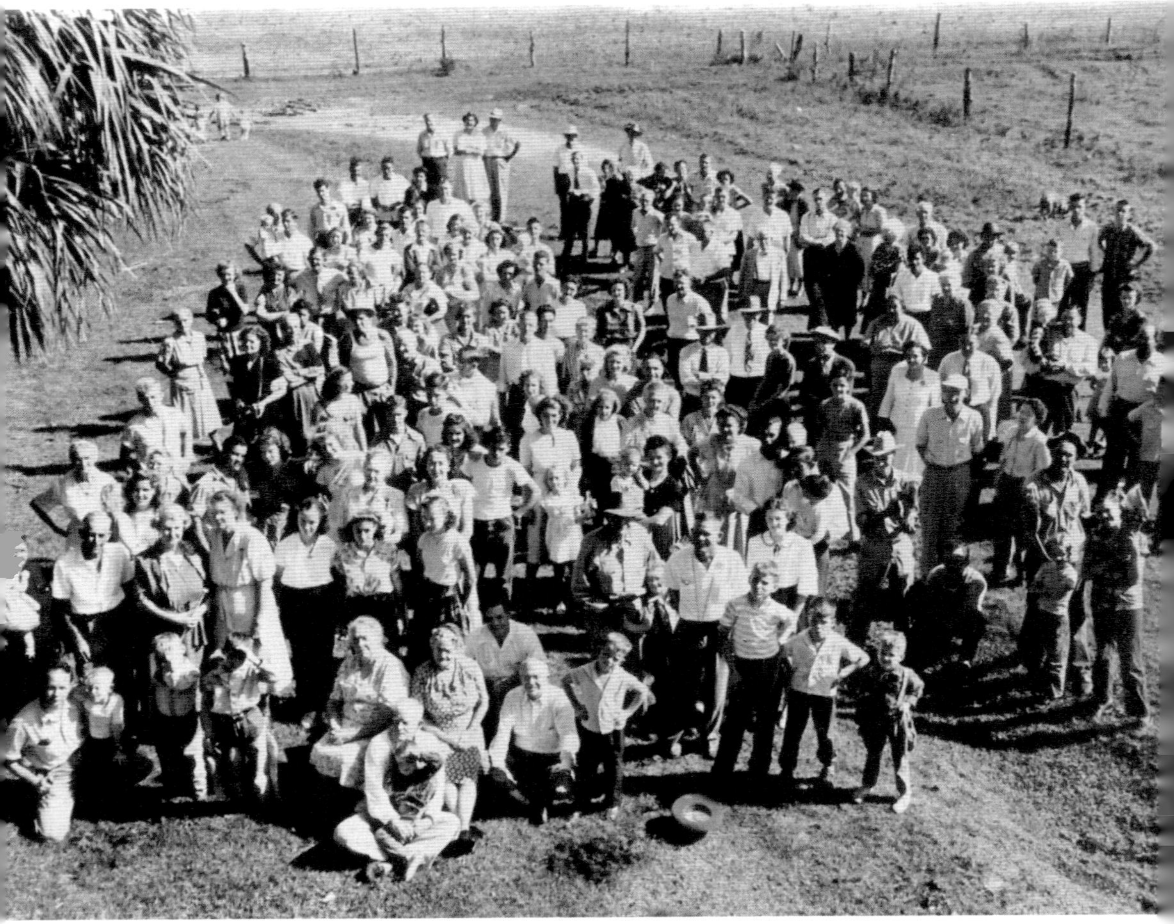

The 1949 Summerlin Reunion
Everybody wants to be a Summerlin when the time comes for the pioneer family's annual reunion. No one can do a fish fry like a Summerlin. This photograph of the Summerlin clan was taken from the roof of the barn at Honeydew Ranch. (Courtesy of the Summerlin family.)

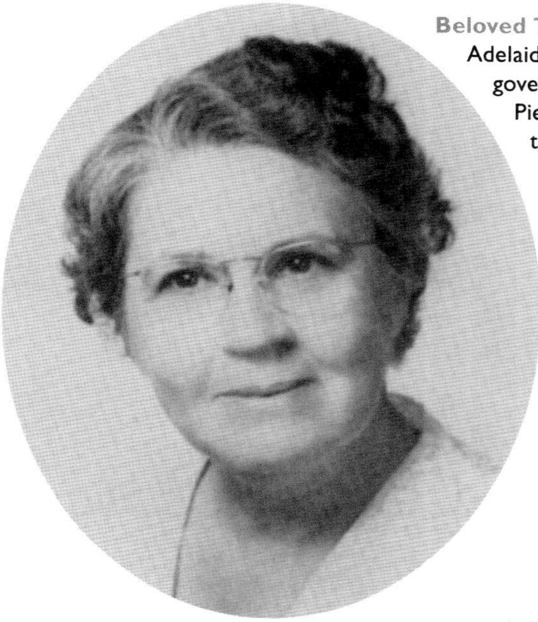

Beloved Teacher
Adelaide Summerlin Scharfschwerdt (1898–1994) taught government and history to three generations of Fort Pierce high schoolers. In the classroom from 1925 to 1968, she inspired her students with a love of country and set many on the road to a lifelong interest in history. She was widowed after only nine years of marriage when her husband, Otto Scharfschwerdt, was killed in a tractor accident. The oldest daughter of Edward and Mary Summerlin, she was valedictorian of the first class to hold graduation exercises in the yellow brick school. The 1958 *Santa Lucian* yearbook was dedicated to Adelaide Scharfschwerdt. (Courtesy of SLCRHC.)

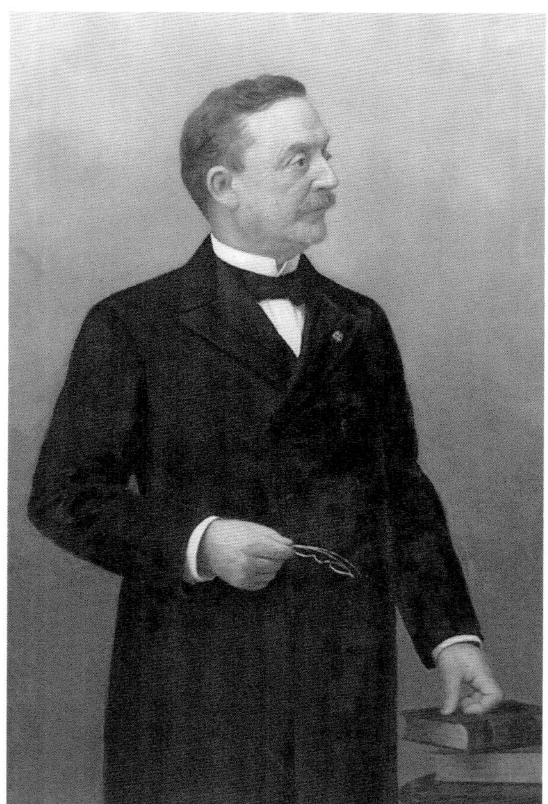

Machiavelli of the Gilded Age
Powerful and politically connected, Sen. Matthew Stanley Quay, of Pennsylvania, loved nothing better than to best a tarpon. Toward the end of the 19th century, he discovered a great spot to practice the sport of tarpon fishing near the Indian River Inlet across from Old St. Lucie. Initially boarding at Paine's Inn, Senator Quay bought property and built himself a house, then a fancier home. The first one burned in 1963, the second, built in 1899, still stands. For years, his cronies and political allies made the pilgrimage to the Fort Pierce area to fish, play poker, smoke cigars, and plot Republican victories. Benjamin Harrison owed his successful presidential election to Matt Quay, and Theodore Roosevelt owed his place as vice president in 1900—and, his subsequent presidency after the assassination of Pres. William McKinley—to Matt Quay. (Courtesy of the State Museum of Pennsylvania.)

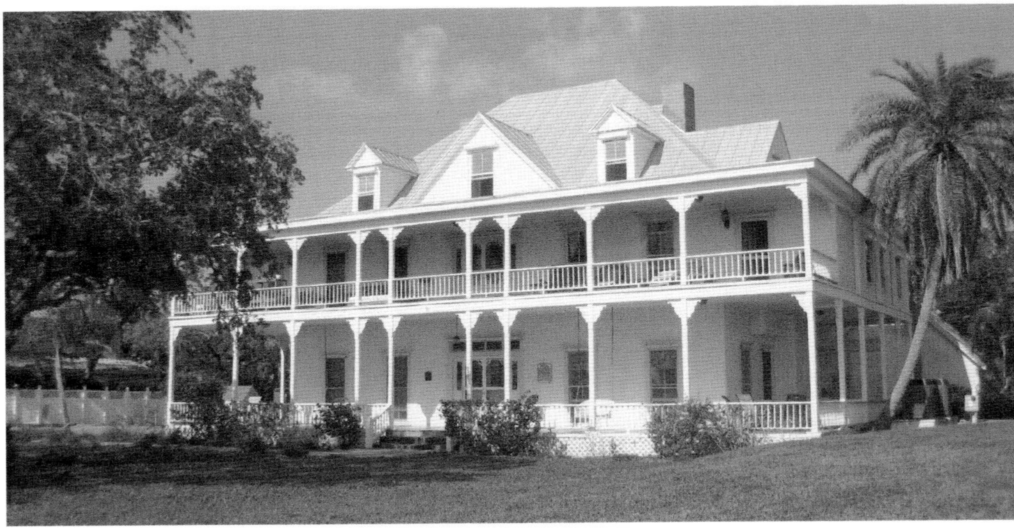

Playhouse for Pennsylvanians

The fishing grounds and hunting fields around Fort Pierce became a popular destination for Senator Quay's friends. In 1902, they built the imposing two-story St. Lucie Club. It was said that a tontine agreement resulted in ownership passing into the hands of US senator-elect William S. Vare, who was never seated as senator, judged to have employed improper means in garnering the win. As to the club, local gossip said the building was used to store illicit whiskey during Prohibition and there was the intermittent presence of fancy ladies. After passing through the hands of several owners, the club was restored and divided into apartments by Susan Grimes in 1989 and was purchased in 2012 by a pair of Californians, pictured here. Robin Hayhurst and Bruno Bornino are refining the restoration with historical integrity including furnishing it with period pieces. The building is listed in the National Register of Historic Places. (Both photographs by the author.)

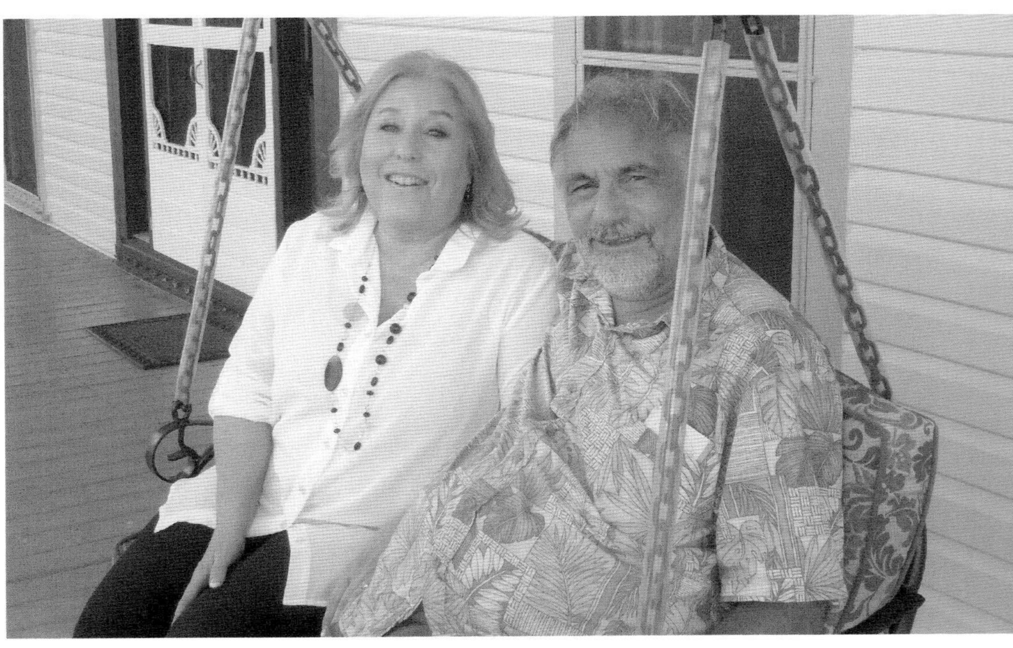

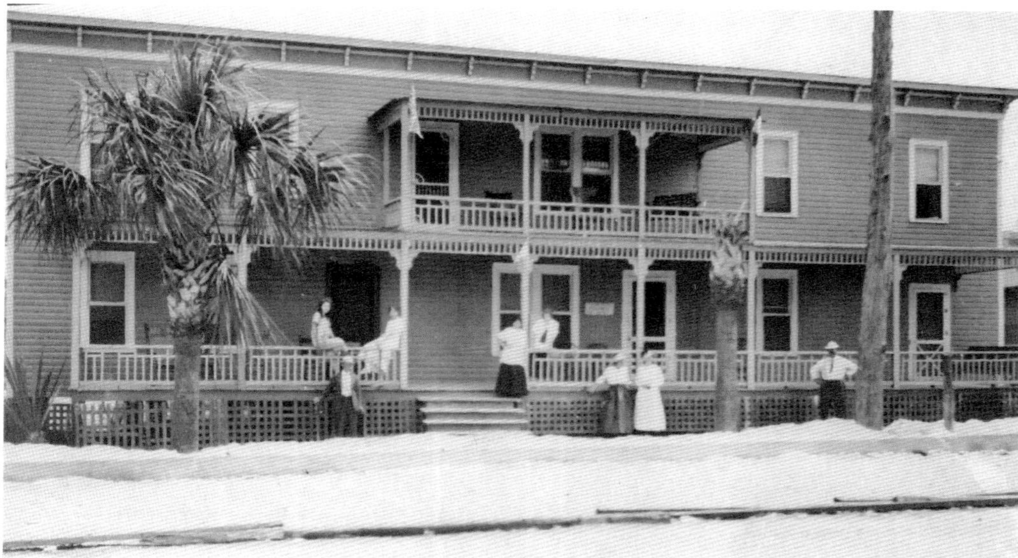

The French Canadian Connection

Joseph T. and Anna Lochapelle Archambault came to Fort Pierce from Canada in 1912. One of their first enterprises was to manage the Stetson Hotel. They are among the figures above on the hotel's porch. What looks like snow is sand. They invested in citrus property west of town. Through their daughter Armande, who married Conrad Forget, also a French Canadian, the Archambaults founded a citrus dynasty with many descendants still active today in agribusiness. They built and operated Forget's store at Okeechobee Road and King's Highway, an early convenience store for rural families. Busloads of farm workers stopped at Forget's before daylight to buy snacks for the long picking day ahead in the fields west of town. There were also small cabins where visiting Canadians might stay and where, during World War II, sailors' girlfriends and wives were housed. Three generations—the Archambault grandparents, the Forget parents, and the Forget children—worked in the store, and it served as a gathering place for all the Catholic families living west of Fort Pierce. (Both photographs courtesy of the Forget family.)

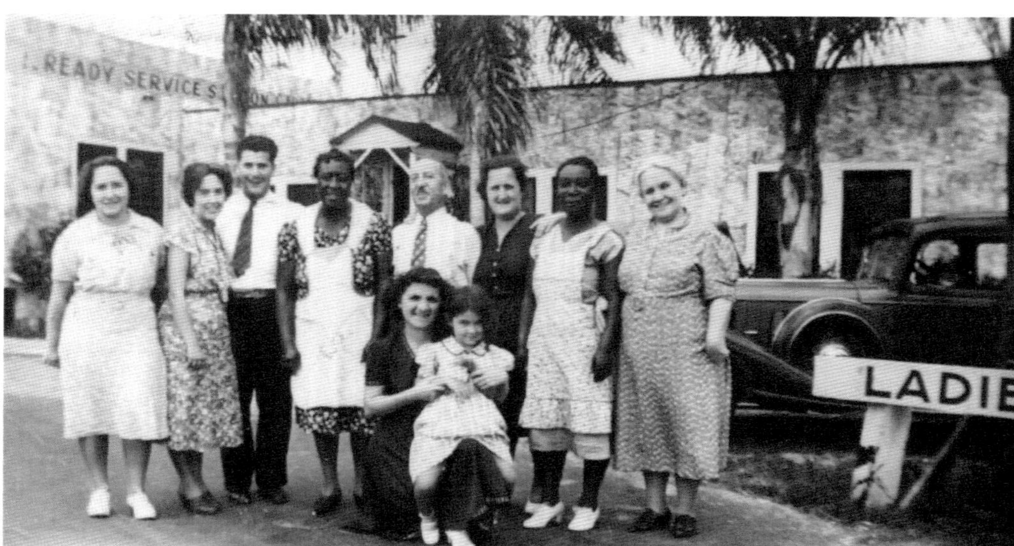

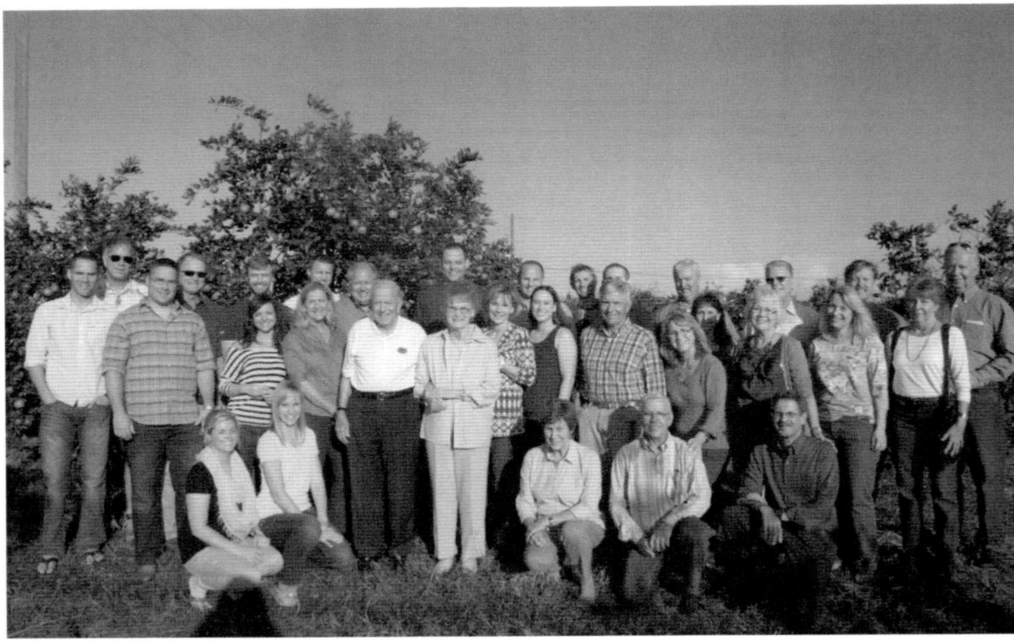

100 Years in Fort Pierce
Louis Forget, prominent businessman and grower, presided over the family's celebration of 100 years in the area in 2012. Louis and Jean Hancock were married by Fr. Michael Beerhalter, St. Anastasia Church's legendary priest, in 1949. (Photograph by the author.)

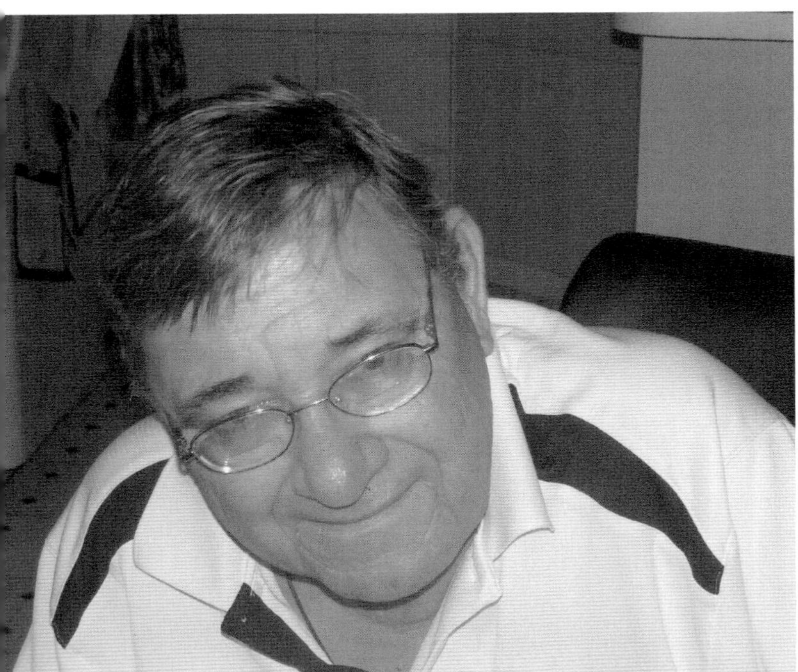

The Educator Priest
Fr. Michael Woodcock, beloved by the Fort Pierce Catholic community, was first assigned to St. Anastasia Parish as a newly ordained priest in 1973. Woodcock is the son of an English paratrooper killed in the D-Day invasion. Throughout his years here, Woodcock served this community as a pastor, teacher, principal, counselor, coach, and friend. A cot for Father Woodcock's rest sat for years at the old Fort Pierce Hospital, where he so regularly responded to calls at all hours to minister to the dead or dying of all religions. (Photograph by the author.)

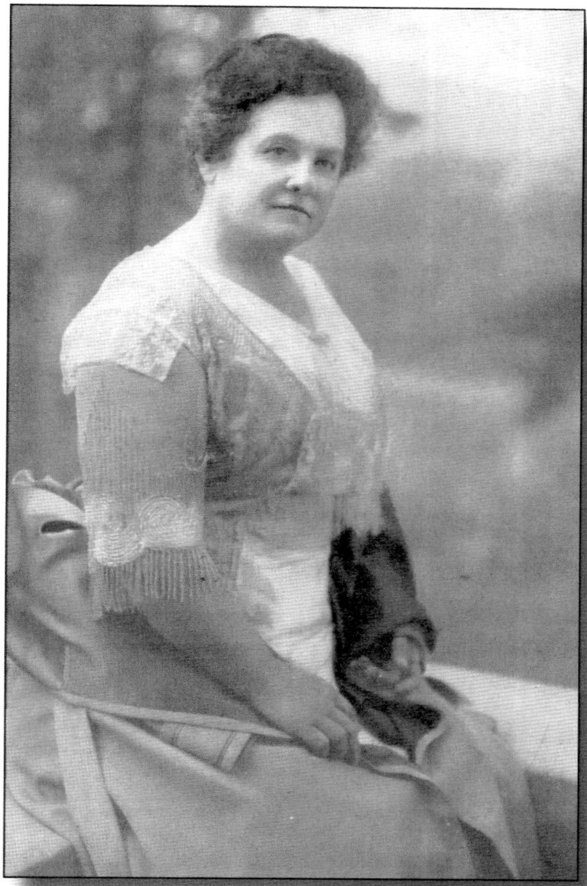

Ankona

Dr. John Fletcher Ankeny founded Ankona, south of Fort Pierce, in 1879. The Ankenys raised pineapples, and when that market faltered, switched to raising commercial ferns. Rose Ankeny Lewis (left), daughter of Peter Ankeny, who arrived in 1882, was a founding member of the local Cora Harper Chapter of the Daughters of the American Revolution. She was elected county school superintendent in 1924 and served as president of the Florida Federation of Women's Clubs for the 1917–1918 term. She was the first woman to serve on a state board in Florida—the board of managers for the Feeble Minded and Epileptic Colony at Gainesville. In the picture below, an unidentified member of the Ankeny family looks over a pineapple crop. (Courtesy of the SLCRHC.)

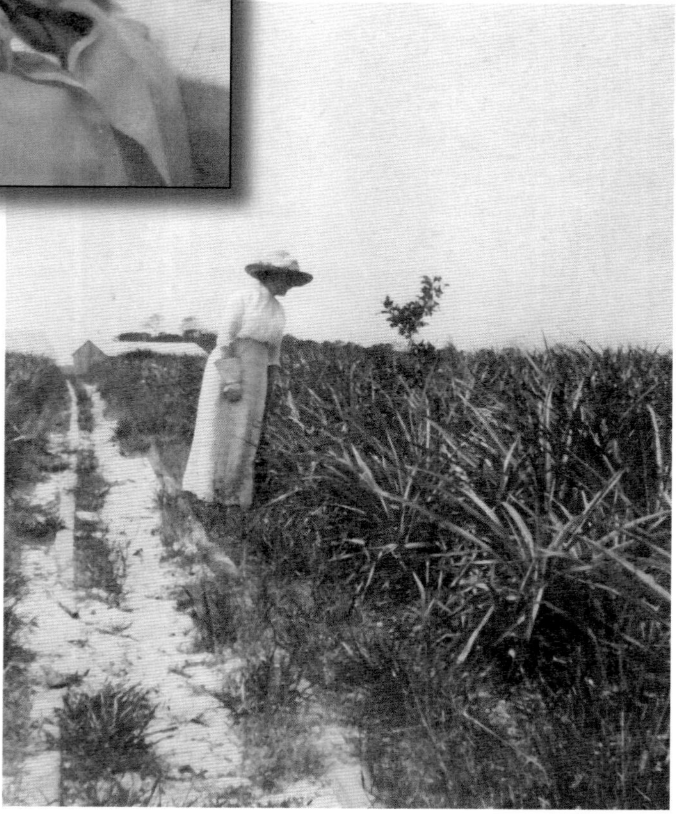

Away All Pests (BELOW AND OPPOSITE PAGE)
William Irwin Fee (1873–1958), "W.I." as he was called (opposite, top left), was the son of Francis Henry Fee (1850–1930), who came to Fort Pierce in 1902 from Melbourne to establish the Fort Pierce Bank. W.I. managed the Fee Hardware and Mortuary. He was a big booster of the booming town and a pioneer in mosquito control. The early settlers considered the mosquito a necessary evil and combated the swarms with netting and smudge pots. There was a time when everyone carried a palmetto switch to brush the pesky insects away. But W.I. Fee believed something could be done about it and sold the county on ditching to eliminate breeding grounds. He was president of the Florida Anti-Mosquito Association and a member of the National Malaria Commission. His leadership put Fort Pierce way ahead of other towns in eradicating mosquitoes, and Fee was in demand all over the state as a speaker to tell other tourist-hungry areas how to do it. W.I. Fee was also an avid historian. He founded the Old Timers Association for settlers who had come to the area before the railroad. He led a group that placed a marker on South Indian River Drive honoring the Florida Armed Occupation Act, and led another effort that resulted in identifying and marking the Okeechobee battlefield where colonel and then president Zachary Taylor fought the Seminoles under Bowlegs on Christmas Day 1837.

The continuity of this old Fort Pierce family is remarkable. Just two blocks west of the old Fee building at the northwest corner of Avenue A and Second Street are the law offices of Frank H. Fee III and Frank H. Fee IV (opposite, top right). On the walls of their office conference room hang the portraits of Attorney Frank Fee II (1913–1983), who represented St. Lucie County in the state legislature (opposite, bottom right), and his father, Attorney Fred Fee (1880–1939), who also had offices in downtown Fort Pierce (opposite, bottom left). (Opposite, clockwise from upper left, courtesy of Bonnie Fee Ludlum, Tom Baumker, Frank Fee III, SLCRHC; below, SLCRHC.)

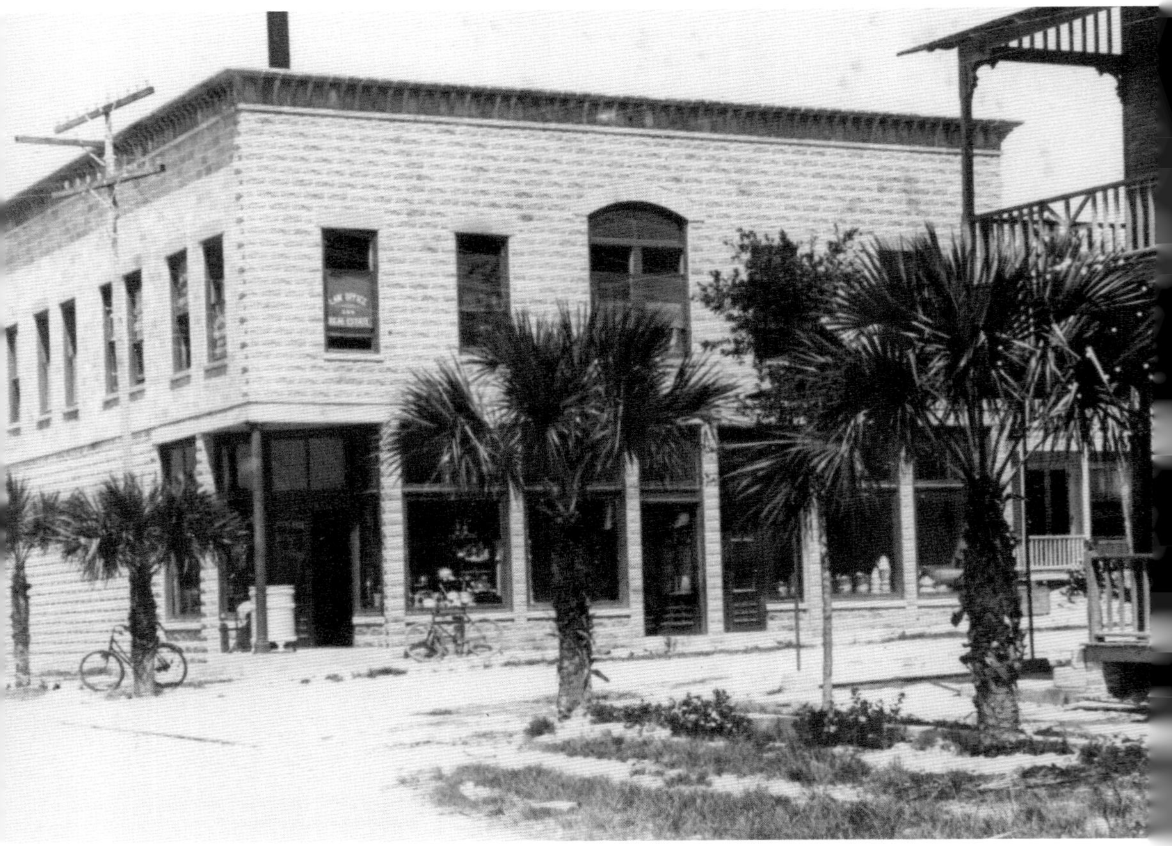

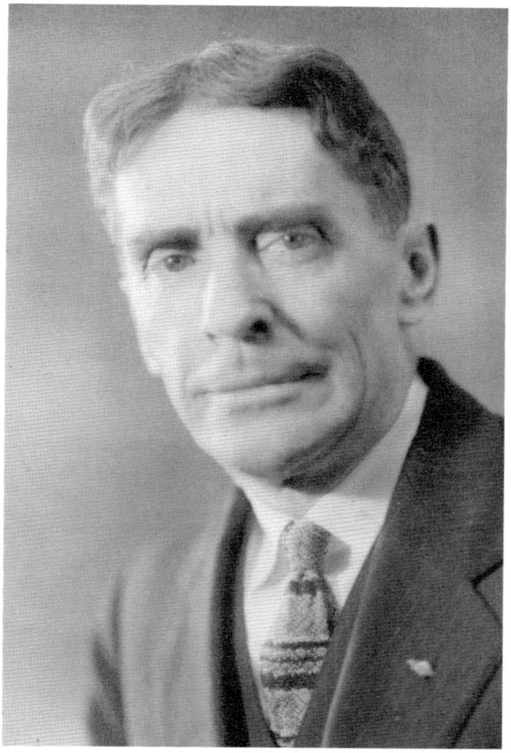

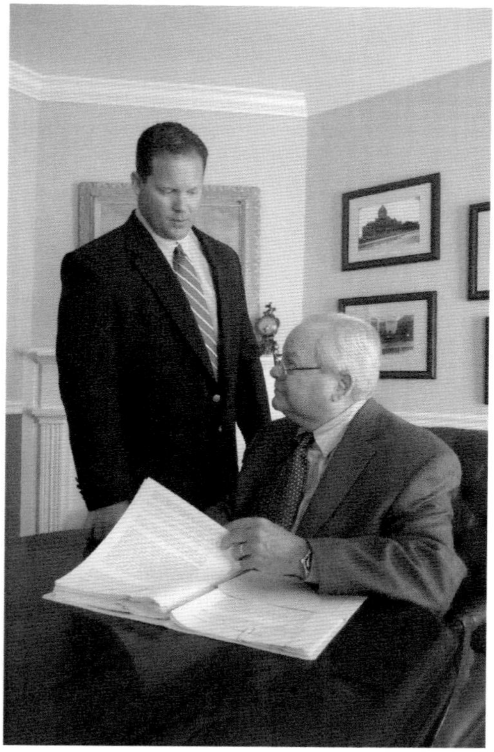

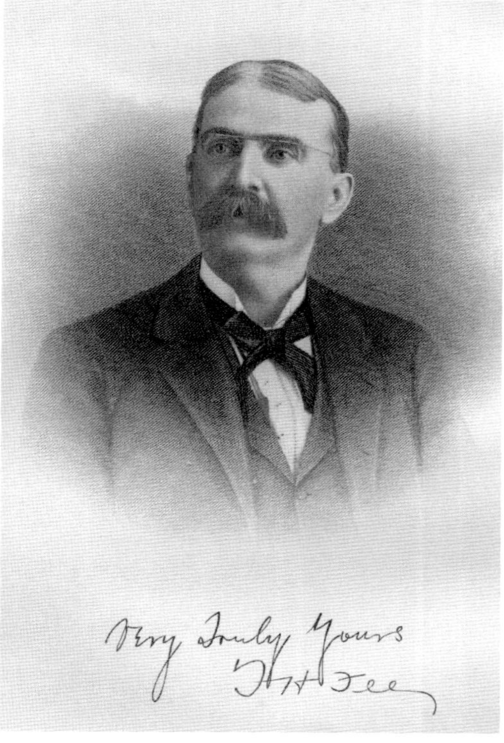
Very Truly Yours

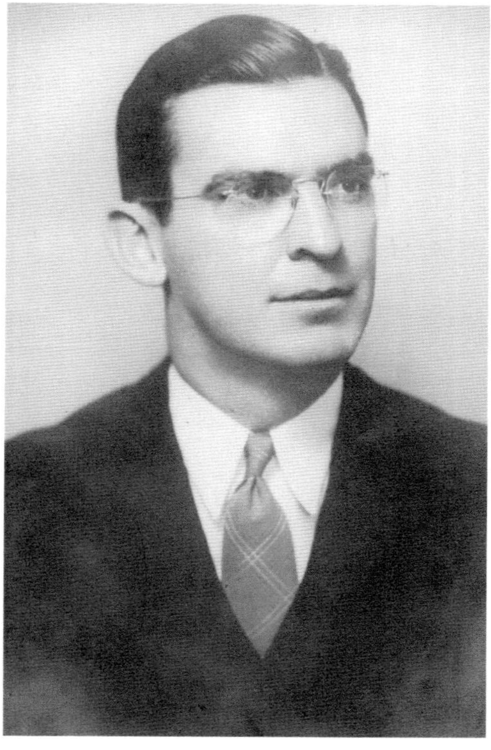

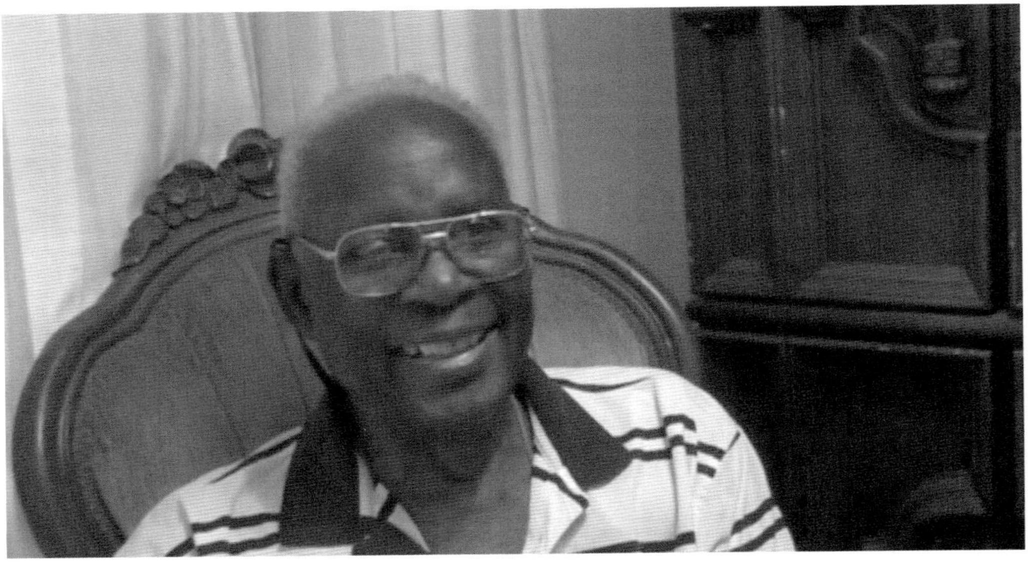

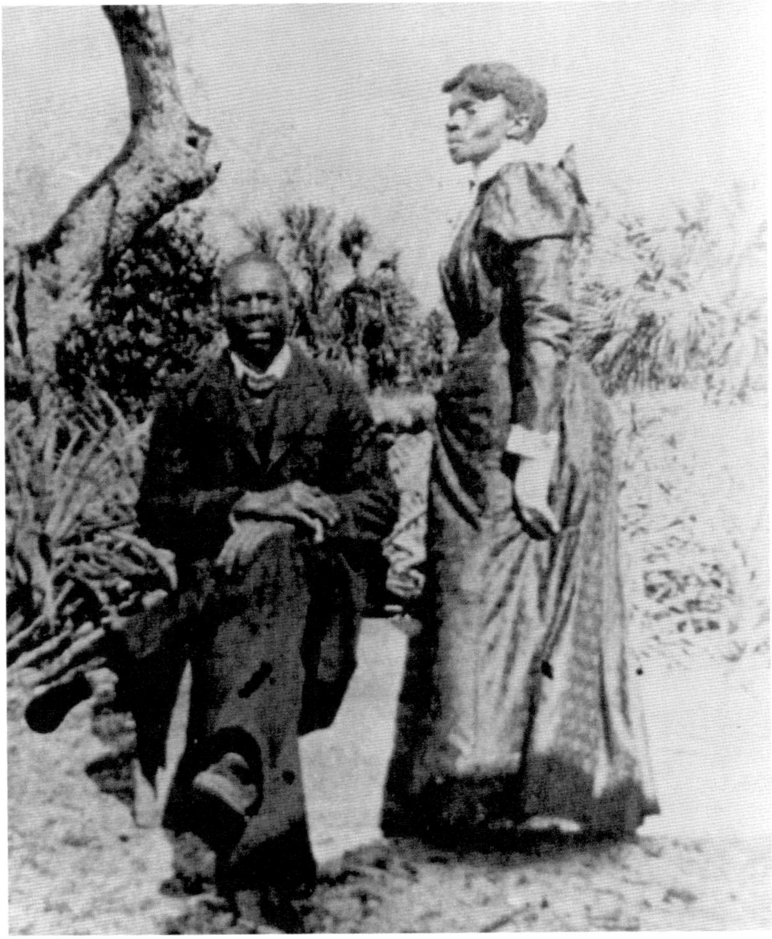

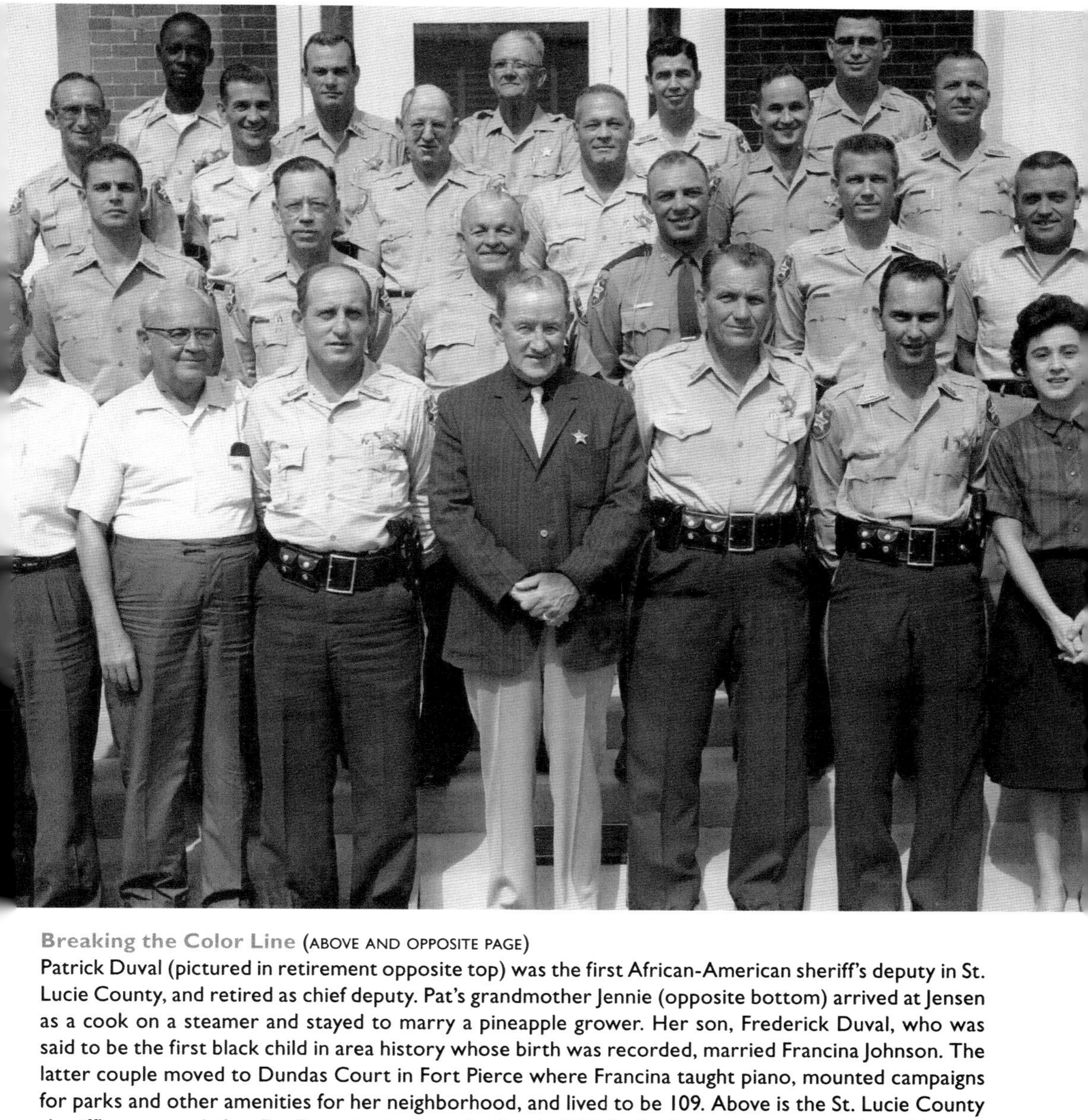

Breaking the Color Line (ABOVE AND OPPOSITE PAGE)
Patrick Duval (pictured in retirement opposite top) was the first African-American sheriff's deputy in St. Lucie County, and retired as chief deputy. Pat's grandmother Jennie (opposite bottom) arrived at Jensen as a cook on a steamer and stayed to marry a pineapple grower. Her son, Frederick Duval, who was said to be the first black child in area history whose birth was recorded, married Francina Johnson. The latter couple moved to Dundas Court in Fort Pierce where Francina taught piano, mounted campaigns for parks and other amenities for her neighborhood, and lived to be 109. Above is the St. Lucie County sheriff's personnel after Pat Duval broke the color line in 1953. In the first row, center, is Johnny Norvell, long-time sheriff; to his left is his son, Lanie, who succeeded him as sheriff and held that office until 1984. (Above and opposite bottom, courtesy of SLCRHC; opposite top, photograph by the author.)

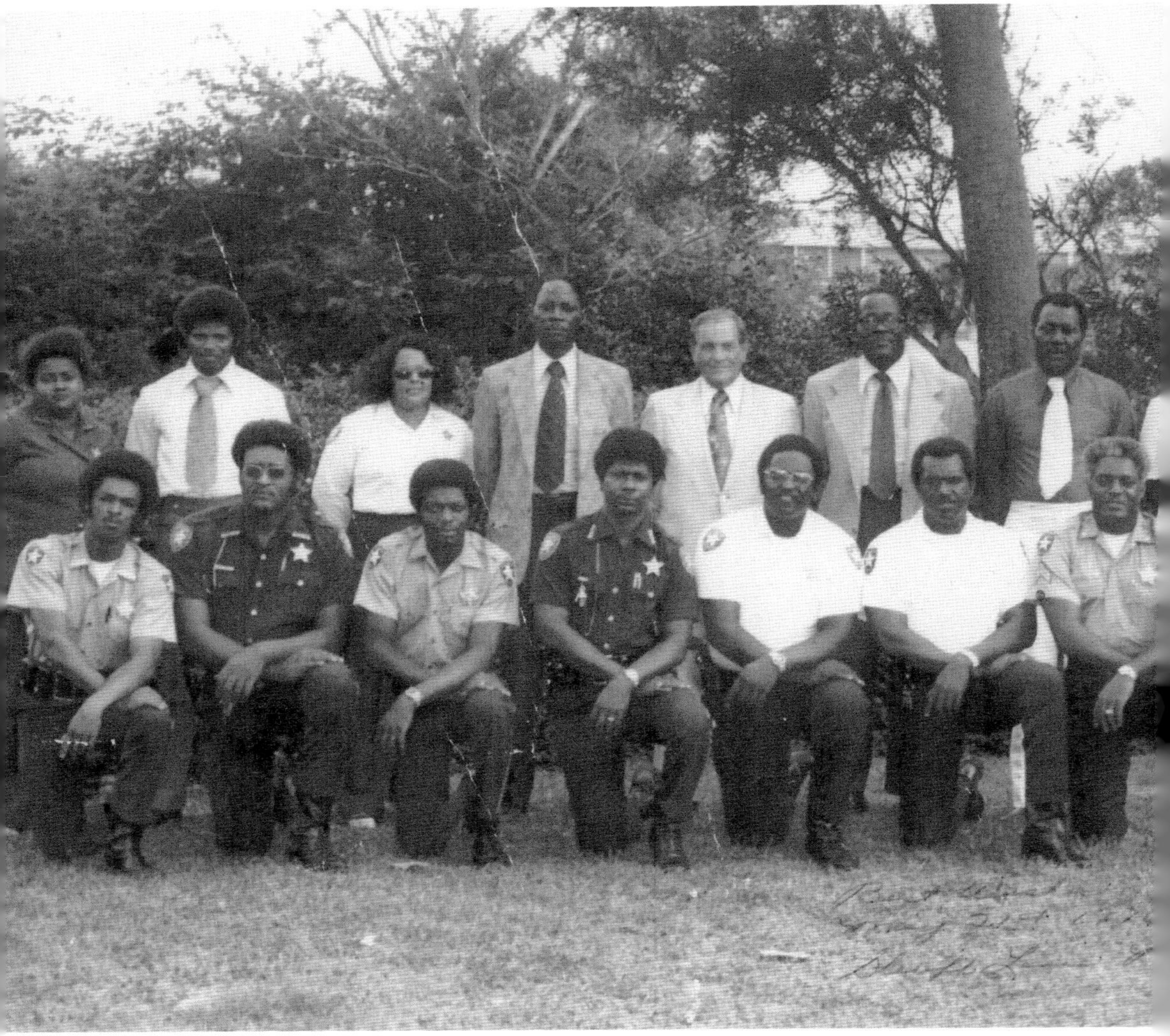

Community Law Enforcement

By the 1960s, the personnel of the sheriff's deputy force more nearly reflected the racial makeup of the community. From left to right are (first row) Percy Brumsley, Lt. Goodson, Frank Smith, Canthony Thomas, Al Washington, Willie Williams, and Eddie Whitfield; (second row) Phyllis Powell, Jimmy Robinson, Margaret Jenkins, Captain Duval, Sheriff Norvell, Deacon Richardson, Wilbert Boatright, and Mally Mae Whitfield. (Courtesy of Eddie Whitfield.)

CHAPTER THREE

Development

Finally, Fort Pierce became a permanent settlement when incorporated in 1901. It continued to have saloons and shootouts, but Carrie Nation visited, an Anti-Saloon League was formed, and churches multiplied. The town became a commercial center where the more affluent ladies from Indian River Drive could buy their hats, where farmers could buy plows and seed, and where housewives could buy salt and canned goods The boom of the 1920s brought a surge of boosterism, construction, and rum-runners amidst the wave of population enticed to Florida by real estate riches. Two visionary entrepreneurs built the foundations of Fort Pierce prosperity: Edwin Binney and R.N. "Pop" Koblegard.

Other "capitalists," as they were unashamedly called in those days, planted the roots of a new generation of old-timers. The Enns developed Maravilla and purchased the newspaper, the Gladwins prospered at Fort Pierce Farms, and Reverend Stone established Stone's Funeral Home.

Alas, the doldrums hit town with the killer hurricane of 1926 followed by the bust of 1928 and the Great Depression of 1929. The grafters and the short-termers deserted; others stuck it out. Curiously, a similar pattern was repeated in the first years of the 21st century. Hurricane Frances hit Fort Pierce on September 5, 2004, followed by Hurricane Jeanne on September 25. A boom in real estate saw housing prices soar in 2005; eager buyers had to search for places for sale, and investors flipped properties and realized inordinate profits. Then came the bust of 2007–2008: residents found themselves in homes with mortgages in excess of value. Fort Pierce found itself having record foreclosures coupled with record unemployment. Local banks were taken over by the government. The city fathers had joined the speculation and faced years of interest payments on land purchased at the high dollar mark of the real estate frenzy.

There Ought to be a Statue

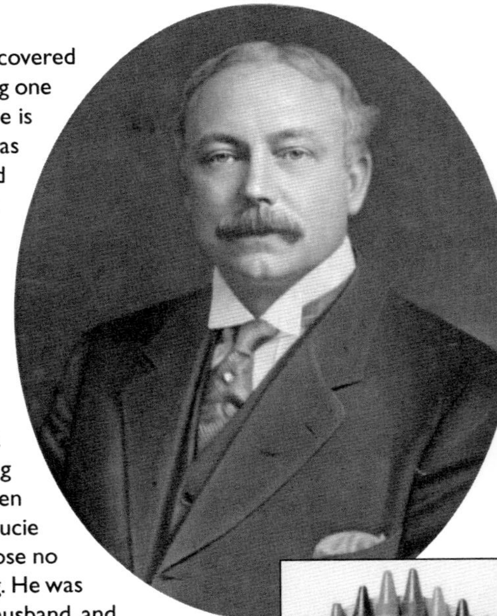

Edwin Binney, the inventor and manufacturer of Crayola, discovered Fort Pierce from the deck of his yacht in 1911. In spite of being one of Fort Pierce's greatest benefactors, the only place his name is remembered is Binney Drive. After his initial visit to what was then a sleepy little village, Binney returned to invest his talent and some of his fortune in its future. His vision included the finest port between Jacksonville and Miami and a beautiful waterfront. He accomplished the former, but local leadership spurned his beautification ideas as well as his offer to donate a modern hospital. So, he took his largesse and built Binney Park in Old Greenwich, Connecticut. Undeterred by local opposition, he made "his beloved Fort Pierce" home. Regardless of business demands in New York or Pennsylvania or family obligations in Old Greenwich, he would come south to vote. He built a home, Florindia, north of town and raised prize-winning citrus on part of his considerable real estate holdings. When the Depression came, Binney stood at the door of the St. Lucie County Bank and assured panicked depositors they would lose no money, and used his own funds to keep the bank from closing. He was a sportsman, visionary, an inventor, a doting father, devoted husband, and humanitarian—the best of good men—and he had a lovely singing voice.

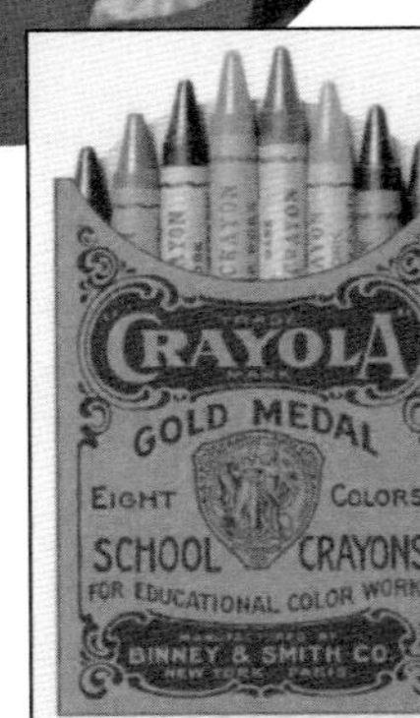

Alice Binney put the French name for chalk, *craie*, with *ola* for "oily" to create the name "Crayola." She was a talented musician and composer and is pictured below at her grand piano with an unidentified companion. She loved flowers and nature and worked alongside her husband and children to save soul-satisfying landscapes and build parks. She purchased the historic Casa Caprona apartments north of Fort Pierce; among her guests was Amelia Earhart. She coined the name "Indrio" for a luxurious city planned but never built. Years later, what remained after "the bust" were sidewalks and streetlights in the weeds, and the name Indrio Road. (All, courtesy of Sally Putnam Chapman.)

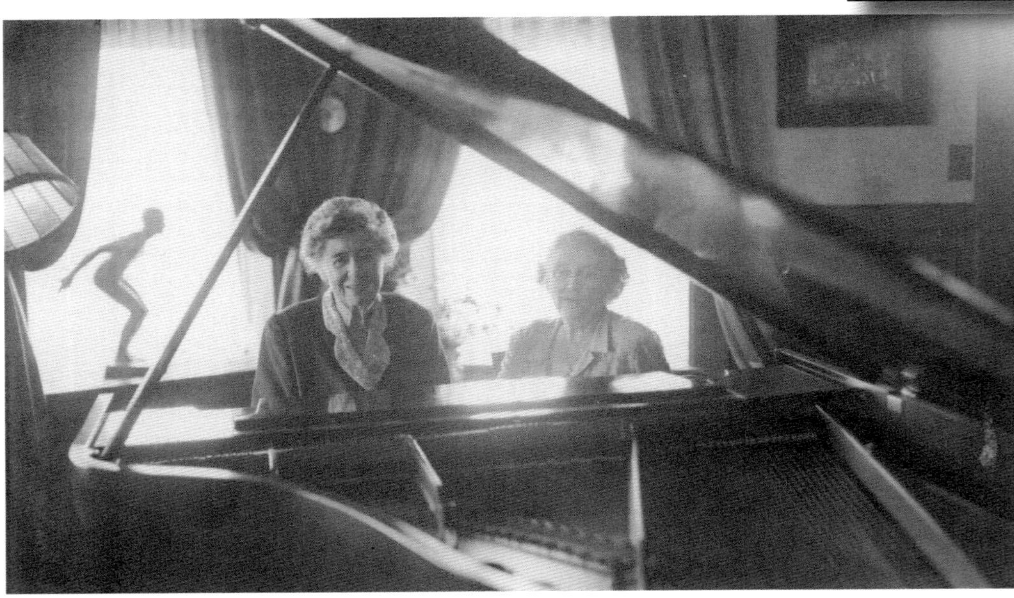

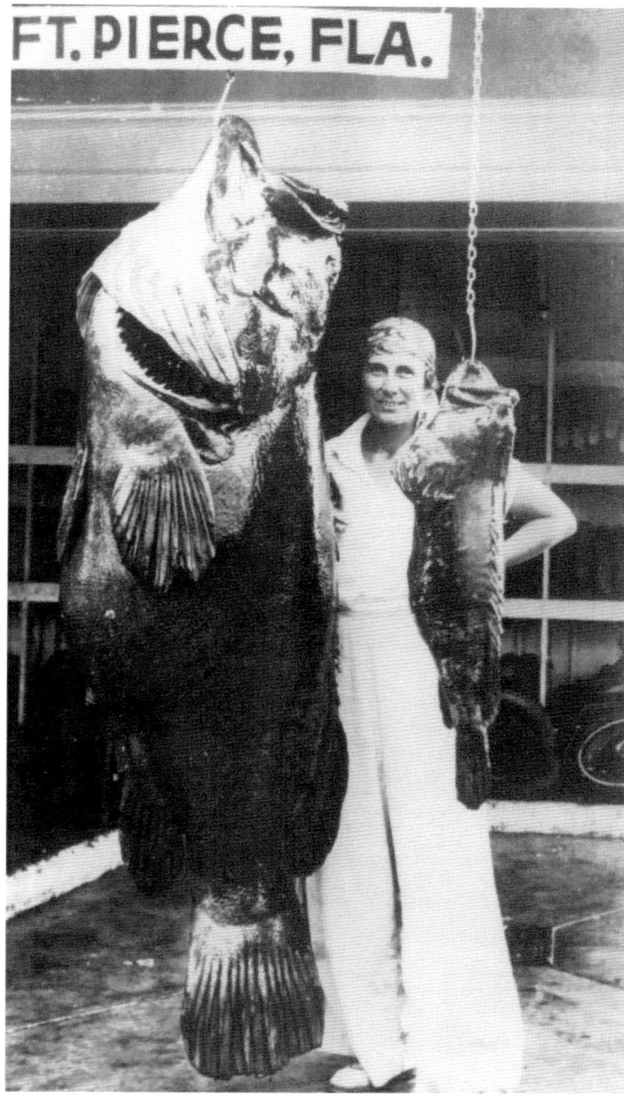

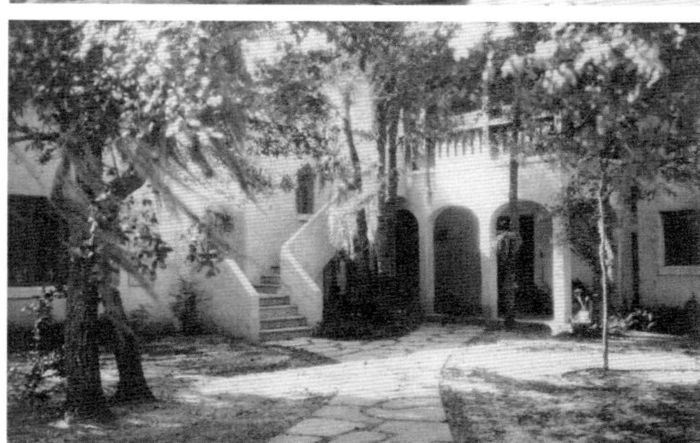

Ah, But She Was a Great Lady
Dorothy Binney Putnam dubbed herself "DDD" for "Devoted Daughter Dorothy." Once the wife of publisher George Putnam, she moved south to make her home in Fort Pierce after her parents relocated there. She built Immokolee, a mansion in a hammock west of town. A champion swimmer, she built a pool above her garage and insisted that guests, including especially invited children's groups like the newspaper boys, learn to swim. Taking her father's charitable lessons to heart, she quietly helped all kinds of local people. Loving nature, even snakes, she nurtured all living things in her purview. This woman, who had traveled the world, set records climbing mountains, participated in scientific expeditions, and done all manner of sophisticated things, became a vital force in the small community of Fort Pierce. She lent her considerable talent to work in the service of the local garden club and wrote a nature column for the local newspaper. She encouraged local artists. She founded the first local Audubon Society in her adopted town and was godmother to the original Sea Scout Troop founded by Edwin Binney. Auntie Mame was a piker next to Dorothy as an example to youngsters—primarily her beloved sons, David and George, and her eight grandchildren, but also many local boys and girls. In the top image, Dorothy Binney Putnam is standing next to an impressive catch, a giant sea bass. Pictured at the bottom is the enchanting entrance to Immokolee. (Both, courtesy of Sally Putnam Chapman.)

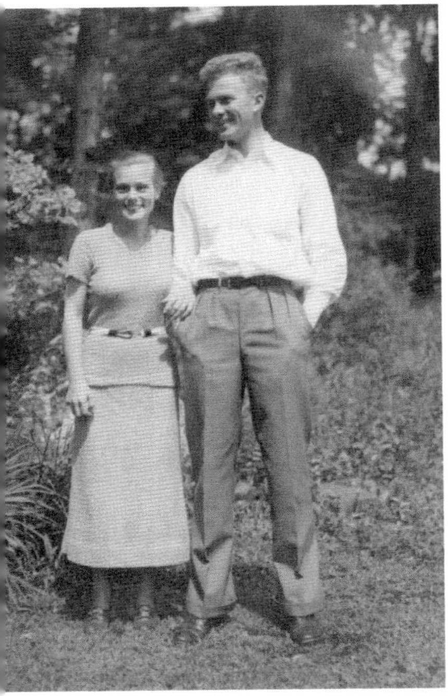

A Very Young Author

David Putnam met Nilla Shields while visiting his mother, Dorothy Binney Putnam, at Fort Pierce at the same time Nilla, a Georgia girl, was visiting a friend. For both of them, it was love at first sight, and they married immediately. David's adventurous life began when, as a youngster, he joined scientific expeditions sponsored by the New York Natural History Museum and wrote about them to become a celebrated juvenile author. He became interested in aviation as a young man, learning to fly as a result of his association with Amelia Earhart, whom his father, George Putnam, sponsored in her famous transatlantic flight and eventually married. David traveled with the famous aviatrix as aide and sometime bodyguard as she prepared for her second flight. He and Nilla had their last glimpse of Amelia when they saw her take off at Miami and David stayed at his father's side in the long days of searching for her lost plane. David's skill as a pilot was put to good use in World War II; when discharged as a lieutenant colonel, he came home to become a businessman and entrepreneur. Among his many ventures were Putnam Mercantile, Fort Pierce Airways, the Ford Tractor agency, real estate, a newspaper, an ice cream factory, and much more. He and Nilla had four children, Binney, Sally, David, and Douglas, who later became the St. Lucie County property appraiser. (Courtesy of Sally Putnam Chapman.)

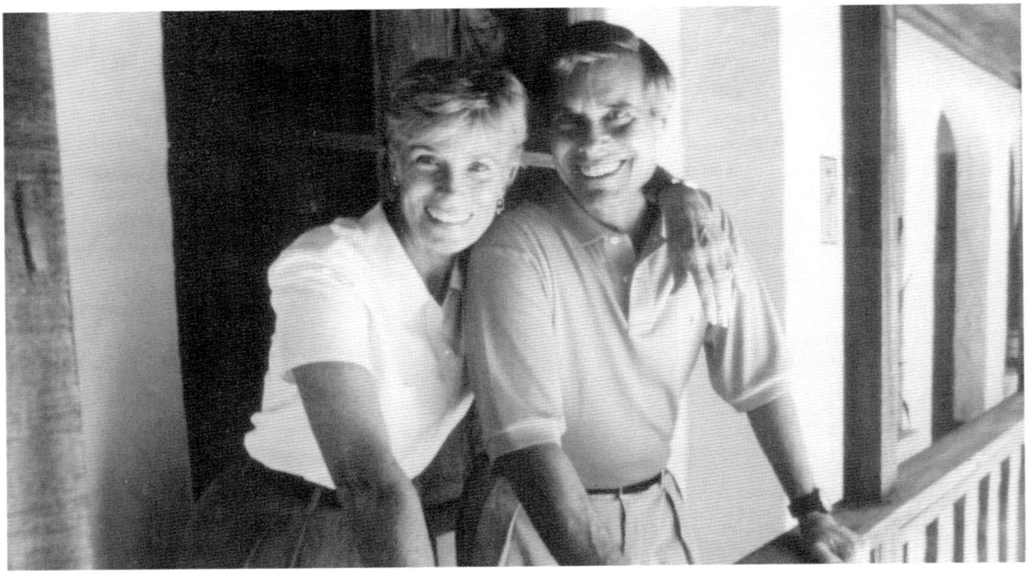

Homage to Dofry

Sally Putnam Chapman, the daughter of David and Nilla, was chosen by her grandmother "Dofry" to take possession of her diaries and other papers and share the most intimate scenes from the older woman's fascinating life. The result was *Whistled Like a Bird*, a biography of Dorothy Binney Putnam and the story of the Binney and Putnam clans. The Chapmans restored Immokolee, Dorothy's home, with all its intrinsic treasures, including art by Don Blanding, the landscaping planted by Dorothy, and the views from the windows that are like paintings. The estate is now listed in the National Register of Historic Places and is often the venue for charitable events. Sally is pictured with her husband, Jack, (Courtesy of Sally Putnam Chapman.)

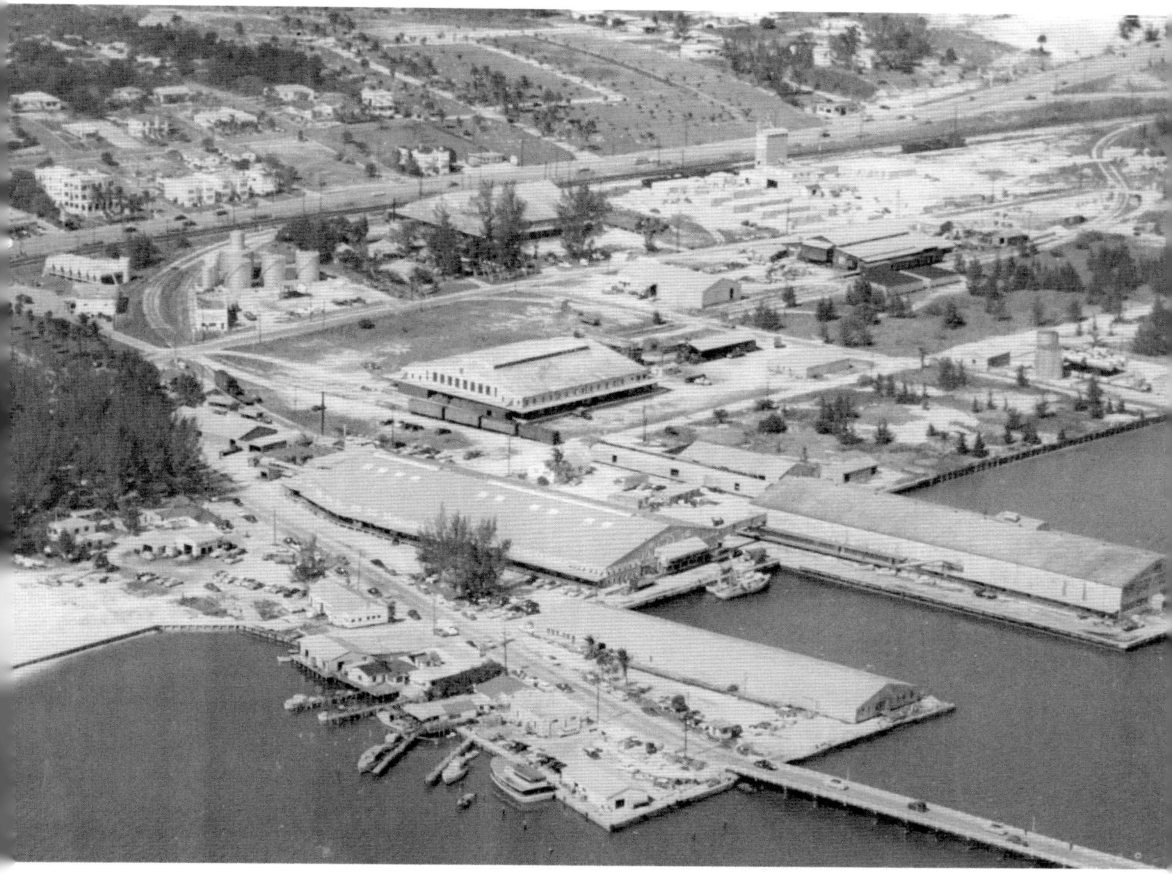

The Once-busy Port at Fort Pierce
Edwin Binney died on December 17, 1934, at Gainesville, Florida, en route to Fort Pierce. He never got to see the port with the refrigeration plant completed, as pictured here. Convinced that mankind needed beauty, even around the workplace, Binney consistently urged the local government to landscape the approach to the industrial area. In the end, what was done, he did himself. Note the line of Washington palms marking the road into the port at upper left. Binney directed and paid for the planting of these trees, five of which are standing today after withstanding several severe hurricanes in the intervening years. (Courtesy of Sally Putnam Chapman.)

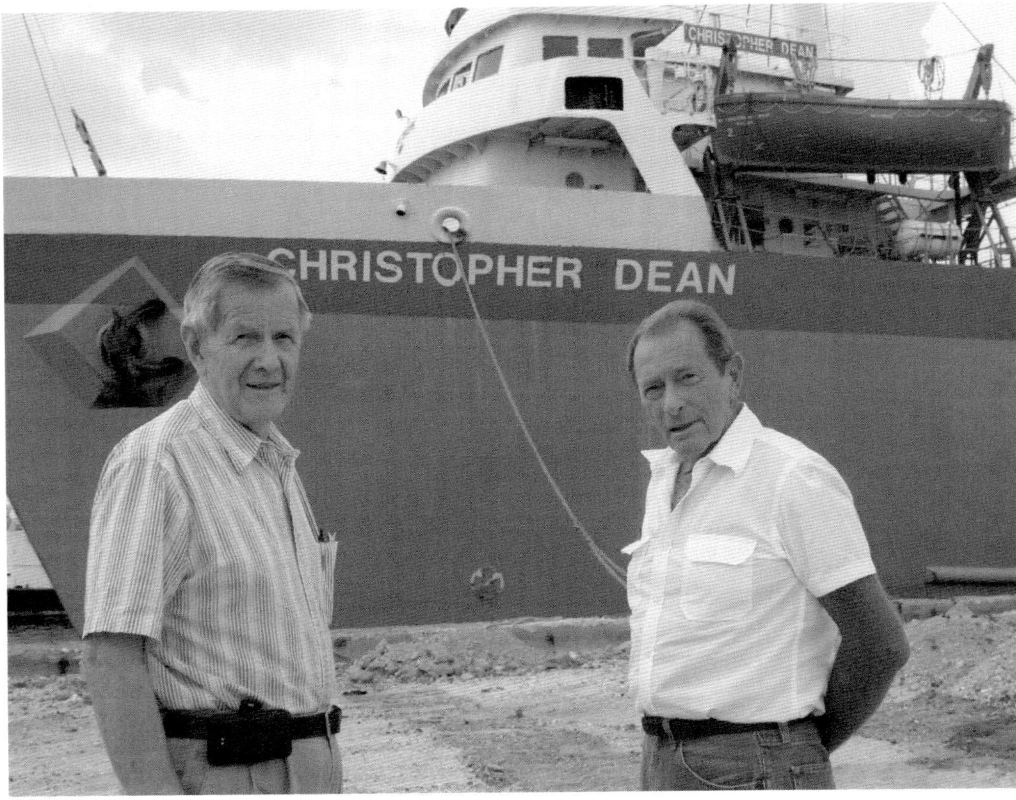

The Port of Fort Pierce, Resting
Dean King (right), chief executive officer of King Maritime Group, is pictured with Kenneth Roberts (left), the organization's Fort Pierce agent, and the ship *Christopher Dean* is in the background. Roberts has been knowledgeable and fair in working with local government entities. The *Christopher Dean* has a history of regularly scheduled trips to the Bahamas and the Caribbean islands. Port activities have been temporarily reduced while innovative owner Dean King contemplates future business directions. The port is a symbol of the conflict of interest plaguing Fort Pierce and many other places: how to balance jobs and the environment. (Photograph by Tom Baumker.)

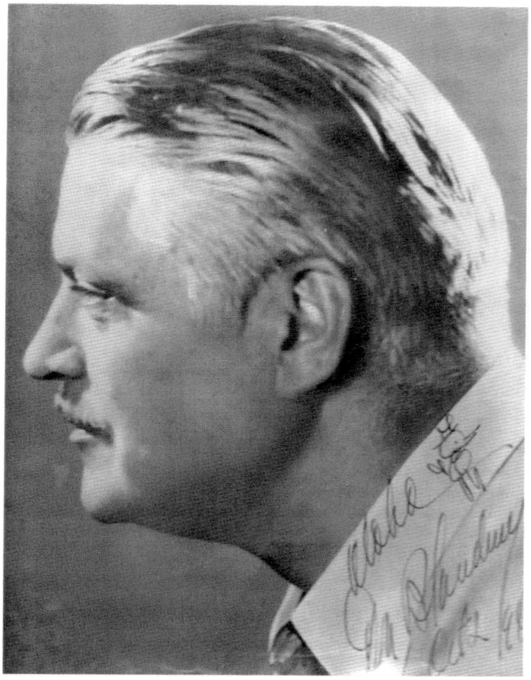

Floridays

What brought urbane Don Blanding—artist, designer, and poet laureate of Hawaii—to pause his wandering life for a time in small-town Fort Pierce in the days leading up to Pearl Harbor? It was his friend, Dorothy Binney Putnam. While there, he wrote and illustrated *Floridays*, a book full of Fort Pierce scenery that was dedicated to Dorothy. He also wrote a newspaper column and befriended a young artist, Beanie Backus. (Courtesy of the SLCRHC.)

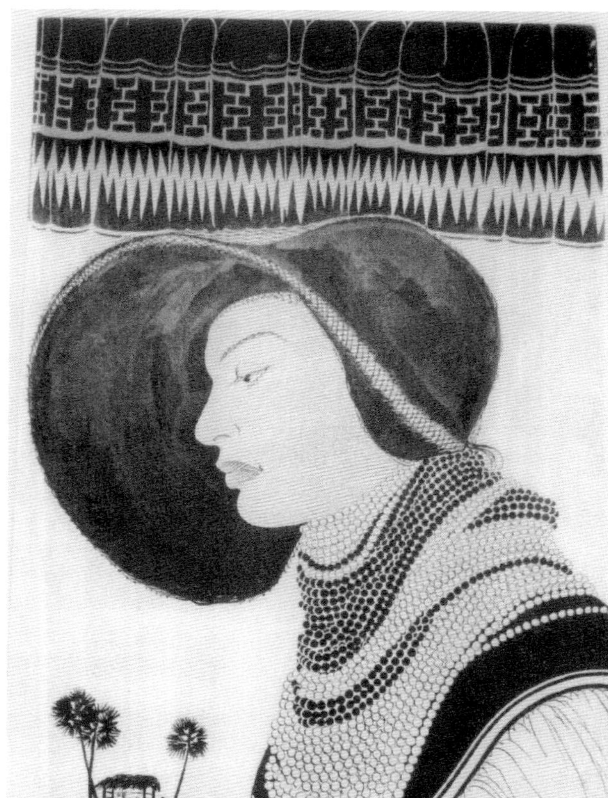

Serene and Seminole

The original of this portrait, included in *Floridays*, hangs in the library of the St. Lucie County Regional History Center. In the early days, travelers remarked at the reticence of Seminole women. Fear of the white man, Seminole tradition, and, mostly, the fact that they neither spoke nor understood English makes it a wonder that interlopers looked on their retiring ways as odd. (Photograph by Tom Baumker, artist Don Blanding.)

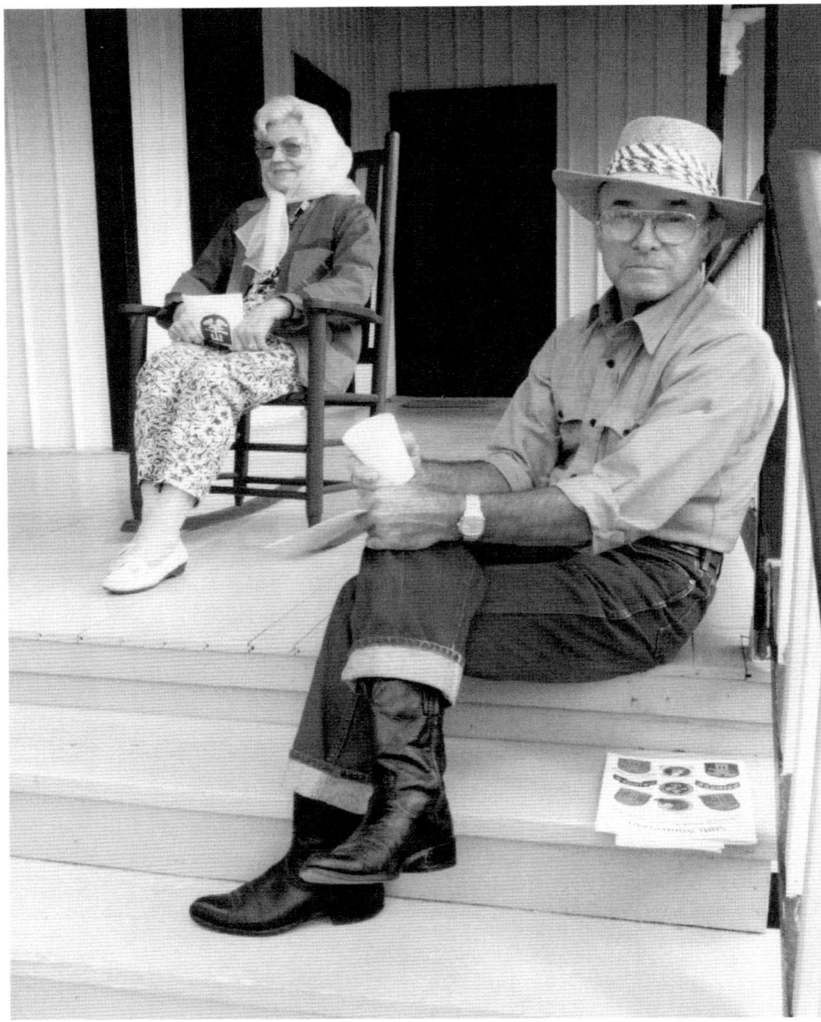

Building Postwar Fort Pierce

O.C. "Pete" Peterson and his wife, Olive Dame Peterson, are on the porch of the restored Gardner house that is part of the St. Lucie County Regional History Center complex. A Wisconsin boy turned World War II flight navigator, Pete first came to Fort Pierce on leave with his pilot, David B. Putnam, in 1942. After the war, Pete came to visit David and decided to make Fort Pierce his home. He joined lifelong friend David in several business enterprises. He married Olive Dame, a war widow and daughter of distinguished Judge Flem C. Dame. Pete became a successful contractor, and many structures in the area testify to his good work. Olive wrote two books about her childhood friend A.E. "Beanie" Backus, a renowned Florida artist. She and Pete were charter members of the St. Lucie Historical Society, and Olive was president of the Florida Historical Society. She named the streets in one of her husband's developments for Spanish explorers of Florida. Pete has served on the school board and the contractor's licensing board. He is a pilot, boat builder, cabinet-maker, and ironworker—he can do almost anything with his hands and has donated countless hours of craftsmanship to the education and beautification of the community, such as the cracker house at Heathcote Botanical Gardens. He did work for Judge Alto Adams, including the judge's impressive library. Never a week goes by that he doesn't visit his best friend Bud Adams. (Photograph by Tom Baumker.)

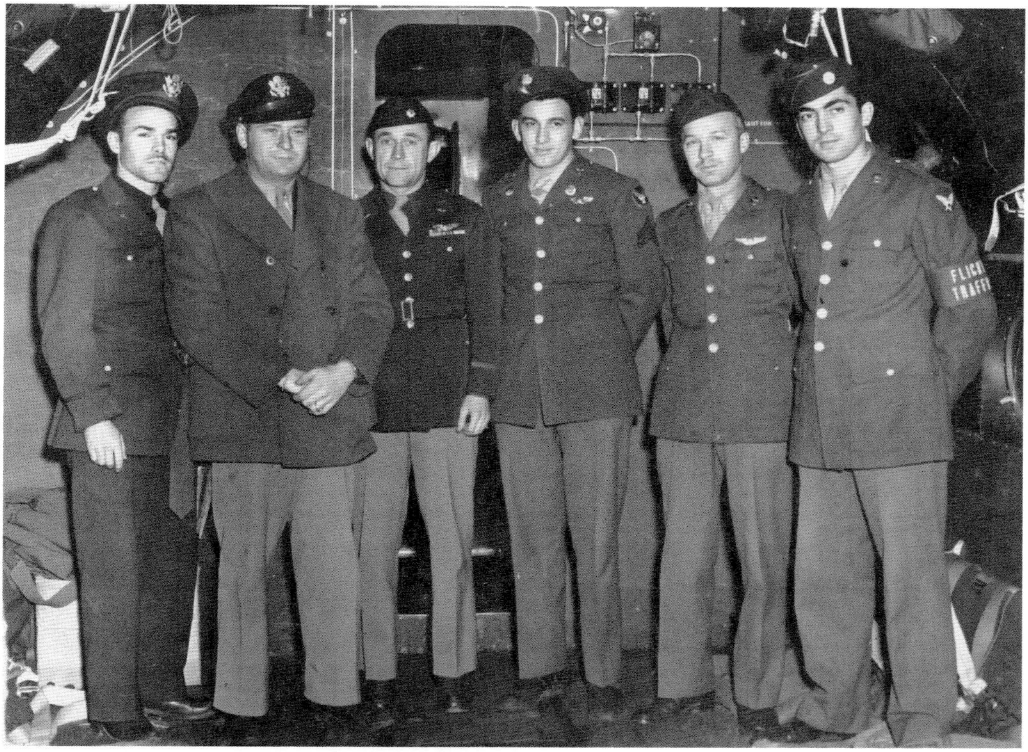

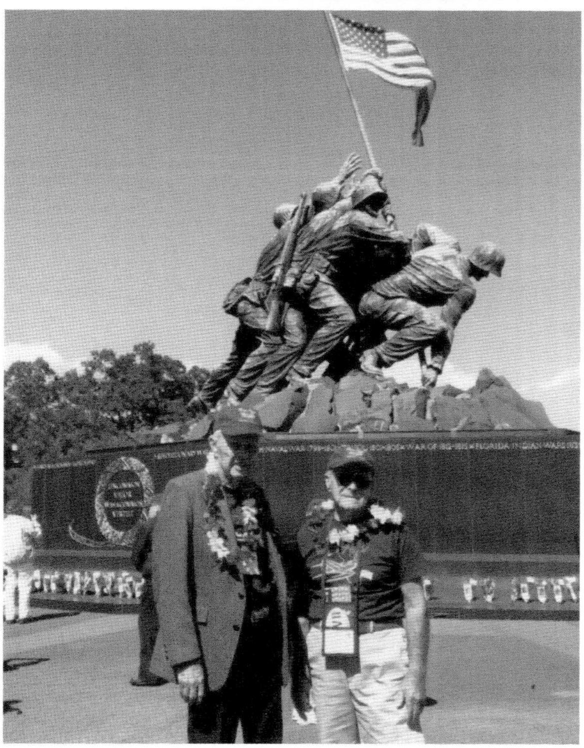

Pete Peterson and Bud Adams
Pictured above is the crew of the first C-54 to fly war wounded over the well-known "Crescent Caravan" route from France to the headquarters of the 2nd Ferrying Group near New Castle, Delaware, in January 1944. O.C. "Pete" Peterson is at the far left. At left, Pete Peterson and Bud Adams are in Washington, DC, during a visit in 2013 courtesy of Honor Flight. (Both, courtesy of O.C. Peterson.)

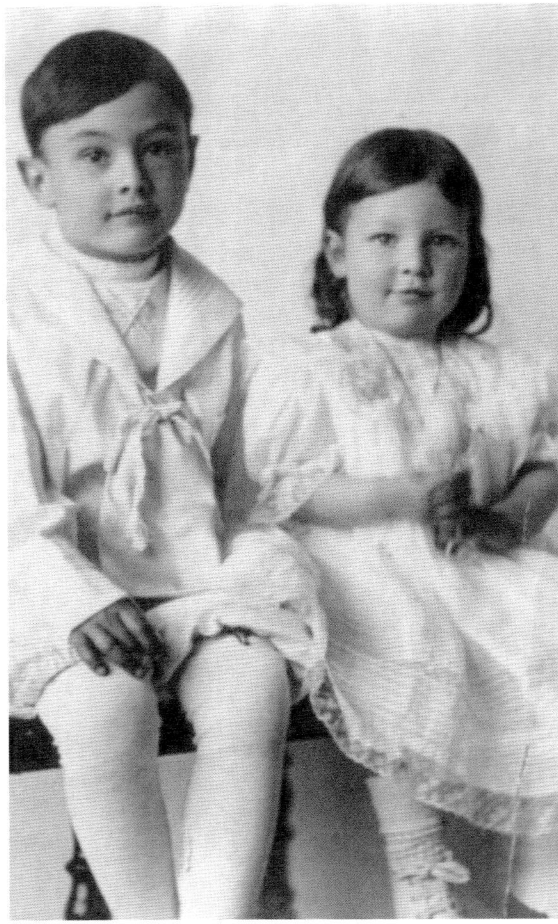

Capitalists Welcome

R.N. Koblegard came to Fort Pierce in 1906 in search of a climate that would nurture his disease-plagued son Ruhl. Already operating successful wholesale food businesses in West Virginia and Washington, DC, he saw the potential of Florida agriculture. He bought large, low tracts that he drained and sold to would-be farmers—Fort Pierce Farms. He built the Sunrise Theatre in 1922, which was turned over to his son Rupert (right) to manage, and he did so with a masterful flair for promotion. Ruhl (left) concentrated on real estate and insurance. (Courtesy of the Koblegard family.)

The Sample Line

Here is young Rupert with his wife, Mary Sample Koblegard. Mary was from a prominent pioneer Fort Pierce family that originated in North Carolina. Adrian Sample came to Fort Pierce to establish a fishing business and was followed by brothers John and Harry. Harry owned and operated an early theater showing silent movies. Among the Sample progeny who made local legendary status are two judges, Jack and Wallace, and Dr. Adrian Sample. (Courtesy of the Koblegard family.)

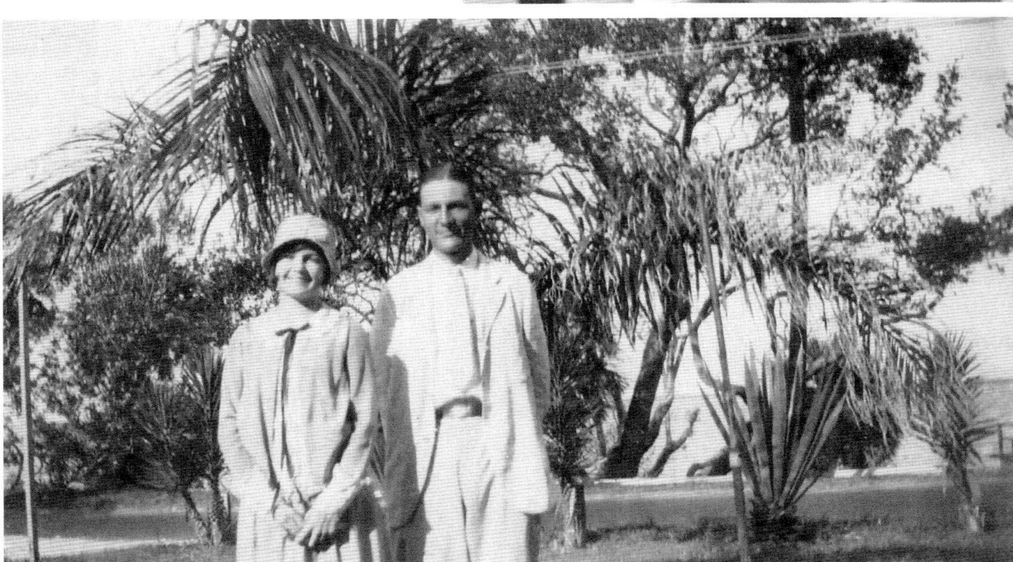

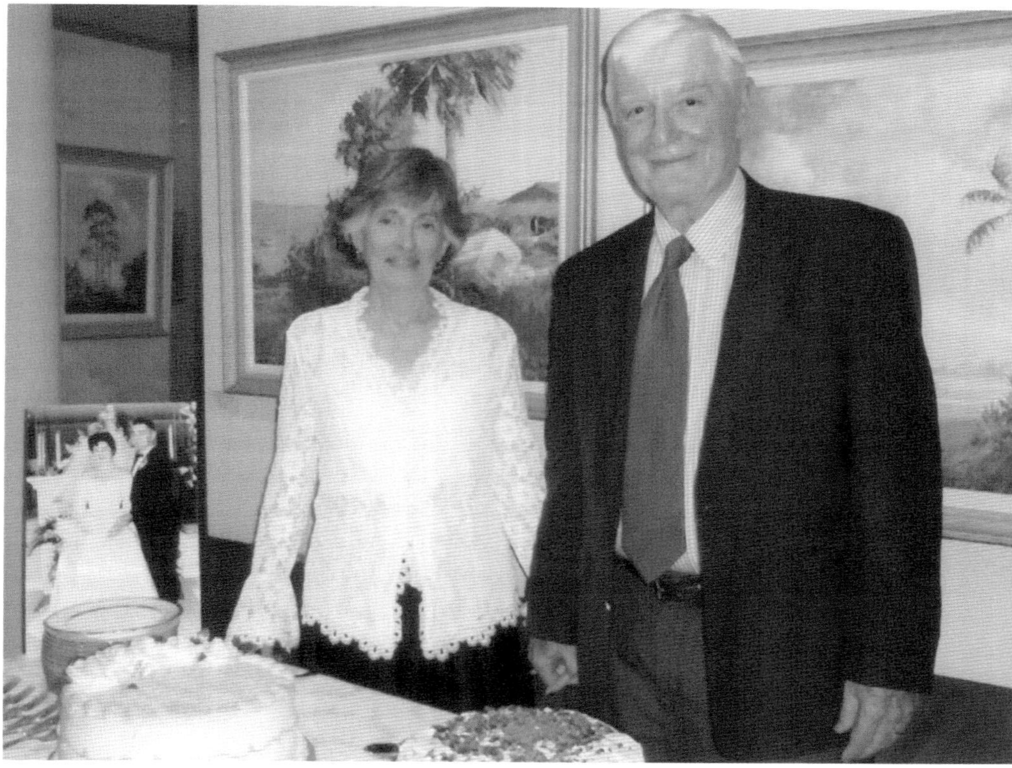

The Third Generation Serves

Mary Ann Koblegard Bryan served as commissioner of the city of Fort Pierce from January 1994 through 2001. Buck Bryan served as mayor from December 1974 through 1976 and as circuit judge from November 1995 through 2009. Pictured above is the couple on their 50th anniversary. Buck's father, Ben Bryan (below), was the principal of Fort Pierce High School, then superintendent of schools from 1956 to 1968. (Above, courtesy of the Koblegard family; below, courtesy of the 1958 Santa Lucian.)

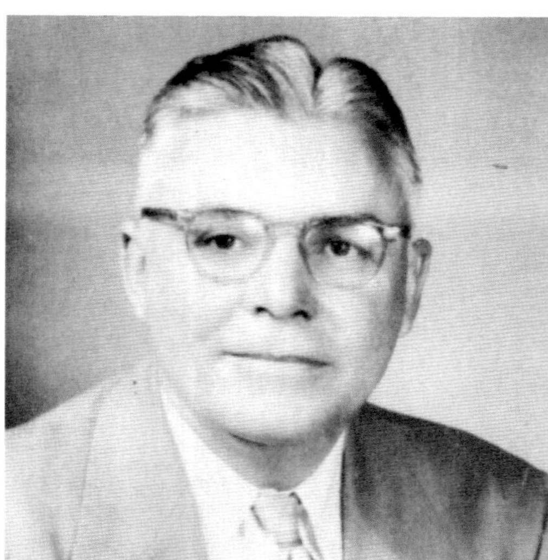

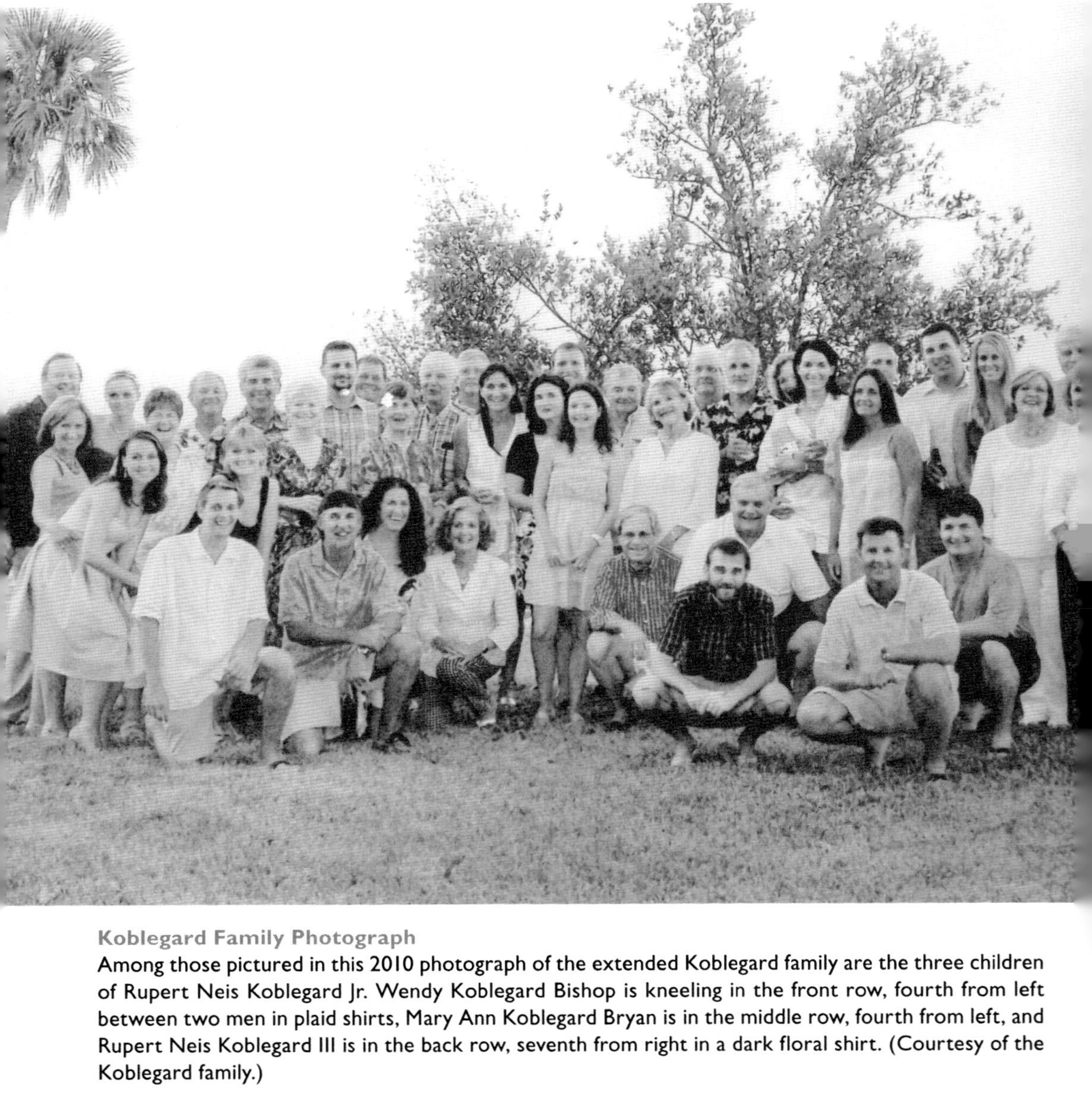

Koblegard Family Photograph

Among those pictured in this 2010 photograph of the extended Koblegard family are the three children of Rupert Neis Koblegard Jr. Wendy Koblegard Bishop is kneeling in the front row, fourth from left between two men in plaid shirts, Mary Ann Koblegard Bryan is in the middle row, fourth from left, and Rupert Neis Koblegard III is in the back row, seventh from right in a dark floral shirt. (Courtesy of the Koblegard family.)

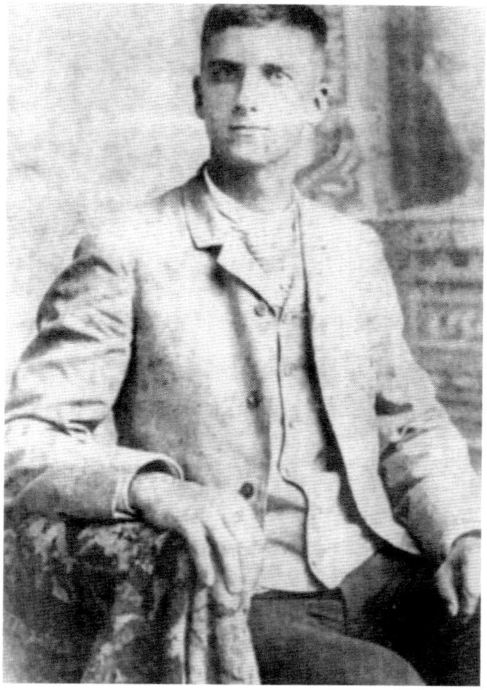

And Still They Came
Robert Reed Gladwin came to the area in 1897 and was mayor and county commissioner of Fort Pierce. He was on the school board when the yellow-brick school on Delaware Avenue was built. The Stephen N. Gladwin American Legion Post was named for Gladwin's son who died in World War I. His was the first military funeral in town. The daughters of R.R. and Florence Gladwin were Marion Gladwin Horton and Margaret Gladwin Enns. Margaret was in the garden club and DAR. (Courtesy of Susan Enns Stans.)

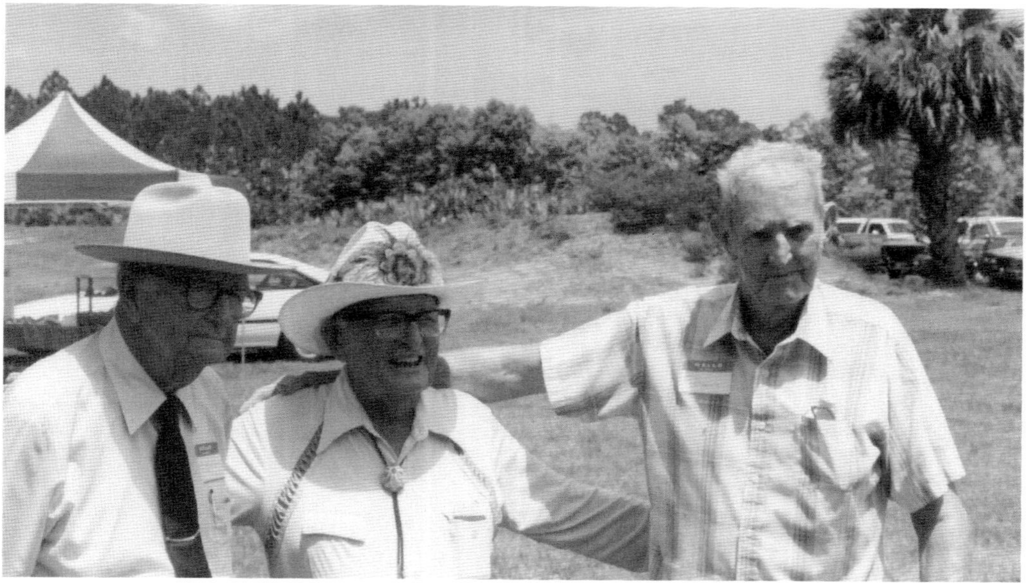

Hero of the Glass Plates
Bob Gladwin, as chief engineer, worked for Edwin Binney in the development of Fort Pierce's port and Indian River Refrigeration Terminal where citrus was stored for shipping. He was the co-founder of the Sea Scouts, organized the first Little League, and labored himself to build the area's first Little League field in 1939. He was also instrumental in organizing the St. Lucie Historical Society. He rescued Hill's collection of photographic glass plates from destruction. From left to right are Judge Trowell, Buck Hendry, and Bob Gladwin on the occasion of Hendry's 85th birthday. (Courtesy of Tom Gladwin.)

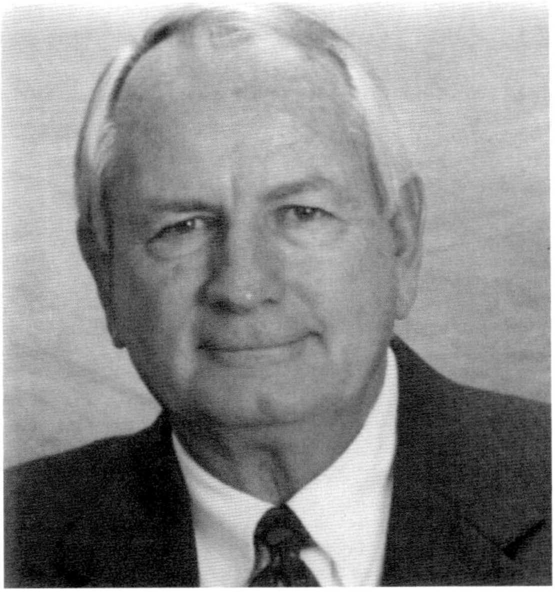

Public Service Genes

The Enns family was prominent in the development of Fort Pierce. Paul, H.T., Nick, and "Putz" Enns migrated from Kansas. Among other endeavors, members of the family developed Maravilla, sold real estate, and acquired the Fort Pierce newspaper. Eddie Enns followed his father, Putz Enns, in the insurance business, and, like his grandfather Robert Reed Gladwin, became mayor of Fort Pierce. Putz was on the local school board and Eddie, surely inheriting the service gene, served as St. Lucie county commissioner for 12 years. His brother Bob Enns was a sports columnist and later editor of the *Fort Pierce News Tribune*. (Courtesy of Susan Enns Stans.)

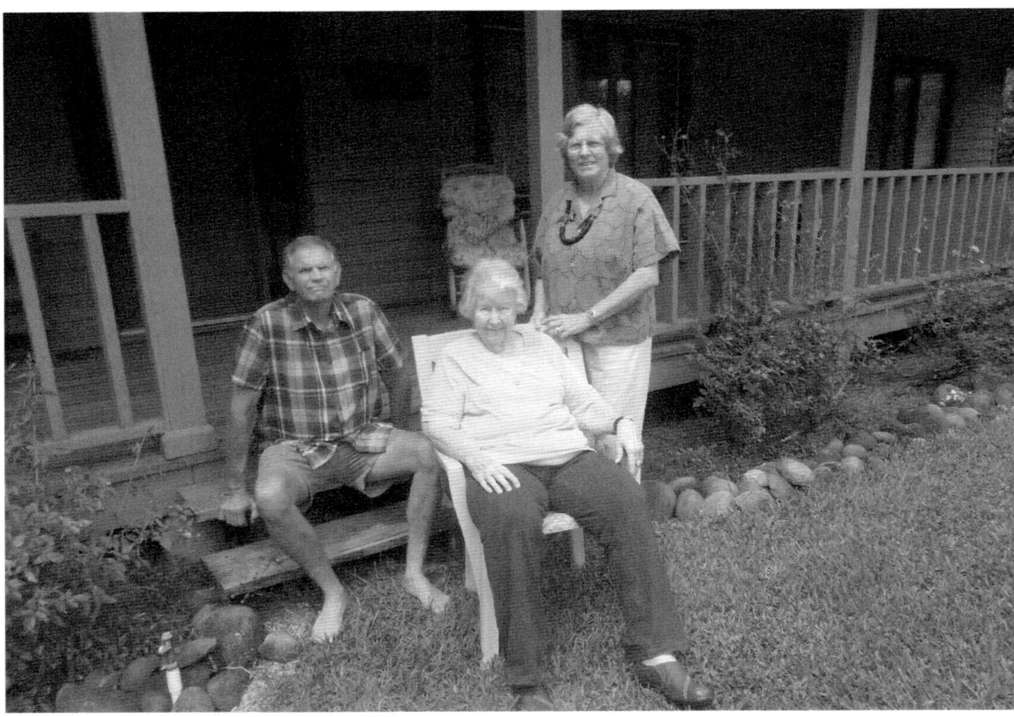

Cousins

Descendants of the Gladwin-Enns families continue to contribute to their community. Tom Gladwin (left) retired as a lieutenant after 33 years as a firefighter. Marijean Horton (center) spent 33 years with the local telephone company. Susan Enns Stans (right) received her doctorate of philosophy for the research she did while living for two years on Brighton Seminole Reservation. She is the author of *Healing Plants: Medicine of the Florida Seminole Indians*. (Photograph by the author.)

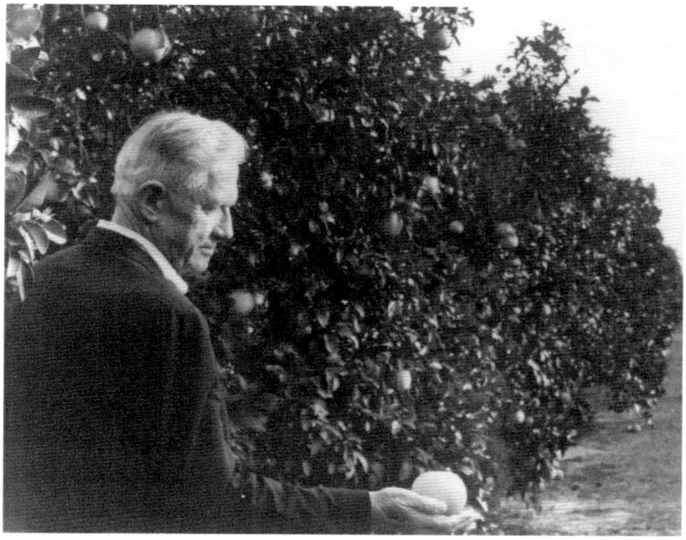

Going International

Bernard Egan (1914–2004) was the chairman of Bernard Egan & Co., which has its headquarters in Fort Pierce. Here, he palms one of his internationally famous Indian River grapefruits. Once affectionately known as the "godfather of grapefruit," Egan was inducted into the Florida Agriculture Hall of Fame in 2002, was appointed by the governor to the Florida Citrus Commission in 1987, and joined the board of the Indian River Citrus League in 1976, serving as chairman and then president from 1987 to 1991. He was one of the first citrus producers to export to Japan. Egan was recognized by Pres. George W. Bush in 1990 with an award for excellence in exporting. (Courtesy of Bernard Egan & Co.)

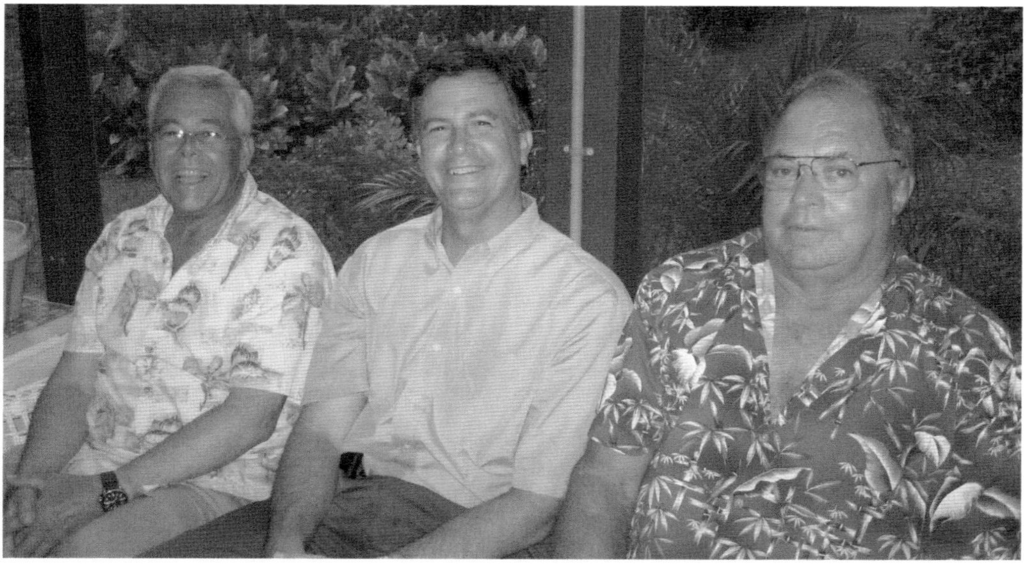

It's a Family Tradition

Ron Rohm, manager of Cow Creek Ranch and groves; Greg Nelson, president of Bernard Egan & Co.; and Mike Emerick, quality control inspector for Egan Fruit, are among the family members who continue to make this privately owned agribusiness an outstanding corporate citizen. (Courtesy of Bernard Egan & Co.)

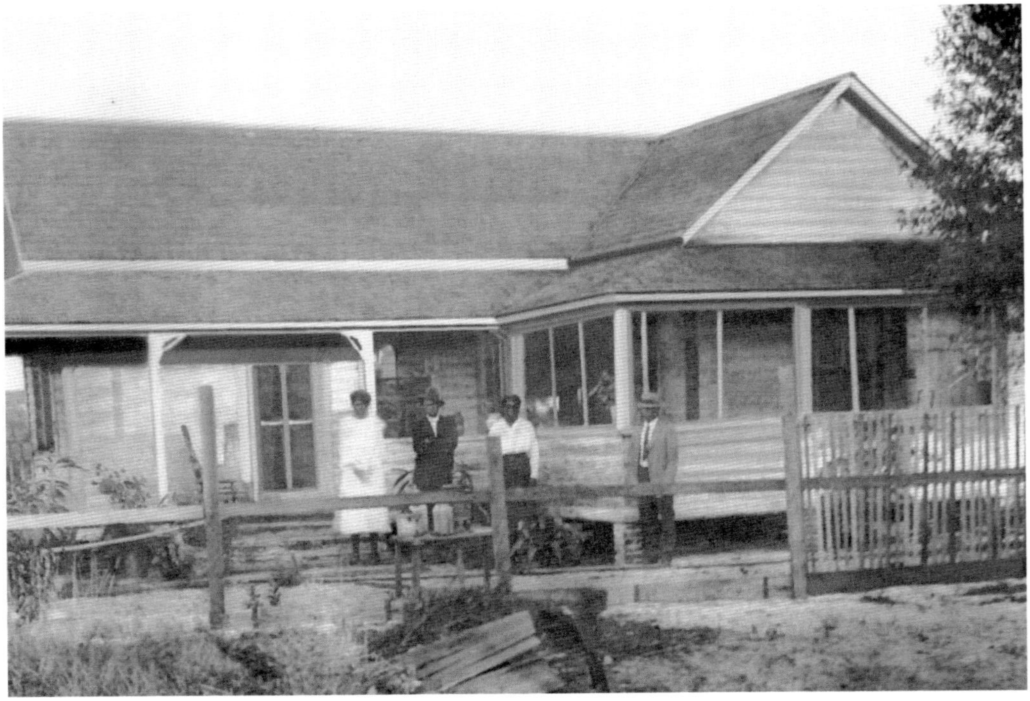

Board by Board

Wilson Lyons came to Fort Pierce in 1903. While working at East Coast Lumber, he hauled material, a board at a time, on his bicycle to the lot he had acquired on Avenue D. At night, he and his wife, Alice, would work on the building they moved into around 1908. Unfortunately, the house, pictured above with members of the Lyons family, was later razed. Lyons went to work for P.P. Cobb, and he and Alice took care of Cobb in his old age. Rufus Alexander, shown below, is a Fort Pierce city commissioner and a descendant of Wilson Lyons. (Above, courtesy of SLCRHC; below, courtesy of Linda Hudson.)

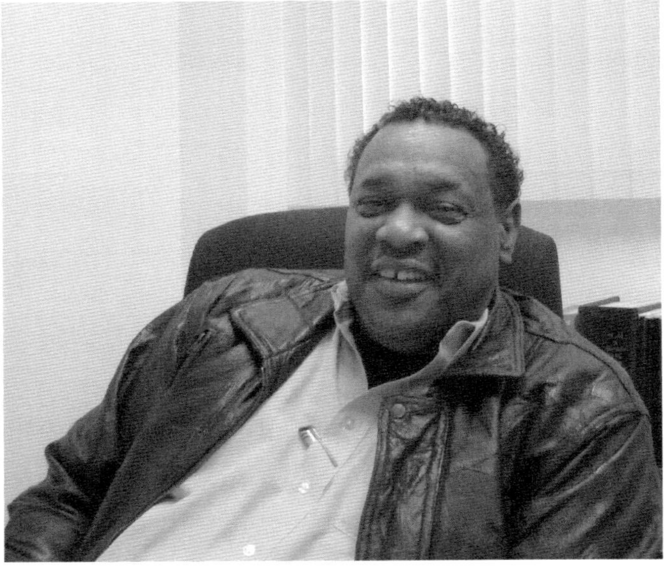

CHAPTER FOUR

Water, Water Everywhere

Going south from Fort Pierce on Indian River Drive, the river lies on the left. Houses, from palatial mansions to modest cottages, can be viewed on the right. Traveling north on Indian River Drive, one can find Old St. Lucie and the location of the oldest house in the county, whose builder was here in the 1840s. William Russell was Fort Capron's landlord and served as speaker of the Florida House.

The bridge that runs from mainland to island allows the tall masts of sailboats to pass beneath and provides a breathtaking view of the inlet, estuary, and ocean to the east. Pleasure boats, both motor and sail, decorate the seascape. West of town, kayakers enjoy the North Fork of the St. Lucie River, a historic river that appears on very old Spanish maps. Others put their boats in at a ramp and ease along, causing alligators to plop into the water from their naps on the bank. White City, on this river, was settled by Socialist Danes and named for the White City of the Chicago World's Fair of 1893. Ten-Mile Creek feeds into the St. Lucie. It, along with the canals dug to drain the wetlands for cultivation, provide the opportunity for fresh-water fishing. South of Fort Pierce are the savannahs, wetlands that furnish the town's water supply. In this subtropic zone flourishes a unique mix of flora and fauna. The Indian River Lagoon, a unique environment, has to be vigilantly guarded from over-fishing, pollution, and invasive species.

In a place like Fort Pierce, nature is a constant of everyday life. Palms of all varieties, bromeliads, century plants, Poinciana, bougainvillea, and oleander are in everyone's yard. Aside from alligators and porpoises, the area is home to manatees, wild hogs, coyotes, deer, opossums, armadillos, land crabs, red-tailed hawks, cattle egrets, and eagles.

Seaside towns have the advantage of being open to the world and a reputation for being tolerant of nonconformity. Fort Pierce is no exception.

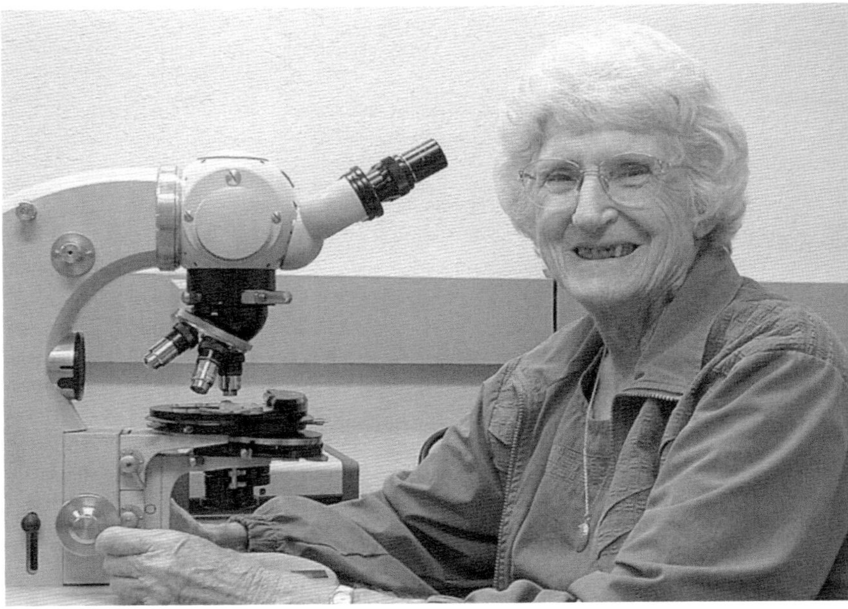

Smithsonian South

Dr. Mary E. Rice is known for her long-term scientific studies of invertebrates of the Indian River Lagoon and offshore waters of Florida and the Caribbean and as the first director of the Smithsonian Marine Station at Fort Pierce. An emeritus senior research scientist since 2002, her tenure as a researcher in the Fort Pierce area began in 1971 when the Smithsonian established a presence in St. Lucie County in offices on a converted US Army barge and on the campus of what was then the Harbor Branch Foundation. Through her efforts, the Smithsonian acquired eight acres of land and moved to its current campus on South Hutchinson Island in 1999. With help from St. Lucie County, the City of Fort Pierce, and other local entities, she brought the living coral reef exhibit of the Smithsonian Institution National Museum of Natural History to Fort Pierce. The 3,000-gallon coral reef system had been on display at the Smithsonian for 20 years and was scheduled for replacement in 2001. Dr. Rice knew it would provide a stunning focal point for what has become the Smithsonian Marine Ecosystems Exhibit at the St. Lucie County Aquarium, educating the public about the wonders and natural beauty of local marine habitats. (Courtesy of the Smithsonian Institution.)

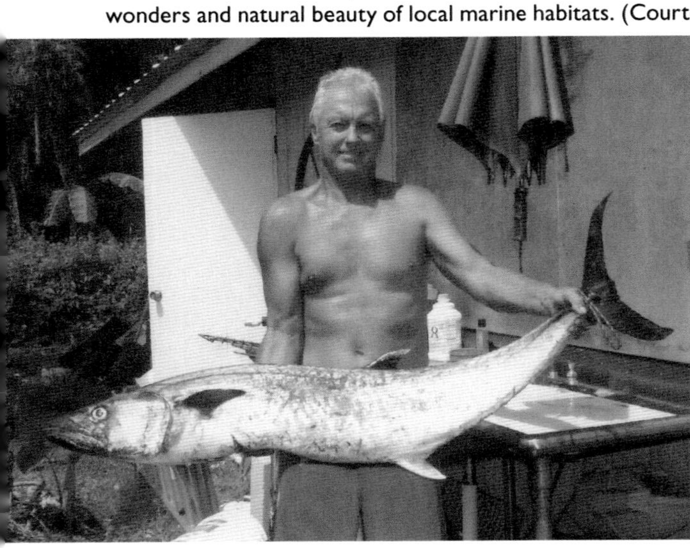

The Smoker

Dennis Macy is a waterman—a diver, surfer, and cast-net fisherman. He lives within sight of the Indian River and has cured his catch for years with a successive variety of smokers. He was laying floors, but when the housing bubble burst, he turned his hobby into a vocation. Now, restaurants along the Treasure Coast feature Macy's smoked-fish dip on their menus. He and his family also sell it at farmers markets. A long-standing member of Grace Family Church, Macy has practiced a jail ministry at the Rock Road County Jail for 25 years. (Courtesy of Dennis Macy.)

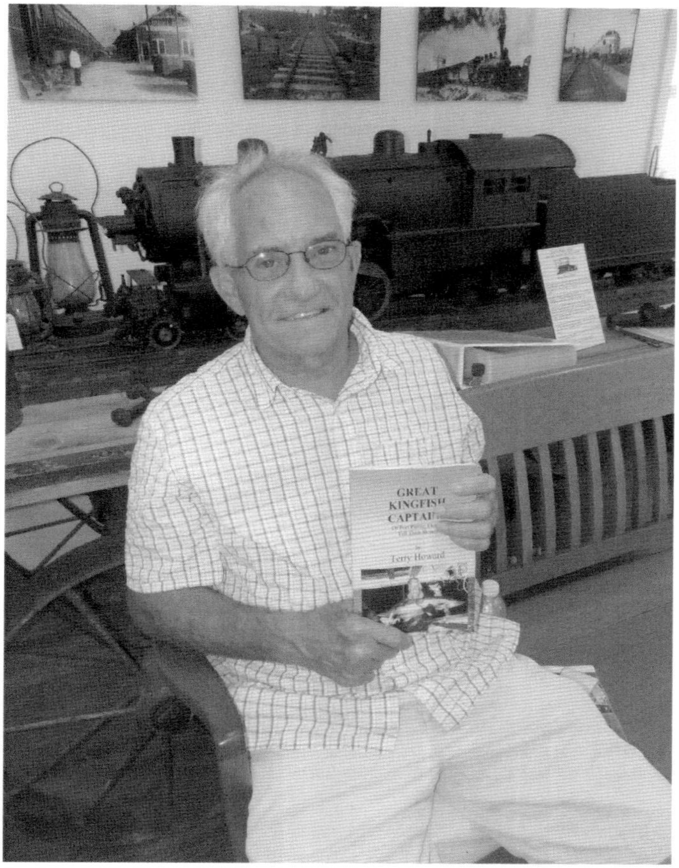

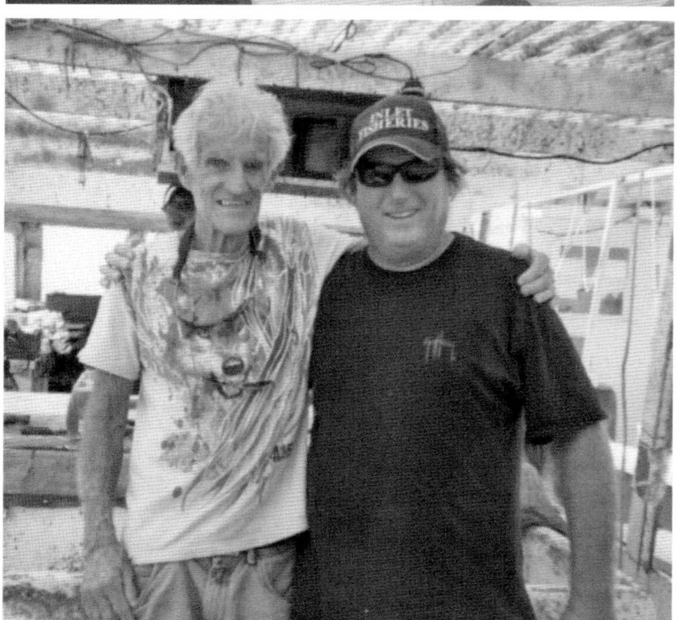

Last of the Handliners
Retired school teacher and commercial hand-line fisherman Terry Howard has preserved the stories of a vanishing breed of seafarers in his books about local commercial fishing captains. Terry's stories recall the dangers and experiences of this brotherhood of harvesters of the deep who navigate and set lines in the dark, negotiate the sudden Florida storms, and handle all the other emergencies that occur out of sight of land and aid. Terry relates their stories of strange phenomena: lightning strikes, waterspouts, a bottomless hole, a spring in the ocean, and much more. The satisfaction of independent living and a kind of spirituality in these seafarers' respect for Mother Ocean pervade his works. Two of the breed are Al Tyrrell (at left below), still fishing at 90, and Jimmy Reeves, another long-time Fort Pierce commercial fisherman. One modern enemy of the hook-and-line fisherman is the porpoise. It is common to see them playing in the wake of a cruising boat, and these intelligent creatures have learned to allow man to catch their fish for them. Several fishermen have been badly hurt hauling in a fish on a taut line when a porpoise snatches his catch and the heavy monofilament line whips back and sometimes cuts flesh. (Above, photograph by the author; below, courtesy of Terry Howard.)

Cleaning the Seabed

Capt. Donald Voss, an Ohio native, is a life-long recycler, environmentalist, and conservationist, and an avid scuba diver and underwater photographer. He retired to Fort Pierce to enjoy the beach and thaw out, but, becoming aware of the overwhelming marine debris choking the Indian River Lagoon, he founded Marine Cleanup Initiative. As its operations director, Don and fellow volunteers have removed more than 375,000 pounds of marine garbage while saving tens of thousands of aquatic animals. Voss was named Oceana International Ocean Hero in 2013. He serves on the Fort Pierce Tourism Board, the board of the American Dream Factory, and the Fort Pierce Ecotourism Committee, and is a leading force in lionfish removal, lionfish being an invasive species that devours native game and food fish stock. (Courtesy of Capt. Don Voss.)

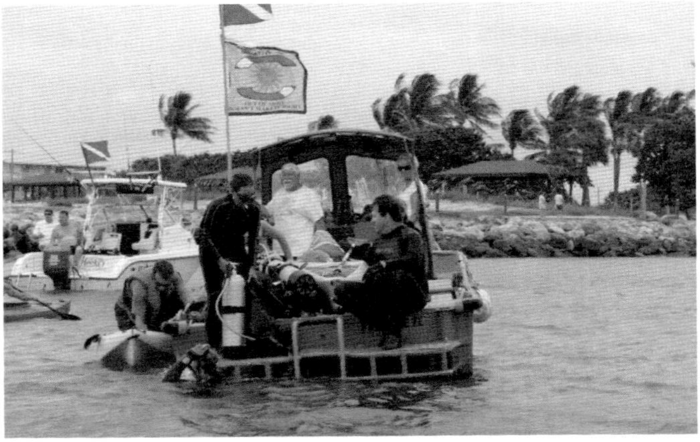

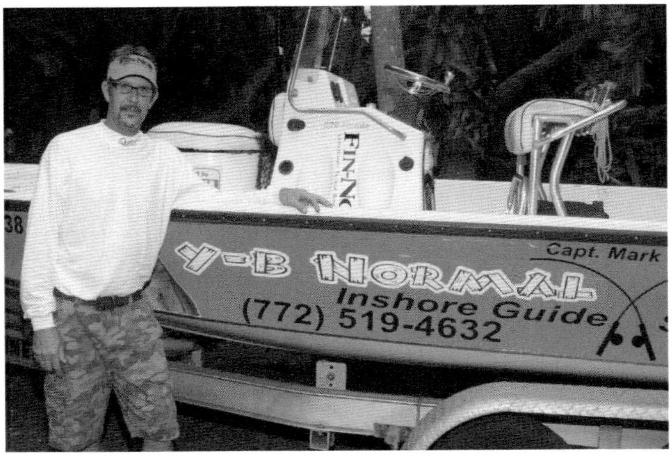

Mentoring Young Fisherfolk

Capt. Mark Dravo has spent his life surfing, diving, and fishing along the Treasure Coast. He runs, operates, and serves as a third-generation fishing guide for Why Be Normal Charters on the Indian River Lagoon. His clients have caught record fish off his boat, including a 15.25-pound margate. One of the unsung contributions of this skipper is that he really enjoys introducing local youngsters into the mysteries of the piscine world via free outings on the river, as well as contributing charters every year to Indian River Keepers, Breast Cancer Foundation, the Coastal Conservation Association, and Wounded Warriors, to name a few. In the waters off Fort Pierce, one can find a gator trout in the double digits or a super snook weighing up to 39 pounds. The only other place in the world where the latter fish can be caught is Costa Rica. (Photograph by Tom Baumker.)

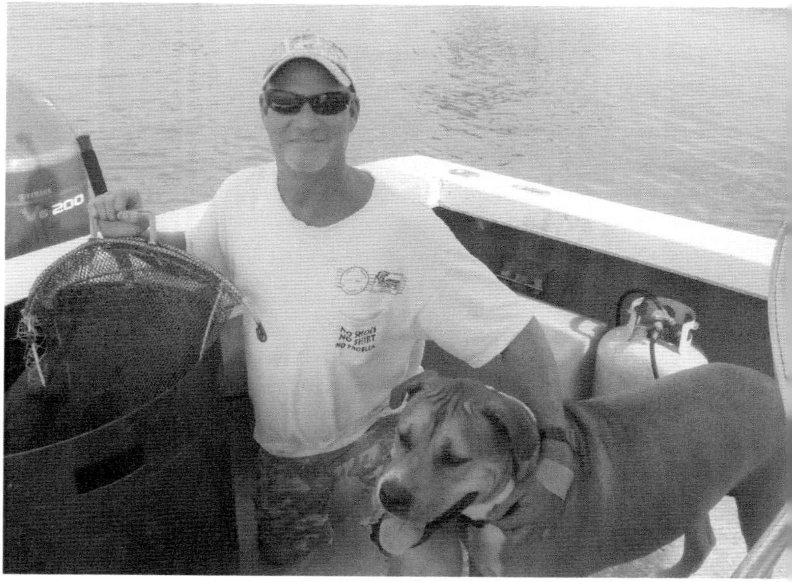

Licensed to Crab

Michael Roberts is the owner of a commercial saltwater products license issued by the Florida Fish and Wildlife Conservation Commission. He sells his stone and blue crab catches to epicures of fresh shellfish. Michael's best friend, Jake, won't chase a squirrel or an opossum but will chase a crab. Michael is a cofounder of the Black Pearl Society, whose salt-life members are pledged to help each other, particularly to provide a tow to land when a boat develops a problem. (Courtesy of Buzz Smyth.)

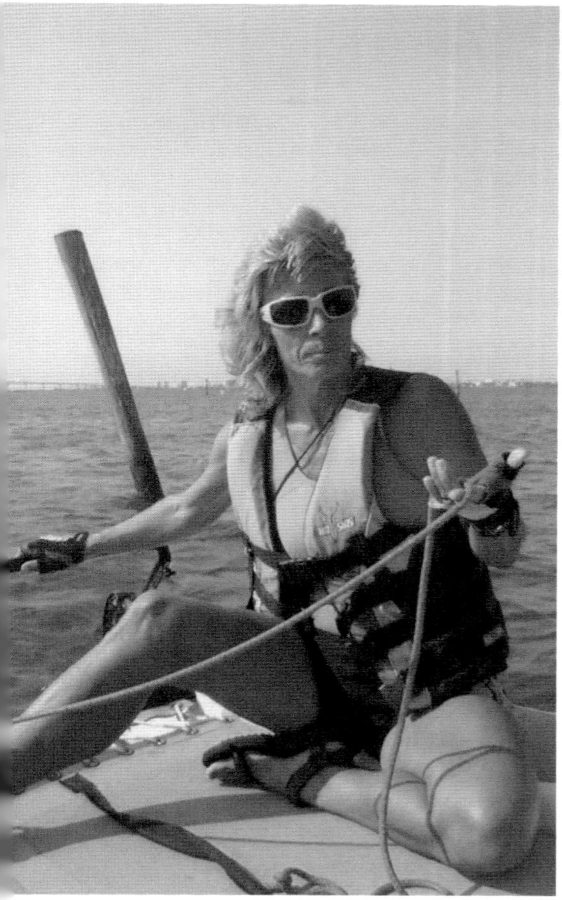

Lisa Fasnacht

Lisa Fasnacht's web site name says what's she's all about: www.getoutsideanddosomething.com. Her mission is to match the person with the activity they will come to love. Lisa believes she discovered paradise in Fort Pierce when she arrived 30 years ago, and her satisfaction derives from helping others enjoy its particular local gifts to the full through kayaking, stand-up paddle boarding, sailing, bicycling, or hiking.

According to Lisa, "When I received my first kayak as a gift, I loved it so much, I wanted to introduce everyone to the sport and relaxation of it. I soon had a line of people who wanted to try it; I bought a second kayak and then a third and—eureka!—I had a business. I needed capital and I lacked a business background, but I had passion and drive." Unaccountably, Lisa was forced to mount a lengthy struggle with city bureaucracy to get a license. Now, Lisa's Kayaks is much more than a place to rent kayaks; she also rents other water sports equipment and bicycles. She also offers guided estuary adventures, and sells items such as paddleboards and inner tubes. Her business is thriving. "I am living my dream," Lisa stated. "I see so many people out doing things both on land and in water and knowing I helped to make this happen is incredible." (Courtesy of Lisa's Kayaks.)

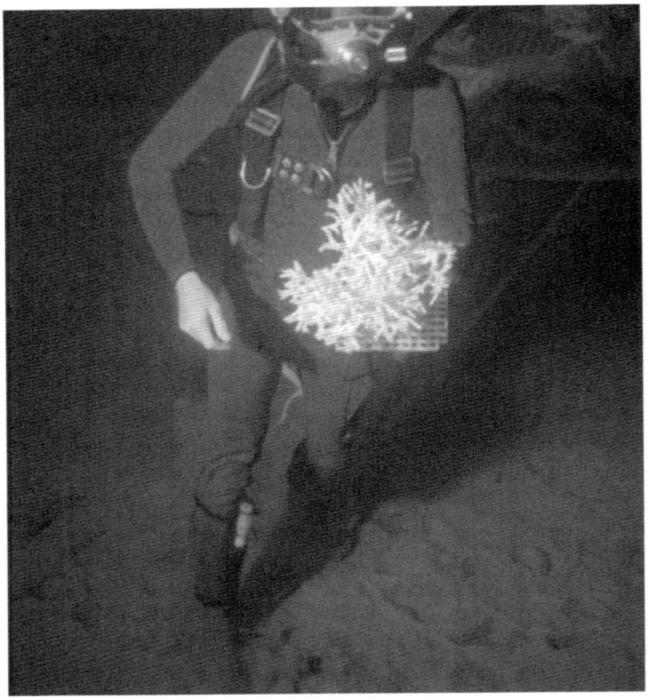

Harbor Branch

John Reed is a research professor at Harbor Branch Oceanographic Institute (HBOI)–Florida Atlantic University and principal investigator for the Robertson Coral Reef Research and Conservation Program. For the past 37 years, John's research and commitment to protect the area's shallow and deep-water reefs have resulted in three marine-protected areas off the Treasure Coast: the 300-square-mile, deep-water Oculina coral reefs that are found nowhere else on earth; the 15,000-square-mile, deep-water coral reefs that reach depths of 1,000 feet to nearly 3,000 feet from North Carolina to South Florida; and the near-shore reefs at the St. Lucie Inlet Preserve State Park. (Courtesy of HBOI.)

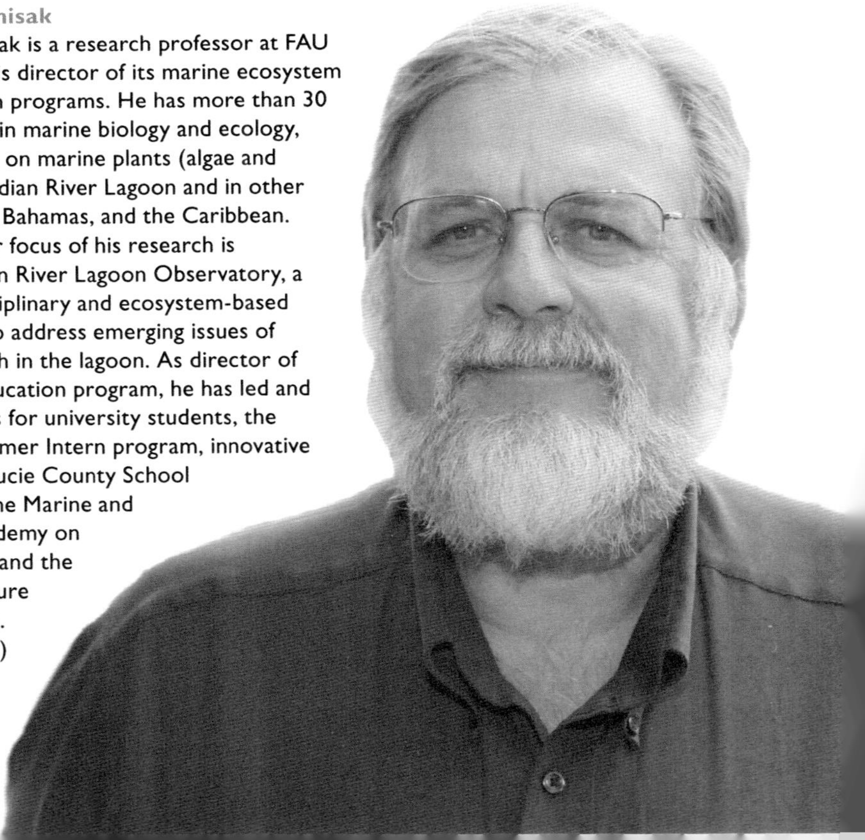

Dr. M. Dennis Hanisak

Dr. M. Dennis Hanisak is a research professor at FAU Harbor Branch and is director of its marine ecosystem health and education programs. He has more than 30 years of experience in marine biology and ecology, conducting research on marine plants (algae and seagrasses) in the Indian River Lagoon and in other parts of Florida, the Bahamas, and the Caribbean. Currently, the major focus of his research is developing the Indian River Lagoon Observatory, a long-term, multidisciplinary and ecosystem-based program designed to address emerging issues of environmental health in the lagoon. As director of Harbor Branch's education program, he has led and developed programs for university students, the Harbor Branch Summer Intern program, innovative programs with St. Lucie County School District (including the Marine and Oceanographic Academy on the HBOI campus), and the Ocean Science Lecture Series for the public. (Courtesy of HBOI.)

Flying High by Flying Low
Pilot Harold H. "Buzz" Smyth and his copilot, daughter Katie, are setting out to take aerial photographs of the water wonderland of Fort Pierce. Taking photographs from his plane, Buzz has recorded the many changes in the area over the past two decades. Buzz doesn't mind being labeled "eccentric." Each day, he believes, is an adventure. For 20 years, when there have been calls for volunteers for a community project, Buzz has been there, taking his girls, Emily and Katie, with him. From planting trees on unsightly lots to using his carpenter skills to build a wheelchair ramp for a friend, he has put his considerable skills to work for city beautification and to aid those who need a hand. The Lighthouse Foundation, which helps seniors pay for medicine, is one of his favorite causes. He is guilty of unabashed boosterism of his Fort Pierce hometown and, for a while, worked for the city of Fort Pierce, guiding entrepreneurs in wending their way through government red tape to startup. He is an appointee to the region's Comprehensive Economic Development Strategy Committee. (Courtesy of Buzz Smyth.)

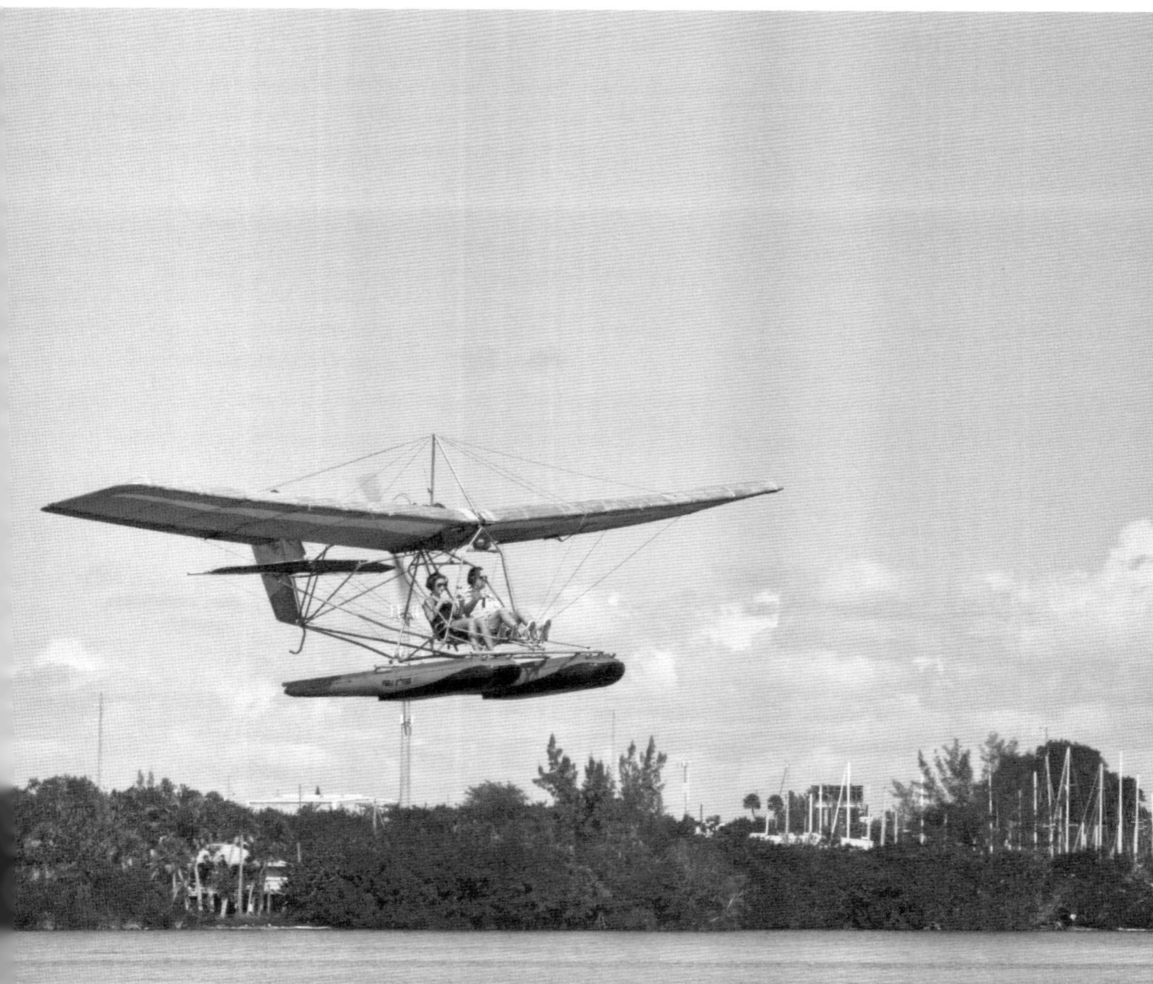

On the Beach

Pictured on Fort Pierce beach around 1950 are the grandparents and great-grandparents of current residents. From left to right are (first row) unidentified, coach Hunk Slay, unidentified, and John McCarty; (second row) unidentified, Bert Bittan, Duke Warren, and Maxwell King; (third row) Martha Keen, unidentified, Mary Louise Lloyd, Binney Putnam, Ann Eden Platt, two unidentified, Dorothy Westbrook, unidentified, and Billie Jean Kemp. (Courtesy of Maxwell King.)

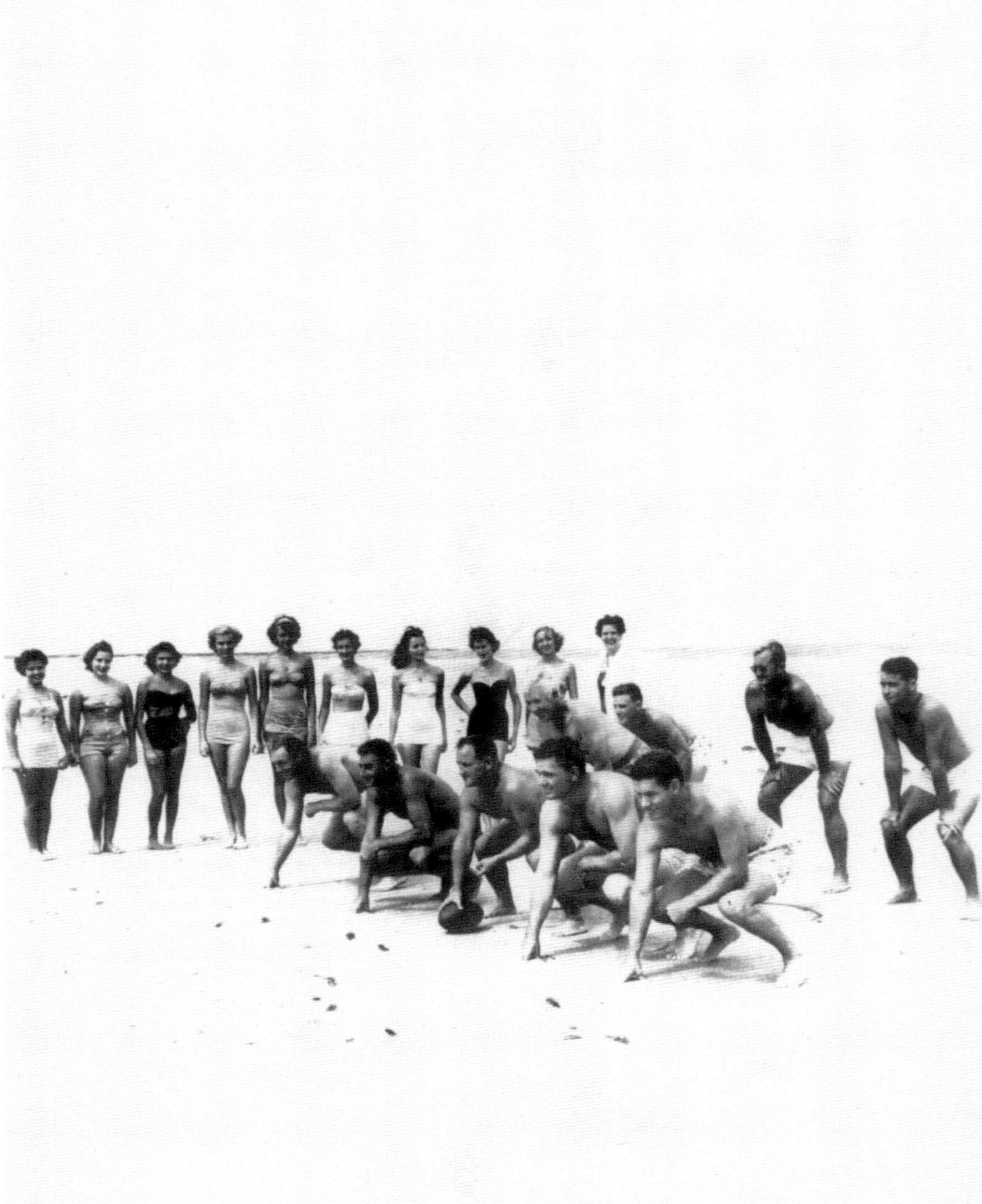

CHAPTER FIVE

Landscape of Enlightenment

Fort Pierce enjoys a wide variety of artistic talent, academic institutions with programs designed to serve its diverse population, entertainment venues from theater to jazz concerts, and masters of literature and photography.

Fort Pierce pioneers enjoyed shows. George and Josephine Sheridan Backus, having come from theatrical backgrounds, were key players in pioneer entertainments. Lucia Zora Card, of future circus fame, shone as a child star in 1898. Later, another Zora, Zora Neale Hurston, worked on her last novel here between teaching school and writing for the *Chronicle*, a newspaper for African American readers. Recitations and skits were organized to raise money for early churches. A bandstand was built at the foot of Avenue A for band concerts. Don Blanding was inspired by the surrounding beauty to write poems and record scenes with his drawing pen. Beanie Backus began his career running a sign shop and painting posters advertising the next film at the Sunrise Theatre. Harry Hill left a priceless gift in the form of his early photographs, a source of endless information about Fort Pierce's past.

The spirit of stretching the intellect toward better things was reflected in the name of the Improvement Club, a structure built by citizens buying "shares" in the project. In addition to serving as an entertainment hall, a corner of the building served as the town's first library. Debating clubs were formed. Learning was prized by the Carltons, who brought a tutor for their children along when they moved into the area. Residents then taxed themselves to build one of the finest high schools on the lower coast, as well as Maxwell King's Indian River Community College, which is now part of the state university system.

Preservation is a mark of a progressive town and a group of men and women with a sense of history formed the Old Timers Association, then, later, another group founded the St. Lucie Historical Society. The St. Lucie County Regional History Center is the culmination of their efforts.

In the days of segregation, Avenue D and the African American community of Fort Pierce was known far and wide as the place to go for entertainment. Baker's Flamingo Bar brought black headliners to its stage. The music from local churches and the jazz musicians were top caliber. Harold Newton began to paint landscapes, and Alfred Hair took his style and founded the Highwaymen, a group of African American artists. Twenty-eight of these men, and one woman, Mary Ann Carroll, have been inducted into the Florida Artists Hall of Fame.

Sports have always been a major interest. Lincoln Park Academy was a powerhouse, winning many championships in the old days. The football team that came together in the year the schools were integrated won a state championship.

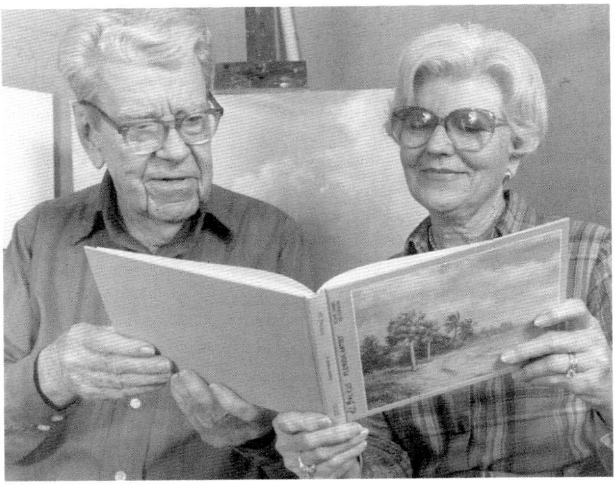

Painting the Landscape

Even though today one cannot buy a Backus for less than five figures, his paintings hang on the walls of modest homes in Fort Pierce, for locals have always appreciated the way his work made them really see the luminous landscape in which they lived. Albert "Beanie" Ernest Backus was born in a small frame house on the banks of the Indian River in 1906 and was never very long away from its shores. As a boy, he started painting signs for Fort Pierce businesses and posters for the Sunrise Theatre. Even after he was discovered by international collectors, became famous, and couldn't keep up with commissions, Backus remained a Fort Pierce boy. His studio, with the river in sight, was open to friends, students, followers, hangers-on, loners, pals, and troubled young people, black and white. His open-house philosophy was modeled on his boyhood home on Boston Avenue where his mother also welcomed everyone, including African Americans and Seminoles, which wasn't the norm in her day. His father, George Tay Backus, operated a boat-building shop on Moore's Creek, and Beanie was introduced to oil paints by painting boats.

After serving on a Navy troopship in World War II, where his commanding officer encouraged him to paint their ports of call in his free time, Backus came home, acquired his father's old boat-building shed, and turned it into a studio. In 1950, he married Patsy Hutchinson, whose brother Jim was an aspiring artist. Jim would later live on a Seminole reservation and paint a series of Seminole Indian portraits. Tragically, Backus's beloved Patsy died five years later and though he went on to live to 84, friends agreed he was never the same. He mentored, and his works inspired a slew of Backus-school artists. He died on June 6, 1990, but it will be many years before the memories of this gentle man working at his easel or relaxing with a libation will fade from the memories of Fort Pierce people. The Backus Gallery, on Indian River Drive in Fort Pierce, features the art of Backus, sponsors Backus festivals, and mounts special exhibitions. This Backus dreamscape was a gift to Charles W. Wilson in appreciation of his many years of service as secretary of Elks Lodge 1520 of Fort Pierce. The lodge building on Fourth Street was dedicated in 1929. (Above, courtesy of O.C. Peterson; below, courtesy of Charles Russell Wilson.)

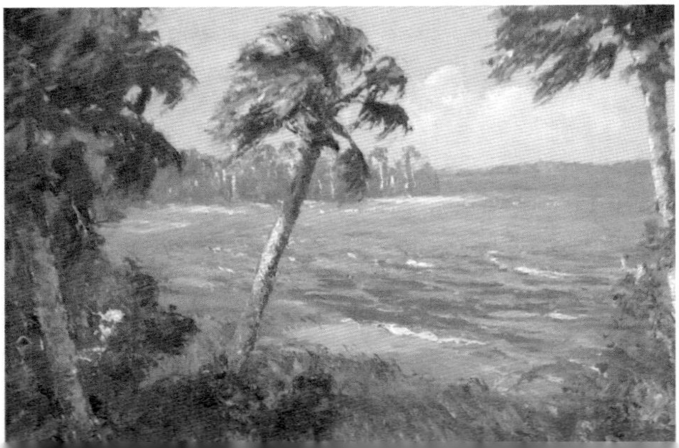

ALFRED HAIR
"Banana Boat"
Football 6; Basketball 2; Baseball 1; Handicraft 3; Science Club 1.
Hobby - Hot Rodding
Ambition - Artist

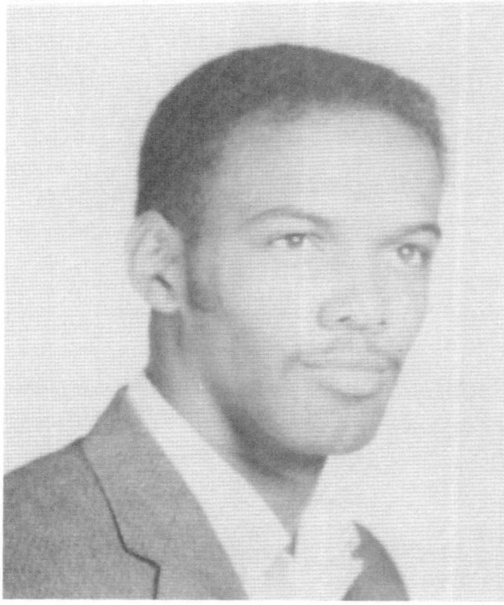

Debonair and Doomed

Zenobia Jefferson, who taught art at Lincoln Park Academy, brought the promising Alfred Hair to the attention of Beanie Backus, who took him on as a student in return for Hair building frames for him. Hair then welcomed talented African Americans to his back yard where he passed on to them what he had learned while they painted and drank beer and traded stories. That was the 1960s when it was still required that blacks go to the back door, but Hair and his cohorts went up and down the highway selling their phantasmagorical paintings to longtime residents who were nostalgic about the old Florida represented in the paintings. A second market for their works was new residents still enamored with the Florida of palm trees, wading birds, and watered sanctuaries that was so different from whence they came. Sadly, the charismatic Hair was mortally wounded by a gunshot in a juke joint on Avenue D by a man jealous of Hair's good looks and charm. The Poinciana tree was a favorite Highwayman subject, and this one was done by James Daniels, who was inspired by Hair to escape poverty through art. (Left, courtesy of the 1961 Lincoln Park Yearbook; below, photograph by the author.)

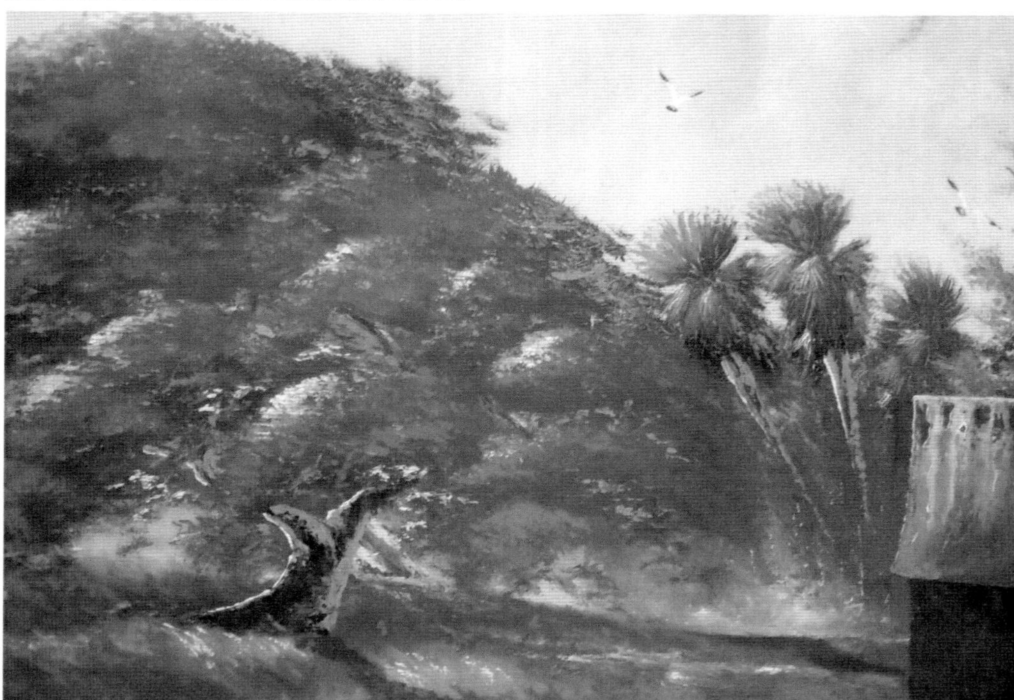

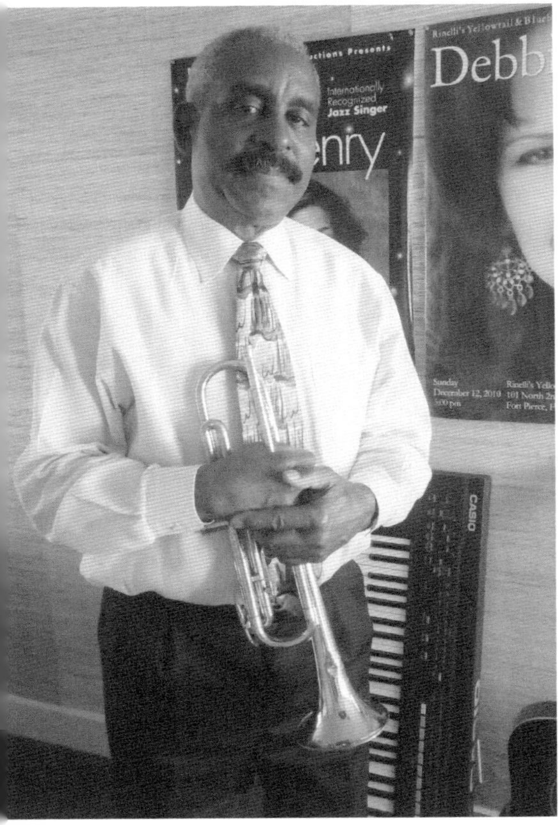

A Jazzed Town

Darryl Bey, cofounder of the Fort Pierce Jazz Society, served as its first president from 1996 to 2006 and as the executive director until 2007. Under his leadership, the jazz society contributed to the rebirth of downtown Fort Pierce by promoting and staging musical entertainment that attracted area residents to visit downtown and patronize local businesses. Jazz society events and sponsorships created by Darryl Bey include weekly jazz jams, the Fort Pierce Jazz Ensemble (which took second place in a national competition in Washington, DC, that was televised by the BET channel's "Jazz Discovery" program in 1998), Members Night Out (held at various downtown establishments), Brown Bag Lunch Concerts at the downtown branch of the St. Lucie County Library, music workshops, jazz art exhibitions at Backus Gallery and other venues, and music scholarships. The society's annual Jazz Week & Tribute to Jazz Masters has featured internationally known artists such as the Duke Ellington Orchestra, Freddy Cole, T.S. Monk, Ramsey Lewis, Ira Sullivan, Little Ed and the Blues Imperials, the Bill Porter Orchestra, David "Fathead" Newman, David Sanborn, Guitar Shorty, Donald Harrison, Christian Scott, Joey DeFrancesco, Melton Mustafa, Zac Harmon, Ana Popovic, Wynton Marsalis, Los Hombres Caliente, Tito Puente Jr., and Billy Branch. (Photograph by the author.)

Learn to Read

Dorothy Brennan sits with John Coleman, who is learning to read. After a child almost died from an overdose because the directions on a medicine bottle were indecipherable to her illiterate mother, Brennan—upset by the near tragedy—founded Learn to Read of St. Lucie County. In a refurbished house on Delaware Avenue, adults learn in the computer lab, on the front porch, in the living room, and in the bedrooms, where a half dozen volunteer tutors work one-on-one with pupils. There are currently 185 active tutors and 450 active students in the program, compared to an initial 20 students in 1983. Funding supports only one salaried employee, Luz Ma Comacho, a former student at Learn to Read. Though Brennan is not as active as she once was (she was injured by a car while crossing the street), she continues to participate as a member of Fort Pierce Main Street, Backus Gallery, Friends of the Library, Heathcote Botanical Gardens, the Conservation Alliance, and the National Audubon Society. (Photograph by the author.)

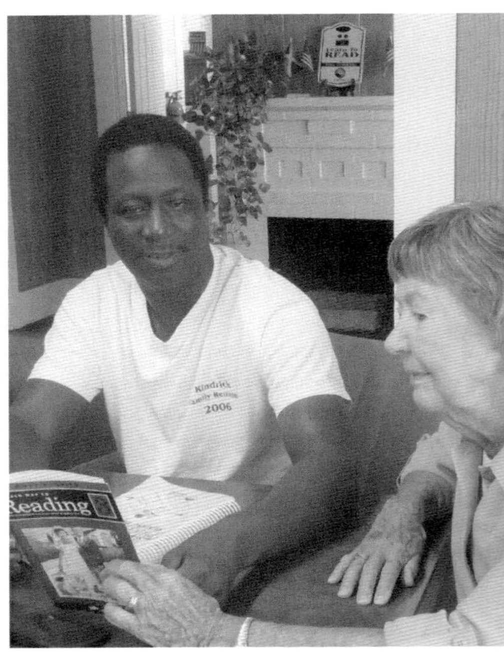

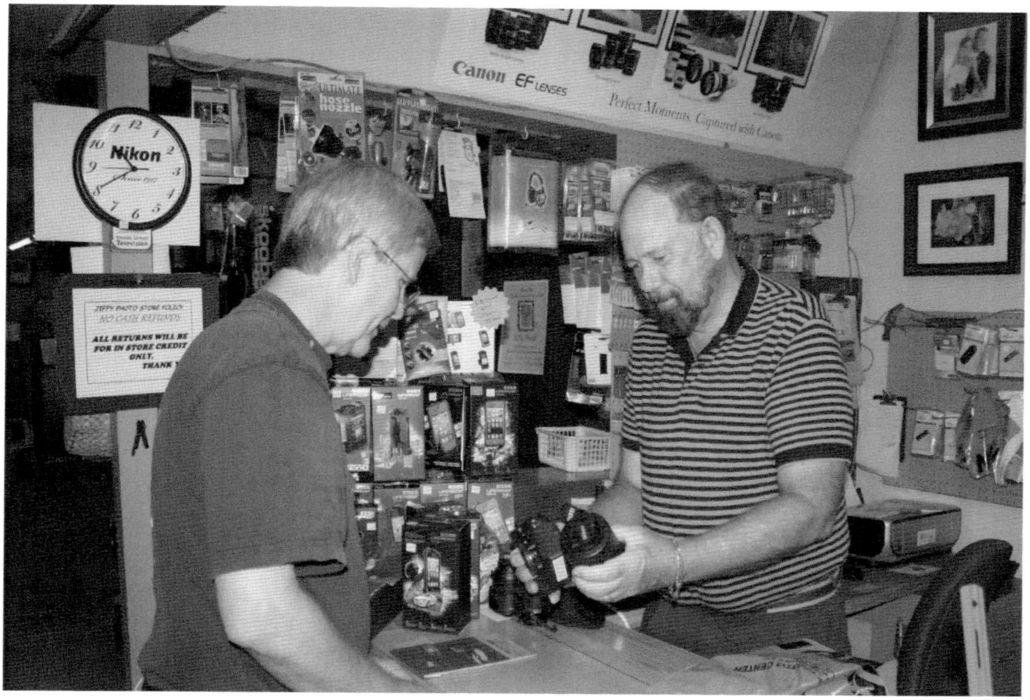

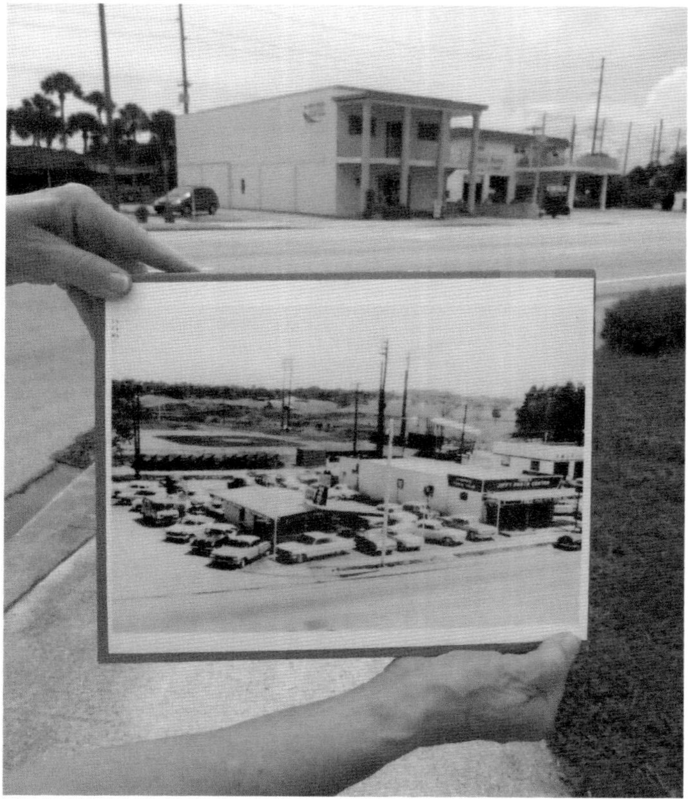

In Aid of Camera Art
Steve Moose (left) consults Mike Hinkle about a lens. The longtime proprietor of Jiffy Photo, Hinkle takes all the time necessary to assist his customers with the mysteries of the camera, patiently demonstrating and advising those who are bewildered by focus to those on the technical front edge. At left, the older photograph of the Jiffy building shows the old Jaycee Field that used to be behind the store. (Above, photograph by Tom Baumker; left, photograph by Tom Baumker with old photograph courtesy of Mike Hinkle.)

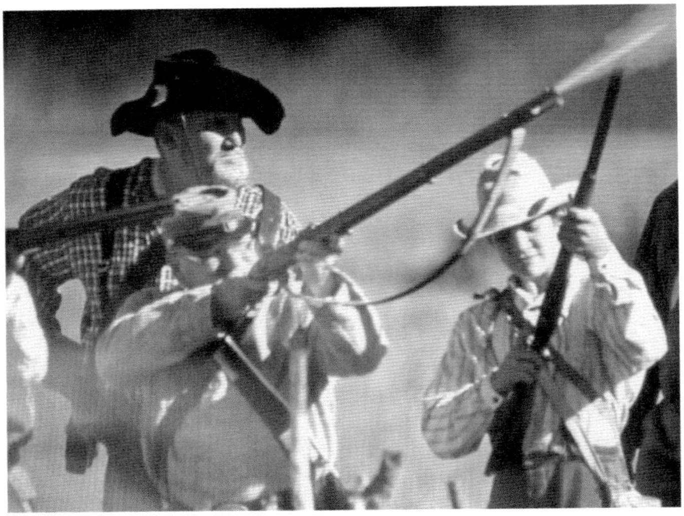

Reenactment as Education
A bearded Jim Odell is taking part in the annual raid on Fort Pierce reenactment. His interest in Florida and military history is underscored by his great-great-grandfather Andrew Jackson Futch, who served in the 8th Florida Infantry in the Civil War. Odell is the adjutant for Camp 1595, Sons of Confederate Veterans. He spent 17 years in the Navy, including assignments on the USS *New Jersey* and the USS *Missouri.* (Courtesy of Jim Odell.)

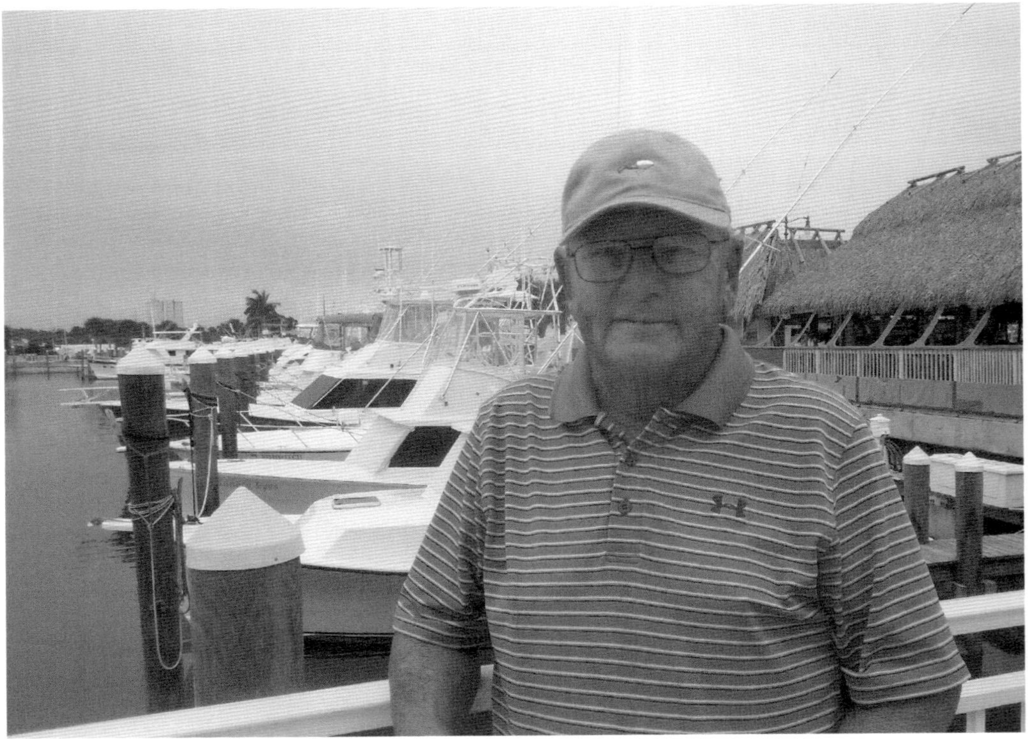

Songhooker
Multitalented Capt. Sam Crutchfield, one of those people who can play any song he hears, has written and recorded several albums including a must for sports fishermen, "Hooked on Fishin'." He has run charters for the big ones out of Fort Pierce and the Bahamas. Captain Crutchfield says, "Fort Pierce has been the perfect place for me: the ocean, the river, the backcountry, and Lake Okeechobee has been a playground for me to enjoy life with my friends. You may not miss me when I'm gone, but I sure will miss not being here." (Photograph by the author.)

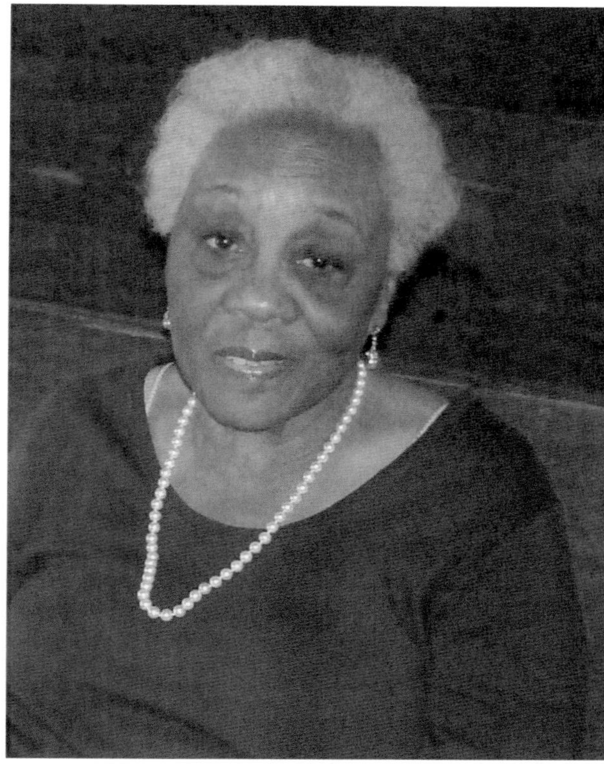

Oral History

Joyce Jackson faithfully supports her beloved African Methodist Episcopal church, including organizing its Law Enforcement Day. "Who's to tell the story?" is her call to remembrance in her oral history project in the black community. She was raised on Avenue B in the heart of the Lincoln Park section of town, back when it was a village that looked after all of its children. Joyce looks back fondly to a time when her world was the streets around her and those streets were safe. (Courtesy of Linda Hudson.)

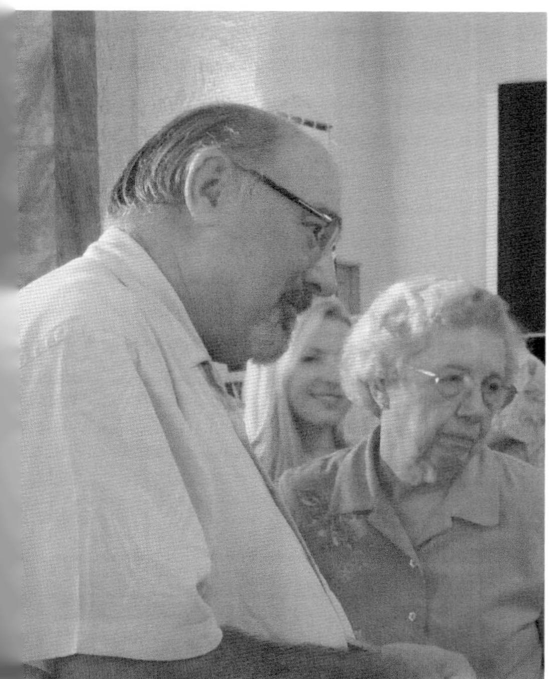

The Everyday Muse

Fort Pierce's most widely read daily columnist, Anthony Westbury came to the United States from England in 1980. After meeting his wife, Joan, in Key West, the two set out to see the country in a 1966 Volkswagen bus. They returned to Florida where Joan's family lived. Anthony has been writing about the Treasure Coast for some 30 years and his subjects, causes, and crusades are informed by a deep familiarity with the community. Westbury, notebook in hand, can be seen everywhere, from public festivities to protest marches. He hosts a public affairs radio program, and is a favorite choice to moderate debates and political forums. Here, he is covering the opening of a time capsule uncovered when a bus hit the corner of the old Methodist church, the lot for which was purchased in 1920. He is talking to Mary Taylor, whose parents were members of the church when the time capsule was buried. Taylor Dairy Road is named for her family; one of her ancestors, John Fultz, settled Spruce Bluff and was the first clerk of St. Lucie County. (Photograph by the author.)

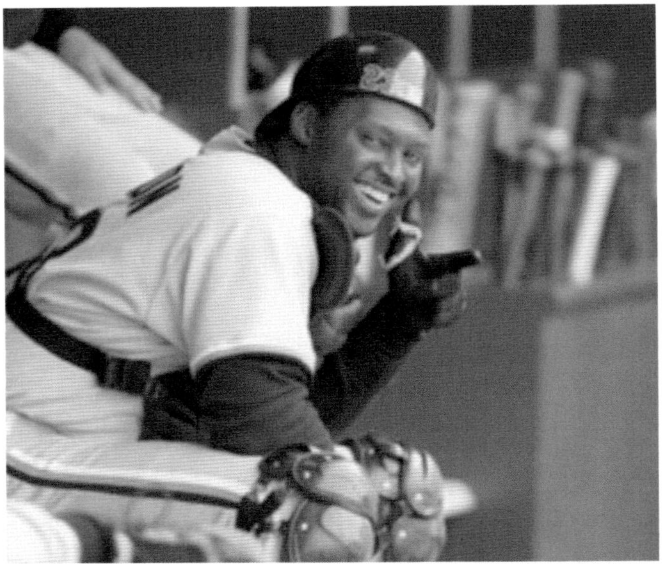

Behind the Plate
Charles Johnson, a graduate of Fort Pierce's Westwood High School, caught 123 games without an error for the Florida Marlins in the 1997 season. One of the all-time great defensive catchers, he helped the Marlins win the World Series that year. Johnson, the son of the finance director for the City of Fort Pierce, won four Golden Glove Awards from 1995 to 1998. (Courtesy of SLCRHC.)

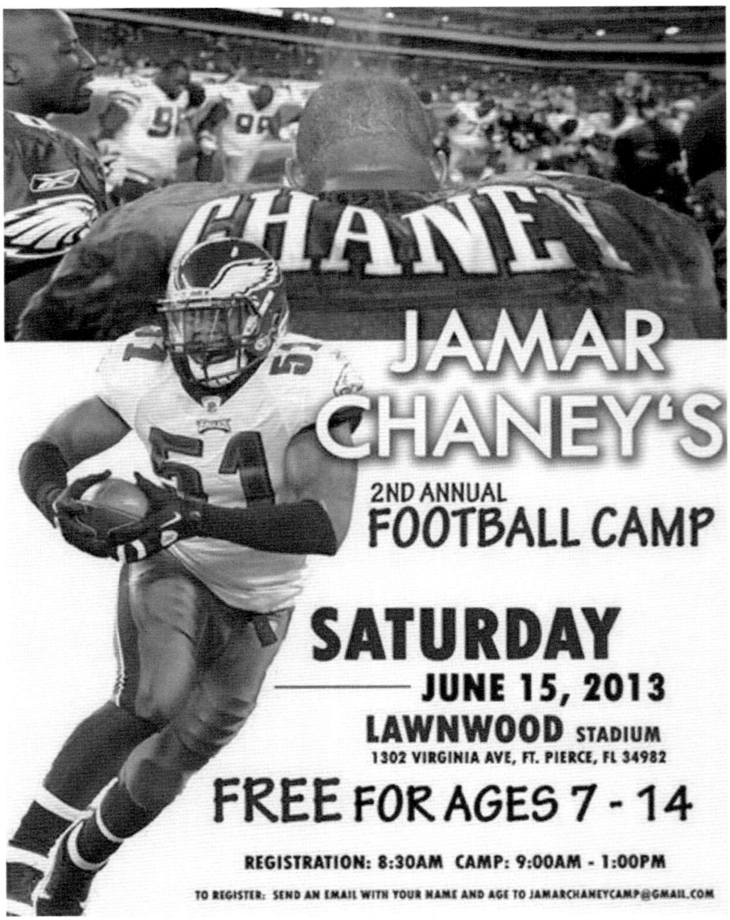

Giving Back to the Community
Pictured is a poster for legendary linebacker Jamar Chaney's football camp. Chaney played high school football in his Fort Pierce hometown, then college football at Mississippi State. He was drafted by the Philadelphia Eagles in 2010. (Courtesy of Linda Hudson.)

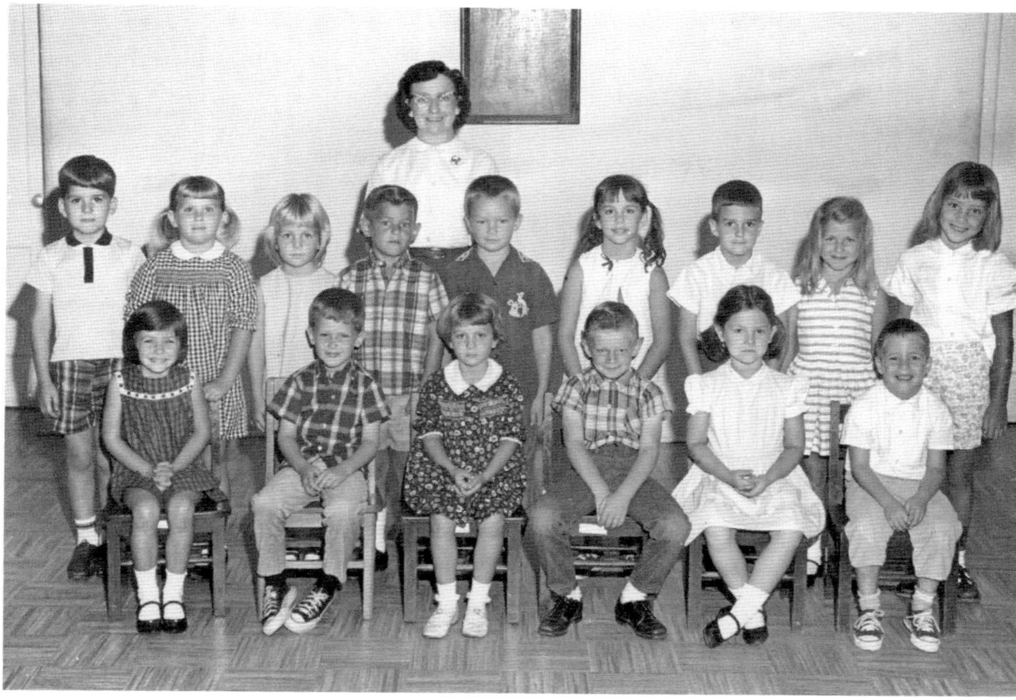

Laying the Foundation

"Good, better, best / Never let it rest / 'til your good is better / and your better is best." This is just one of the rhymes Elizabeth "Betty" Uhl taught children at the First United Methodist Church in Fort Pierce back in the 1960s. In her 47 years at the preschool and kindergarten, she taught these children and some of their children. A high school valedictorian once told Uhl, "I was not a bit afraid when I stood at the podium to speak—because you put me on stage when I was five years old." On the eve of her retirement (below), Uhl noted that children today have been exposed to much more than their parents. Still, she never compromised her insistence on discipline and good manners. "I always met them at the door with a hug," she remembered. Nowadays, she gets those hugs returned when former students bend down to hug her. At less than five feet tall, Uhl has a heart tall enough to reach the shyest child. (Both, courtesy of Elizabeth Uhl.)

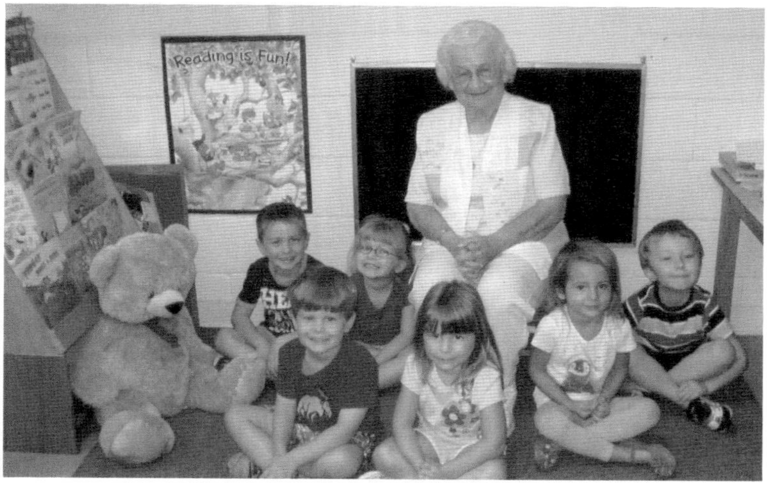

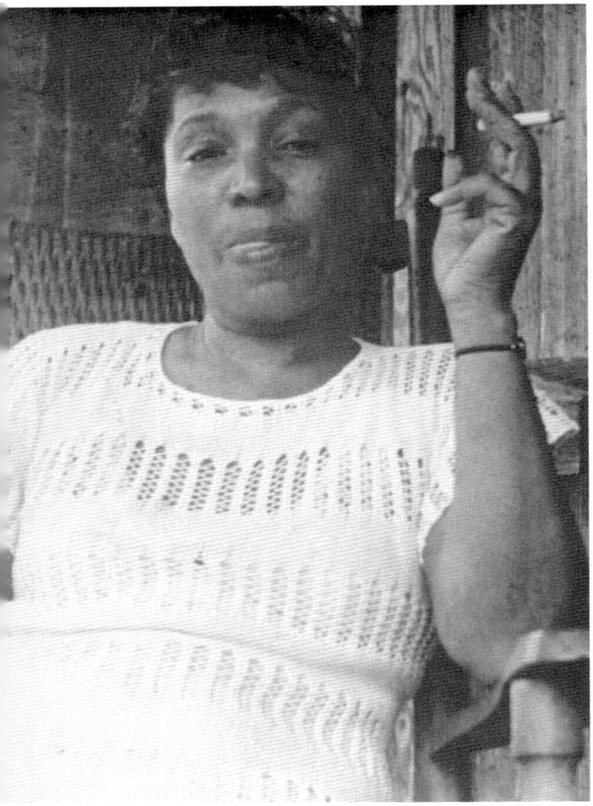

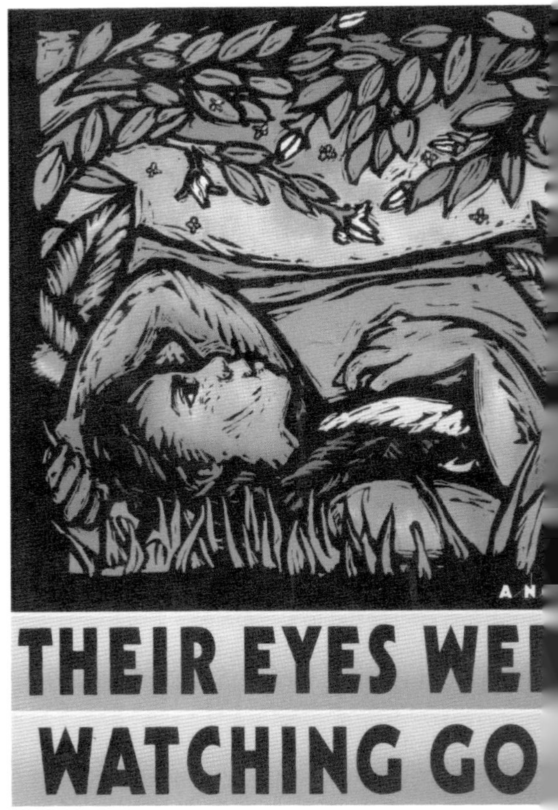

Her Eyes Watched God (ABOVE AND OPPOSITE PAGE)
Young Zora Neale Hurston grew up in Eatonville, Florida, a predominantly African American community. With persistence, sponsors, and luck, she earned an anthropology degree, after which she collected folklore about Florida and the Caribbean, became a luminary in the Harlem Renaissance, and authored books and plays. Published in 1937, her book *Their Eyes Were Watching God* is considered a classic.

The popularity of her work eventually waned, and she found herself in a trough of what-ever-happened-to. She ended up in Fort Pierce, writing for the *Chronicle*, a newspaper aimed at a black audience. She also did some teaching; some locals remember being in her class. She had friends among both races. "Sometimes I feel discriminated against," she wrote, "but it does not make me angry. It merely astonishes me." Pictured opposite is Zora's last home at 1734 L Street in Fort Pierce.

Zora died in January 1960 and was laid in an unmarked pauper's grave until Alice Walker came to Fort Pierce to insist the former "Queen of Harlem" be honored in death. Walker's enthusiasm for Hurston's literary legacy helped restore the author's works to the attention of a new generation. Today, her books are bestsellers, and her stories and articles are taught in literature classes. She has become internationally popular once more, and she has a well-marked grave. (Above left, courtesy of SLCRHC; above right, photograph by the author; opposite top, photograph by Tom Baumker; opposite bottom, photograph by the author.)

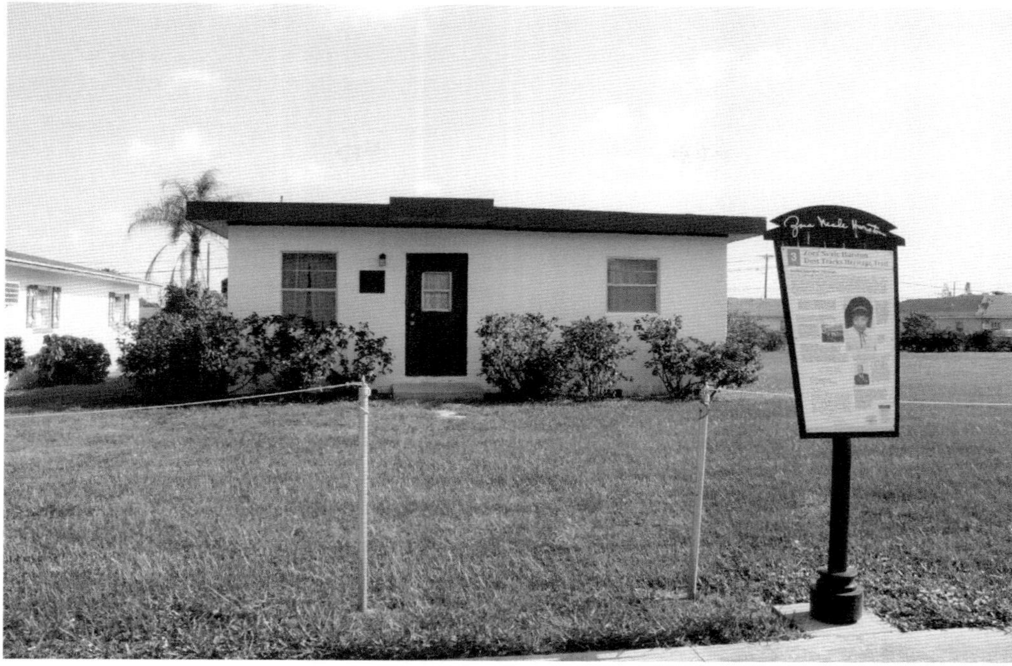

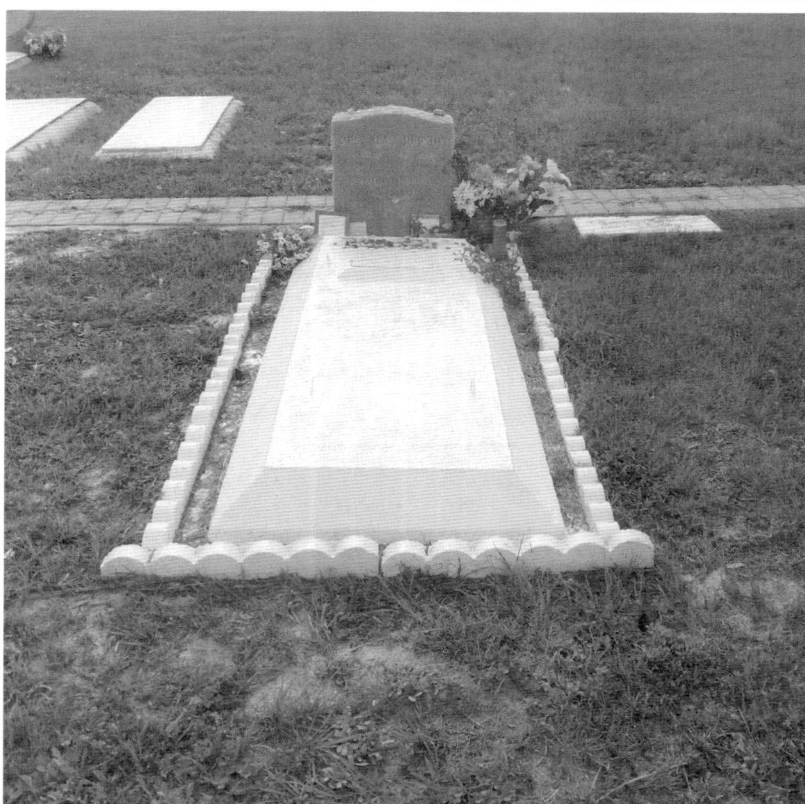

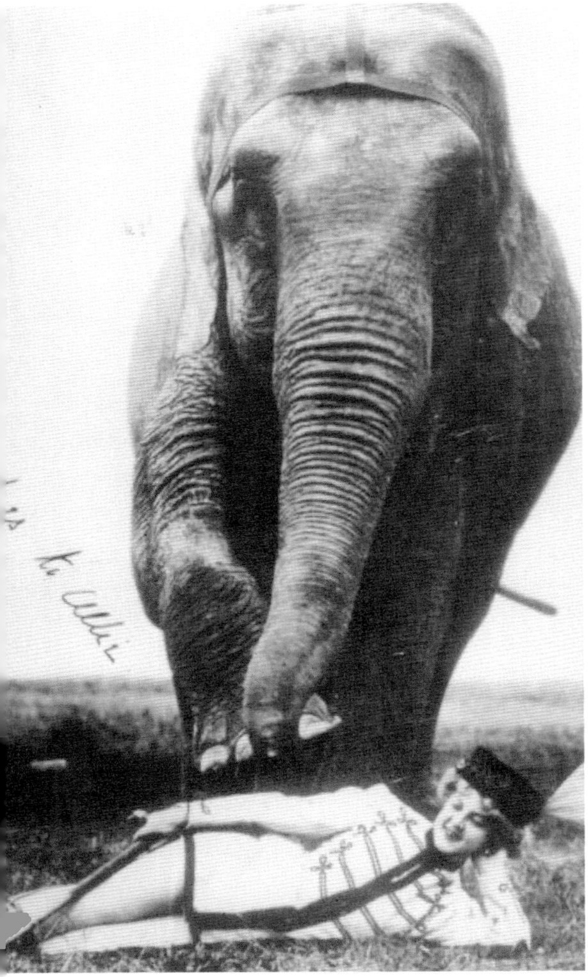

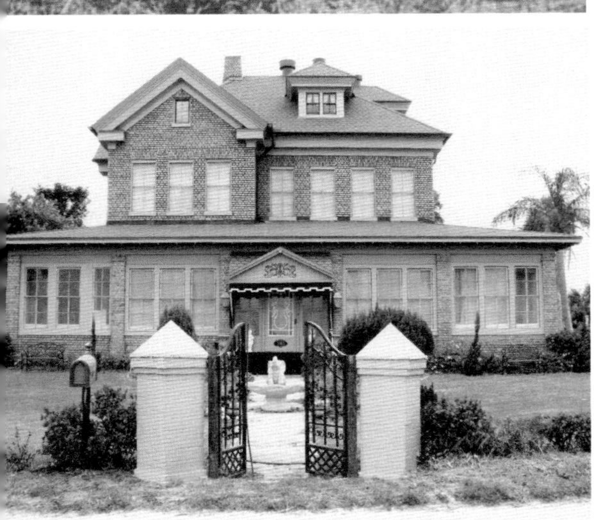

The Bravest Woman in the World

Lucia Zora Card was trained for the opera but ran away from home to join the circus and became known as the "Bravest Woman in the World." As this photograph with Old Snyder proves, Lucia could rest comfortably under an elephant's foot. An animal trainer with skills she learned from her trainer husband, Fred Alispaw, she became the first woman to enter a cage with both lions and tigers. She had shown her vocal talent as a girl when, in 1898, she wrapped herself in a Cuban flag and entertained Fort Pierce residents to raise money to top the sand road with shell. Tears were shed by members of the audience when little Lucia sang "The Cuban Captive," followed by much laughter when she belted out "The Fort Pierce Home Guard," a comic piece she composed about the local home guard under Capt. Adrian Sample. She authored a book about circus life, *Sawdust and Solitude*, which was published in 1924.

Milton Card, Lucia's father, first came to Fort Pierce to hunt. In search of his own vine and fig tree, he returned, purchased land, and became a pineapple planter. In the early days of the automobile, locals would go out for a drive down the road by the Indian River, and the Card house, pictured, was one of the highlights of the tour. Note the small elephant statue on the front walk. It is said that Lucia Zora Card acquired a pet elephant, and it roamed the grounds for a while but ate too many of the neighbors' plants.

Lucia was at her father's bedside when he died in September 1927. She and her husband, Fred, moved to Fort Pierce from Colorado, where they had homesteaded after retiring from the circus. They bought an orange grove, and Lucia took care of her mother, Myra. It was reported in her obituary that she died in a hospital in north Florida, most likely Chatahoochee, Florida's mental hospital. Zora and Fred moved into the Card family home in 1932. Lucia's exotic past did not prevent her from fitting into small-town life. She became involved in community affairs, chairing the Indian welfare division of the Florida Federation of Women's Clubs and serving as vice president of the local Business and Professional Women's Club. She was also a member of the St. Lucie County Democrat Party Committee. She died, well mourned, in 1936, and was buried in the local cemetery in a grave still unmarked. (Top, courtesy of SLCRHC; bottom, photograph by Tom Baumker.)

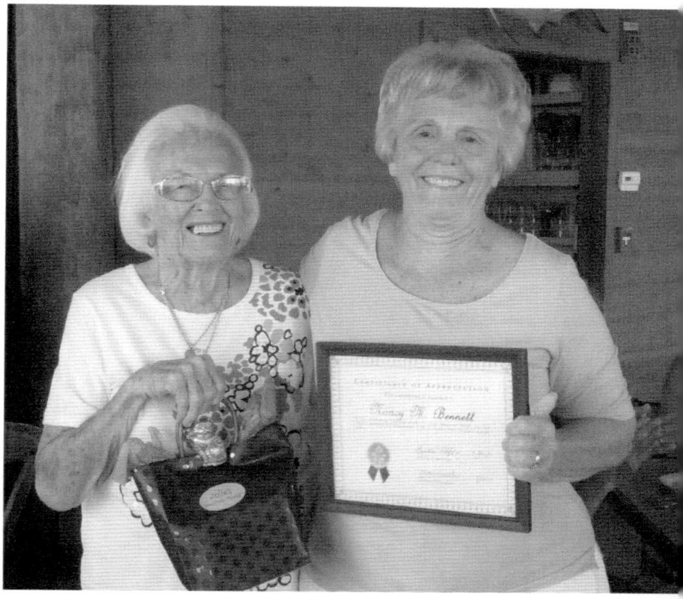

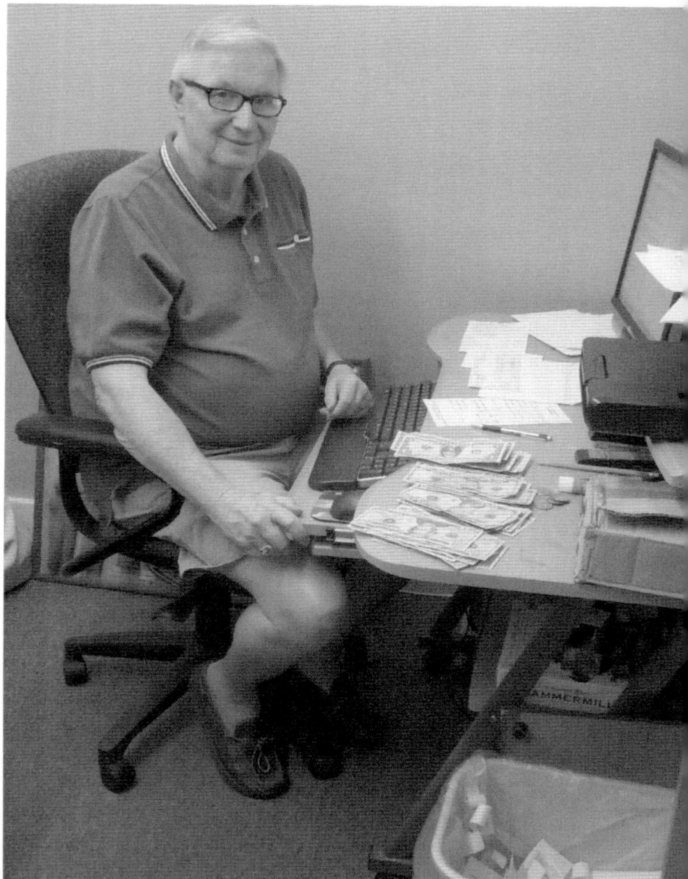

They Kept It Open

When the economy dived in 2008, one of the options for county leaders to save money was to close the St. Lucie County Regional History Center. After long and arduous negotiations, Nancy Bennett, president of the St. Lucie Historical Society, signed a contract allowing the museum to reopen with all volunteer labor. Nancy manages the center, and hundreds of primary school students take field trips there to learn about Florida and local history. Nancy is there every day, tending to everything from dead opossums in the garden to blown fuses in the attic. She has a friendly greeting for every visitor. Her first lieutenant, Lucille Rights, trains the docents and answers history questions. She is the premier historian of the Treasure Coast and author of *A Portrait of St. Lucie County*. The third lieutenant is Mose Saunders, who keeps the books and money accounts. His computer skills also allow him to contribute to the center in other ways, such as cataloging the new books that are donated.

A cadre of devoted volunteers put in half-day shifts so that residents and tourists can view the exhibitions. Among the offerings are the treasure room with Spanish artifacts that were recovered from the ocean, a model Indian camp that illustrates the Seminole way of life, and a room that interprets the World War II Navy experience at Fort Pierce.

The photograph above of Nancy (right) and Lucille was taken at the annual volunteer luncheon. The photograph of Mose Saunders was snapped in his office. (Both photographs by the author.)

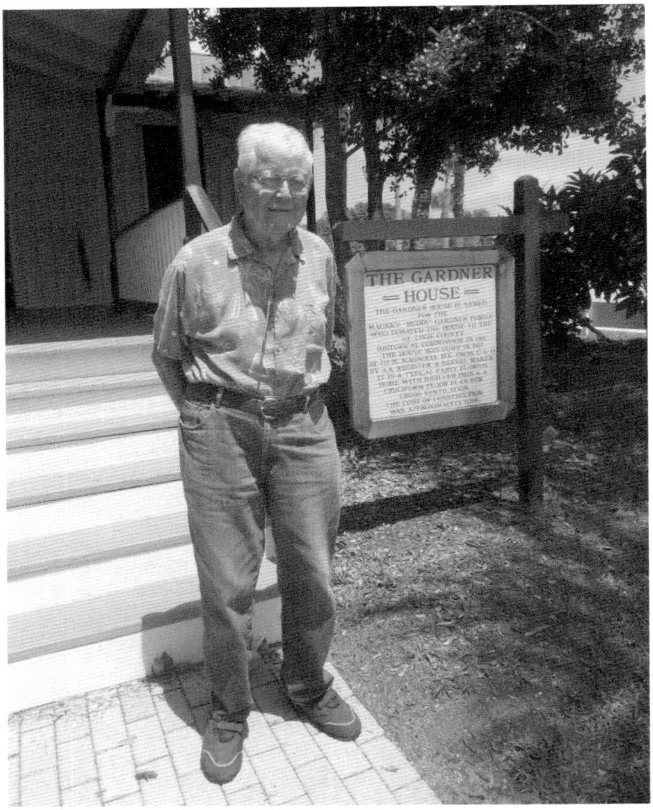

The Gardner House
Donated by the family and furnished with period furniture, the Gardner house is now a part of the St. Lucie County Regional History Center and illustrates how people in Fort Pierce lived in the early nineteenth century. It is a special privilege when Dan Gardner, a museum volunteer, leads a tour group through these rooms, telling his personal stories of growing up in this house. (Photograph by the author.)

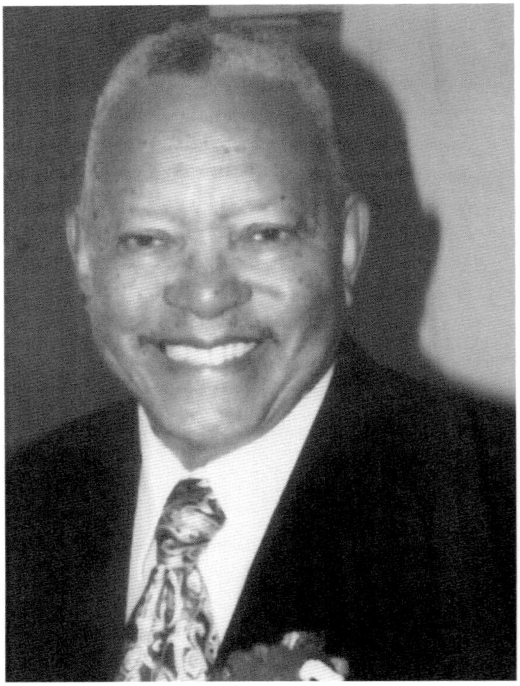

Classical Master
Prof. Earl Little, a 1945 graduate of Lincoln Park Academy who attended Hampton University, a college founded in 1868 to educate newly-freed slaves, has taught thousands of young people in local schools to perform and appreciate music during his academic career from 1951 to 1991. In 1985, Little was named Teacher of the Year at Fort Pierce Central. In retirement, he works as the music director at the Jensen Community Church and produces the church's annual Christmas concert, which is a must-see for music lovers. In 2012, he was inducted into the hall of fame by the Florida Vocal Association for "excellence in the teaching of music and renown in the area of vocal and choral music education." He plays several instruments and is an inspiring vocalist with a repertoire that includes opera. He was the choral director for the Fort Pierce Opera Society (it is now inactive). His wife, Alice, is also a graduate of Hampton and a violinist of note. (Courtesy of Earl Little.)

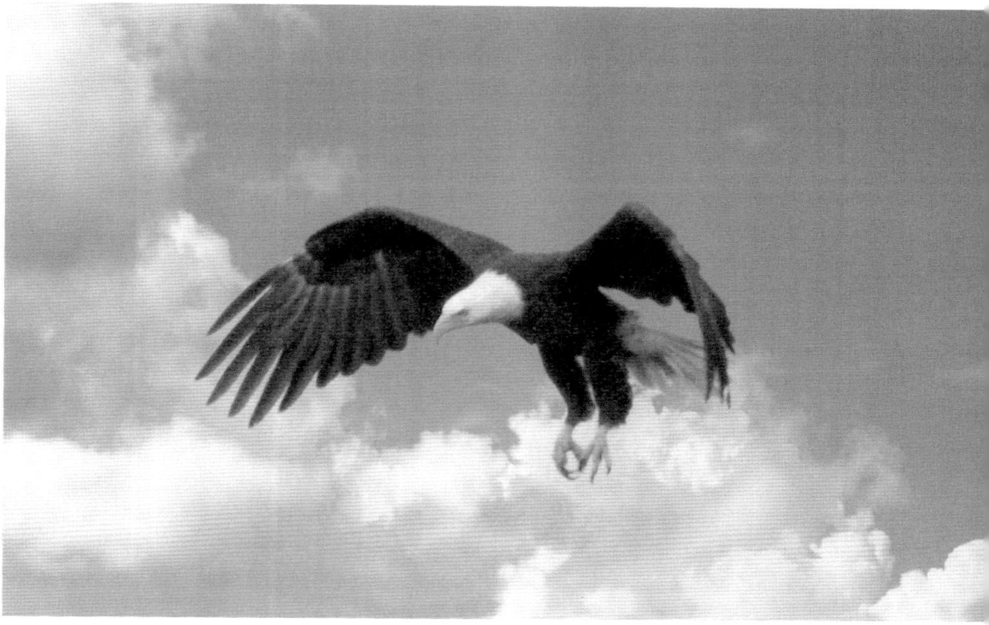

The Eagle Man

Tom Baumker has been a welder, policeman, citrus grower, and forest ranger. He worked at the city power plant and the Florida Power and Light nuclear plant. He was the fire marshal for the Atlantic Undersea Test and Evaluation Center in the Bahamas and the supervisor at Harbor Branch Oceanographic. Ever since his mother gave him an Ansco camera at the age of 10, he has been taking prize-winning photographs. Beanie Backus, from whom he took art lessons, praised Tom's singular talent for composition. In retirement, Baumker Photography has become a full-time pursuit. Tom is known as "the Eagle Man" because of the 13-year photographic chronicle he produced showing the life of a family of those proud birds that were living in the nearby savannah. He also has a considerable collection of vintage photographs. His photographs of Florida flora and fauna earned him 150,000 hits in 2012 on his website, www.redbubble.com/people/tombaumker. (Above, photograph by Tom Baumker; below, courtesy of Tom Baumker.)

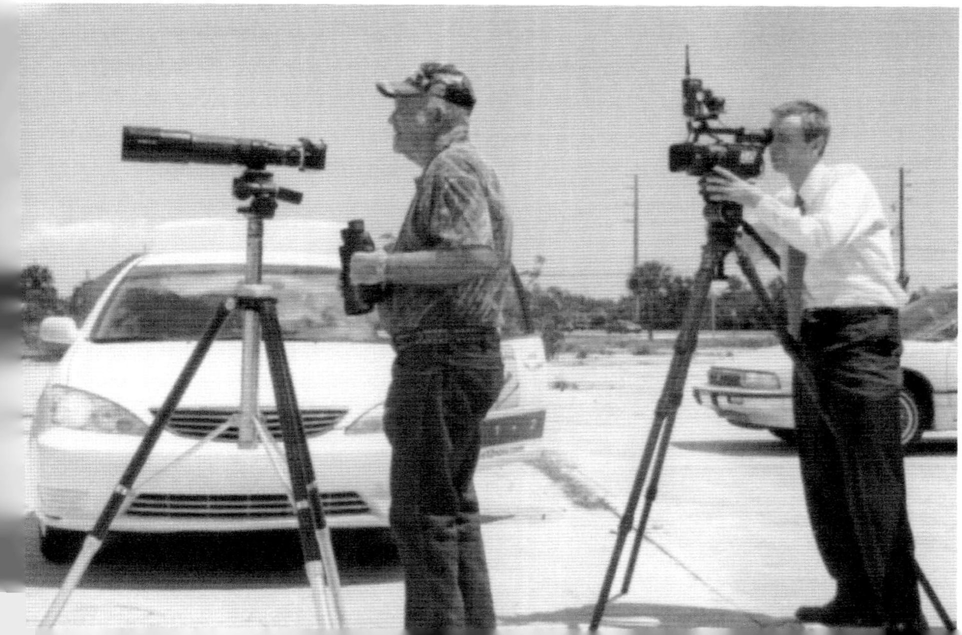

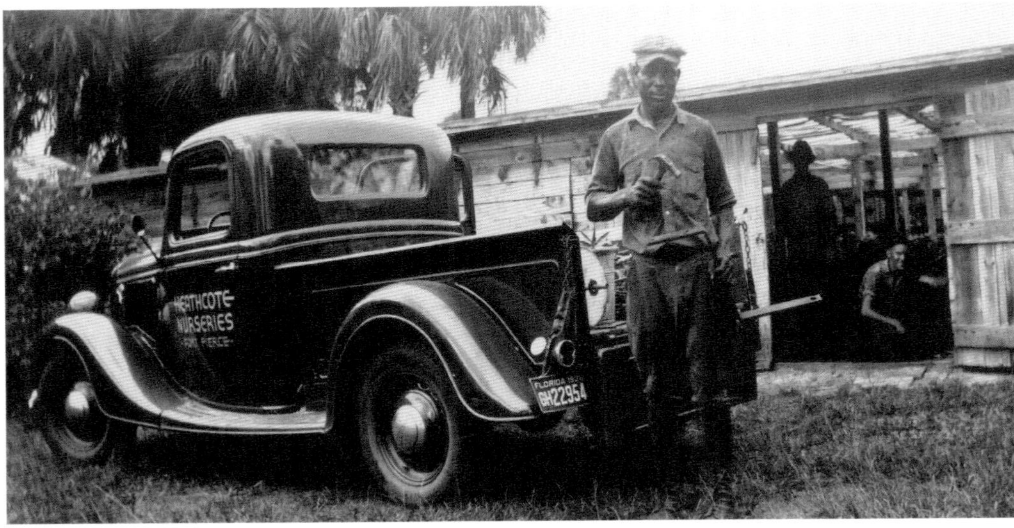

Heathcote Botanical Gardens

Larry, Clements, and Martin Baumker worked at Heathcote Nurseries. There, Martin is said to have developed the first bougainvilleas with color other than the traditional scarlet, such as purple. Above, Larry Baumker is pictured inside the doorway of the shed; the gentleman in the foreground is unidentified.

The nursery originated in Scarsdale, New York, and in 1926, a branch of it was established on Orange Avenue in Fort Pierce. After a few years, the local branch was managed by Jim and Mollie Crimmins, the latter of whom was a talented landscape artist. The couple purchased the enterprise in 1957 and moved it to Savannah Road. In addition to cultivating native plants, the Crimmins collected plants from around the world. Jim and Mollie retired after 60 years in business.

In 1985, the City of Fort Pierce, St. Lucie County, 9 businesses, 13 organizations, and 66 individuals donated funds to purchase the nursery property and establish the Heathcote Botanical Gardens, a nonprofit 501(c)(3) operated by volunteers. Gardener Marian Moore Charles and groundskeeper J.D. Collins are seen in the photograph below taking a midday rest on a nursery bench. Marian is the daughter of the late Gloria Moore, who was the steadiest of the founding members of the public garden. Today, visitors who enjoy the peace and beauty of Heathcote Botanical Gardens do so largely due to the dedication of Gloria. The grounds contain palms, herbs, ornamental and tropical plants, and a replica of a cracker house built by Pete Peterson as well as a 1922 Victorian house. In 2010, bonsai master James J. Smith, founder of the Treasure Coast Bonsai Society (which has contributed to the US National Arboretum), donated 100 tropical bonsais, giving Heathcote Botanical Gardens the largest public collection of bonsais in the United States. (Above, courtesy of Tom Baumker; below, photograph by the author.)

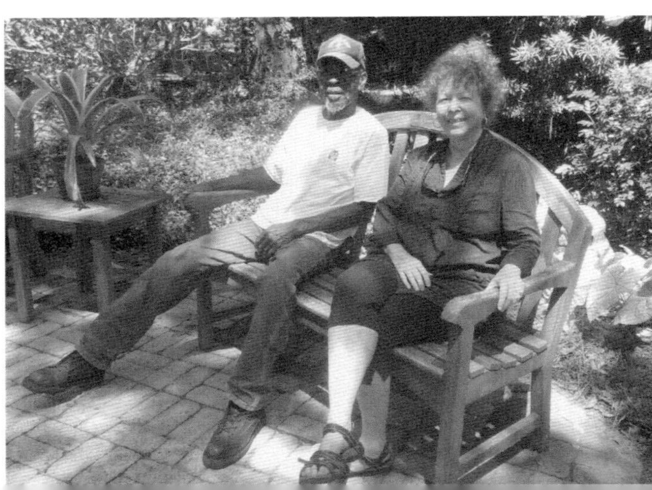

CHAPTER SIX

The Enterprise Zone

Fort Pierce has the longest history as a trading center of any town on Florida's lower east coast. When Annie Hogg was selling tobacco to Milton Card in 1880, hers was the only store between Titusville and Miami. Her husband, Capt. Ben Hogg, took Roseate Spoonbill feathers that were gathered by Seminoles to Jacksonville to satisfy the ladies' hat industry and traded them for a cargo of flour and canned beans his wife could sell to yachters and homesteaders.

By the 1890s, Peter P. Cobb was ensconced in the store at the end of Avenue A in Fort Pierce where he continued to trade knives and such for Indian deer hides and supplied settlers with "Everything to eat, wear and use." As trade boats, supplied by the canning company that bought out the Hoggs, had carried floating stores to the settlers up and down the river, Cobb's delivery wagon supplied his customers. Harry Hill began to take photographs in 1897 and soon occupied a house in Edgartown. In 1902, the Fee family set out from Melbourne, Florida, to begin their long sojourn as Fort Pierce residents.

In 1912, the Holtsbergs established a department store on the main street, and, in 1919, a grocery store next door. In 1926, as part of the building boom, the Arcade Building, an early mall with cool, inside corridors, was completed, and its stores rented to tenants.

On Saturday afternoons in the 1940s and 1950s, Fort Pierce streets were crowded with shoppers. Kids came to watch the newest cowboy movie. McCrory's, Rubin's, Odom's Bar, Penney's—all these and more supplied the town.

Like other small towns, Fort Pierce has struggled to keep its downtown relevant in the age of malls and big-box stores. Most of the old landmarks are memories.

Bud Adams, possessing a sense of history like his father, Judge Adams, purchased the P.P. Cobb building to assure its preservation. It is the oldest continuously operating commercial building in the area. Customers can still buy groceries there and can also get their hair cut or clock repaired. For the first time in 130 years there is no bank on Second Street, but Rosslow's remains on its downtown corner and is still the preferred destination for discriminating ladies in the market for a new outfit. The old Florida Photographic Concern studio and Hill residence has been converted into a microbrewery, Sailfish Brewing Company.

The Sunrise Theatre has been revamped and standing-room-only audiences today enjoy headliners like Willie Nelson and Tony Bennett. The Downtown Fort Pierce Farmers Market has become a Saturday tradition and Friday Fest attracts a happy crowd on the first Friday of every month. East Coast Lumber is still headquartered on Avenue A; it is the oldest family-owned business in Florida. Other longtime businesses do a brisk trade outside downtown: Boudrias Groves is by the turnpike, Roy's Liquors & Fine Wines and Jetson Appliance & Electronics Experts are on US 1, Carter's Grocery is out in cowboy country.

But Archie's, the iconic beach bar whose first customers were the Navy skeleton-crew workers left to close the World War II base, is thriving.

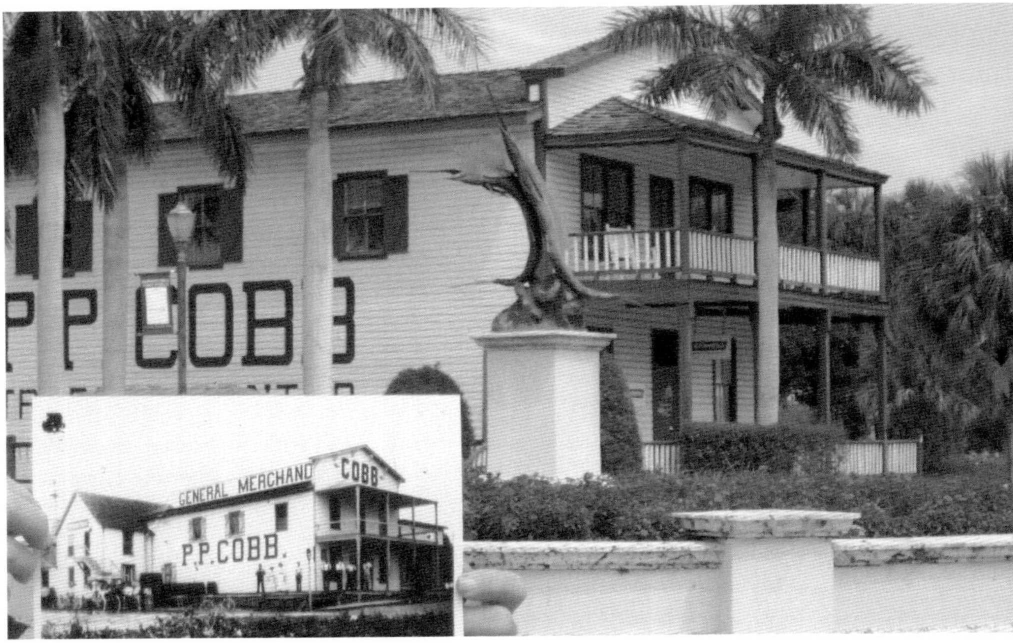

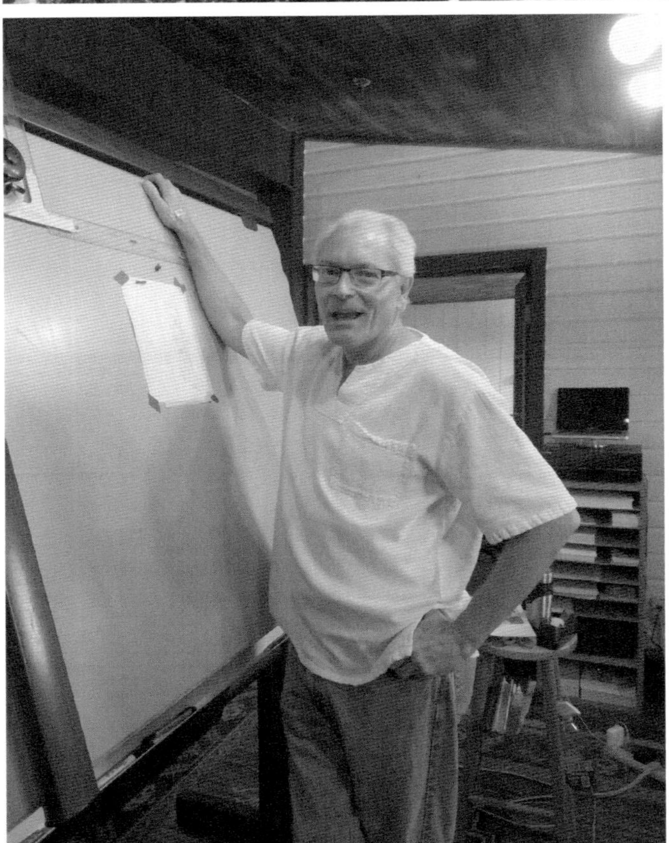

An Indian Trading Post
Pictured is the oldest commercial building in Fort Pierce. On this spot, a series of bold entrepreneurs—such as Frank Smith, Capt. Benjamin Hogg, and P.P. Cobb—traded ammunition and thread with the Seminoles in exchange for deer hides and feathers. (Courtesy of Buzz Smyth.)

Architectural Preservationist
David Cleveland is a stickler for truth in architecture. Pictured at his board, he is investigating old Fort Capron with a Google map overlay of an old military map. Among buildings he has restored are the Arcade Building, the Boston House, and the P.P. Cobb building, where he has an office upstairs. (Photograph by the author.)

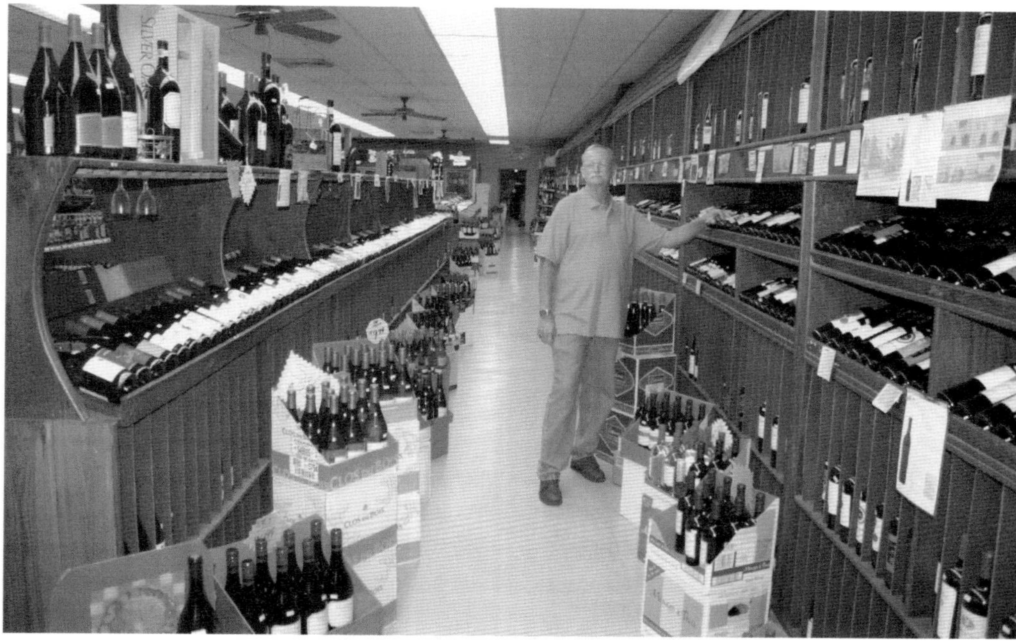

Nothing Stopped Him

Roy's Liquors & Fine Wines is located streetside with the Boozgeois Saloon in the back. Roy Andersen opened the first Roy's Liquors in 1955. He was on crutches, having contracted polio the year before. After 25 years at Food Fair shopping center where he opened the original Boozgeois Saloon, the business moved to this location on US 1 and Georgia Avenue. During the last decade of his life, Roy operated his business from a wheelchair. Keith Andersen took over his father's business in 1975, adding a stock of wines to establish the store's reputation of having the finest collection on the Treasure Coast. Keith can be counted on to produce a wine tasting to raise money for any good cause, and he is prepared to advise a savvy hostess about the wines she should serve dinner guests. Keith is a longtime board member of Learn to Read in St. Lucie County. (Photograph by Tom Baumker.)

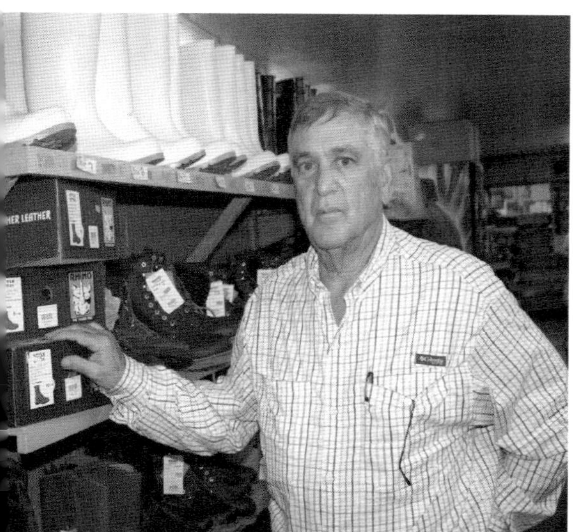

More Than a Grocery Store

Carter's Grocery offers an array of goods: chewing tobacco and chains, hats and hardware, sunglasses and groceries, and more. In the back of the store are hot lunch choices: fried chicken, barbecue sandwiches, Mexican spicy soup, collard greens, ribs, fried fish and hush puppies, baked beans, and corn. Craig Carter has been the proprietor for 35 years. Oftentimes, working men with clipped beards and camouflage caps can be found eating at the grocery's tables where jugs of water and rolls of paper towels are conveniently at hand. Cowboys and grove hands can be heard guffawing over the latest tales while they eat. Craig's daughter, Tobi, posts the daily specials for the store's hundreds of friends on Facebook. (Photograph by Tom Baumker.)

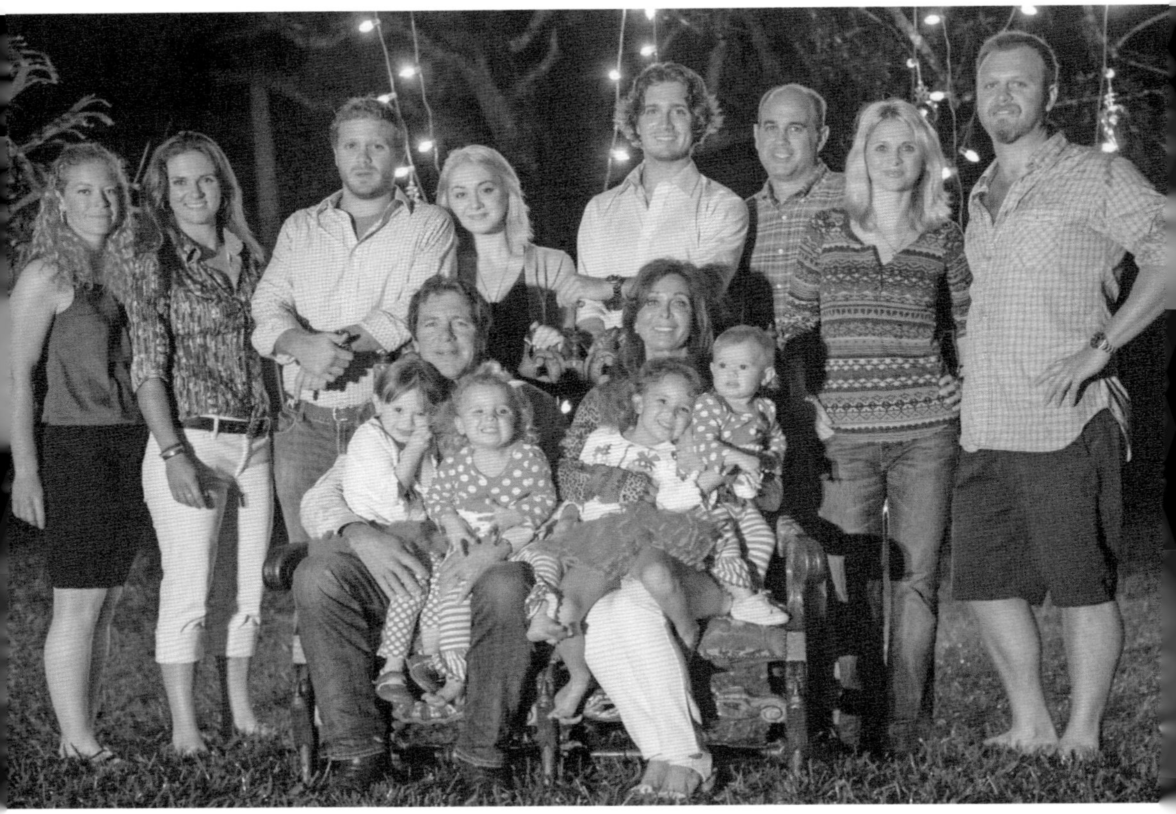

German Beer, Southern Style (ABOVE AND OPPOSITE PAGE)
Peter W. Busch, a descendant of Adolphus Busch, a visionary brewer and founder of Anheuser-Busch, moved to Vero Beach in 1984 to take over ownership and operation of the local beer distributor. Southern Eagle Distributing has flourished over the past 29 years and become the Treasure Coast's leading beverage distributor.

Peter's belief has been that "we all must give back to the very people who help keep us in business and survive." He has made enormous strides in providing for charitable causes. Aside from all that he has contributed, citizens within the community view Peter and his family as ultimate givers, not only of monetary and beverage donations, but of their time, hearts, and minds. The Peter W. Busch Family Foundation was founded in 1991 with successful intentions of supporting initiatives that improve the quality of health, education, and family in the community, as well as the preservation of Florida's indigenous animals and landscape.

Peter's son Philip A. Busch (pictured opposite), now president of Southern Eagle, plans on keeping the family legacy alive with innovation, growth, and, of course, philanthropy. Making friends will always be their business. Pictured above are members of the Busch family, from left to right: (first row) Beatrice Dunford, Peter W. Busch, Julia Busch, Joan Busch, Kate Busch, and Gertrude Dunford; (second row) Christina Clark, Tiffany Busch, Philip Busch, Martina Busch, Jacob Busch, Eddie Dunford, Julia Busch-Dunford, and David Busch. (Both, courtesy of Southern Eagle Distributing.)

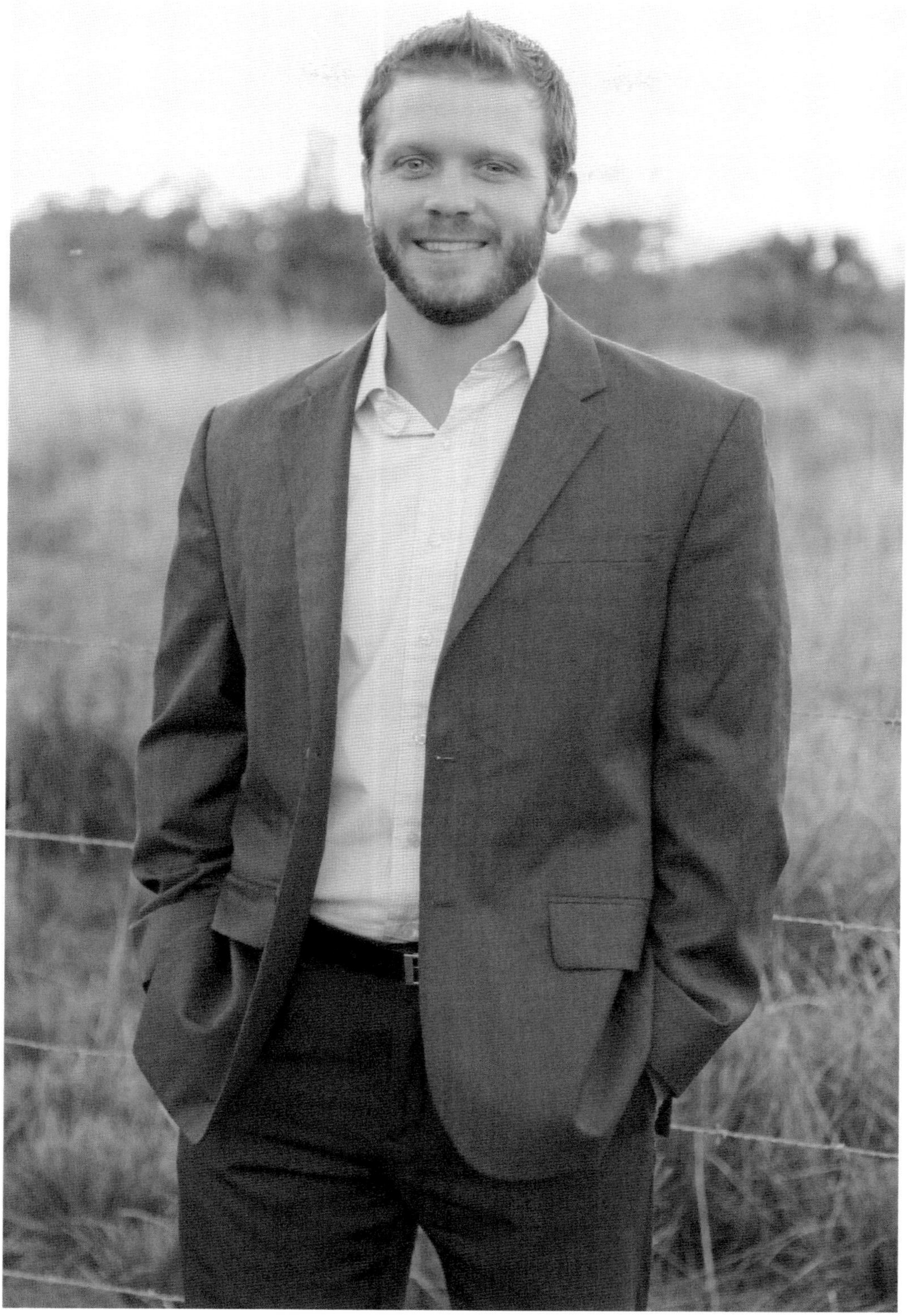

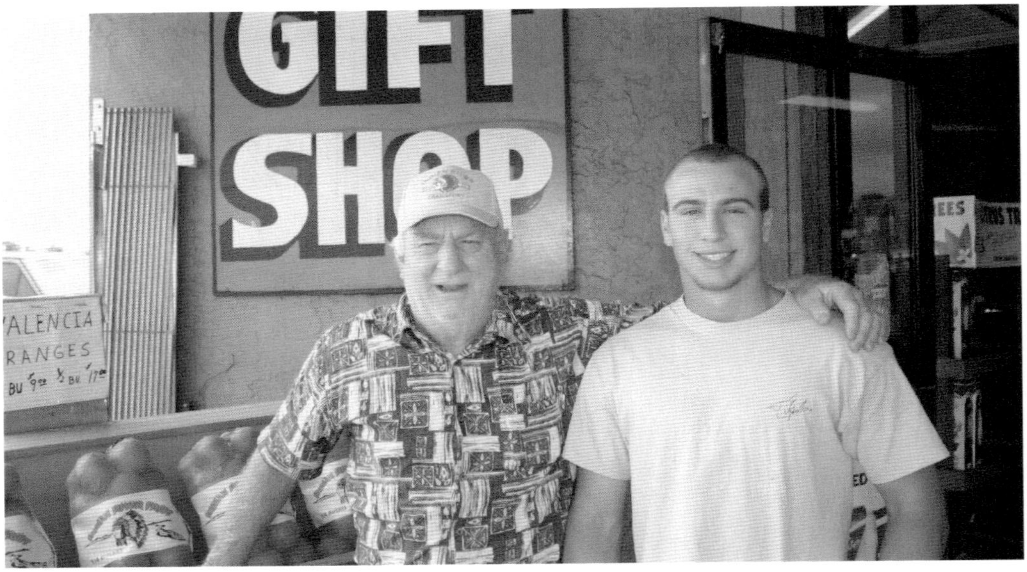

Location, Location, Location
Roland Boudrias, pictured here with son Douglas, is one of the French Canadian clan in Fort Pierce. Roland sells oranges, grapefruit, orange-blossom honey, and souvenirs like coconut heads at one of the best locations in the state: where I-95 and the Florida turnpike have adjacent exits at cross-state Okeechobee Road. A hard worker, Roland labors in Florida-style work clothes—a cotton shirt and khaki shorts—to produce the orange and grapefruit juice prized by locals as the freshest and best. Boudrias Groves is situated where Forget's, an early convenience store, once stood. (Photograph by Tom Baumker.)

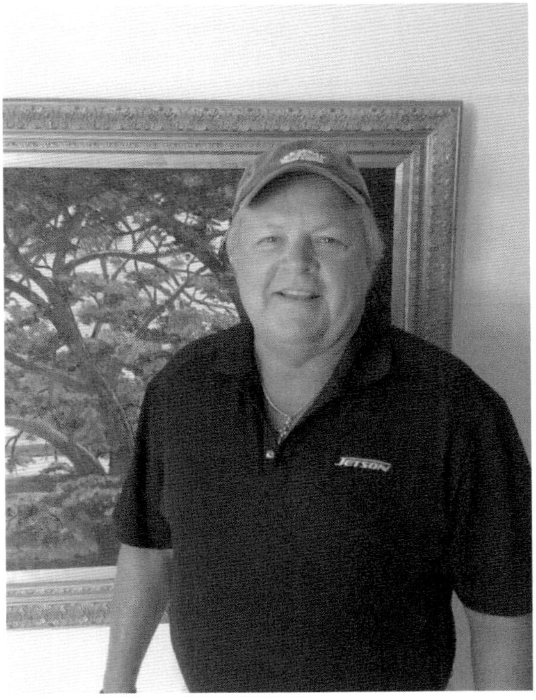

The Patriotic Appliance King
Starting with one Fort Pierce Jetson TV and Appliances store in 1974, John Jetson now has seven locations stretching from Vero Beach to Stuart. John has always supported products produced in the USA, as well as supported the local community. American-made Serta mattresses recently joined the electronics and appliances lineup sold at Jetson Appliance & Electronics Experts. John enthusiastically supports local artists—he collects the colorful landscape art of the Florida Highwaymen and, in this photograph, he stands by a Highwaymen Poinciana. John has 174 pieces of art that were made by the group, and they are displayed in his stores. In his spare time, he enjoys the fishing opportunities in the water off Fort Pierce. (Courtesy of Susan Harris of Jetsons.)

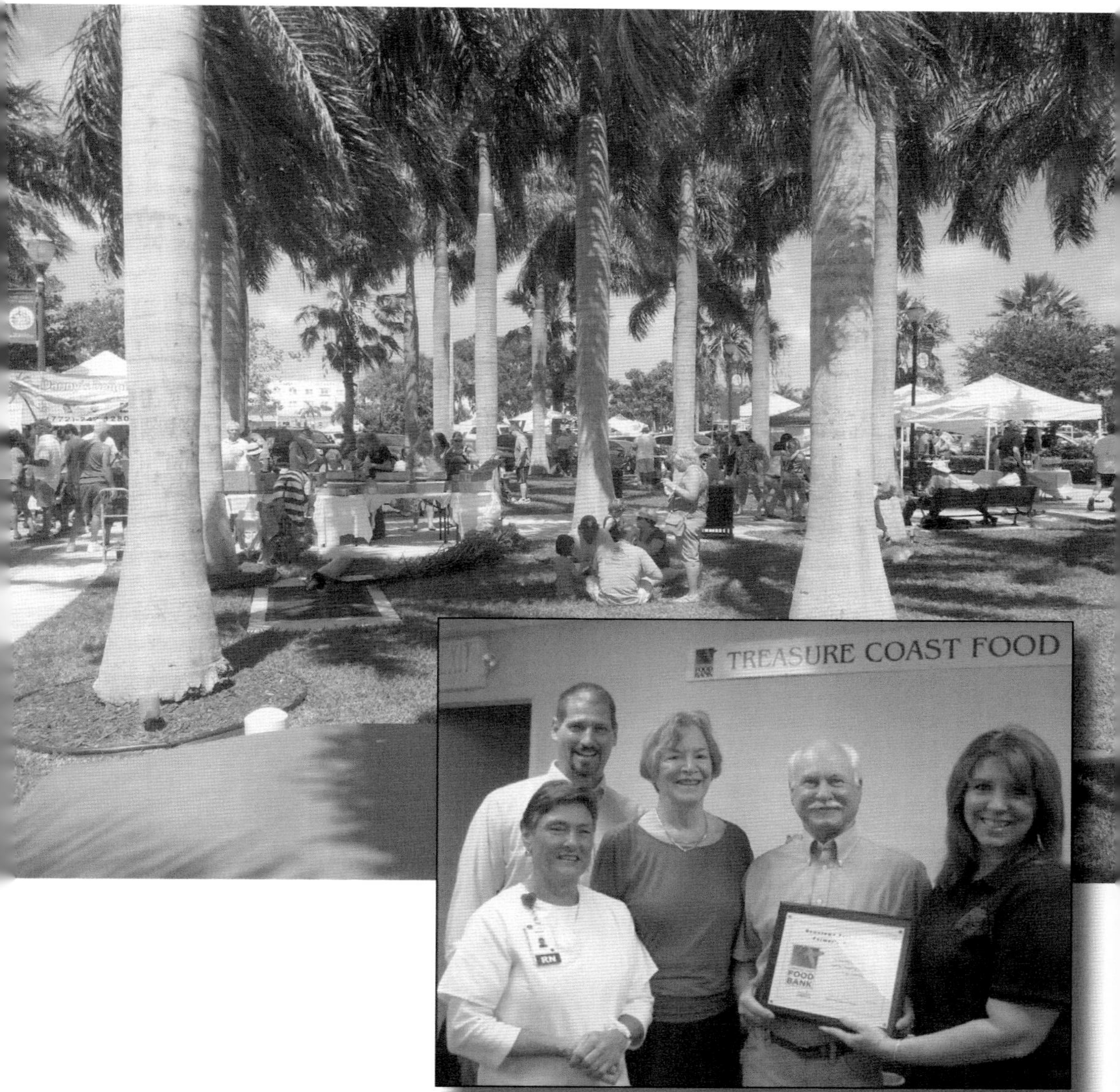

A Saturday Morning Tradition

Patrons come—rain or shine—from all over the Treasure Coast to the Downtown Fort Pierce Farmers Market. A typical visit to the market might go like this: getting a fresh sweet roll from The Bread Man and a specialty coffee from a vendor of choice, then sitting on the seawall and eating and drinking while visiting with neighbors and listening to the live music of the week. Next, one might purchase fresh vegetables; fish dip and guacamole; orchids and potted herb gardens; loaves of just-baked, whole grain bread; a bag of oranges or a gallon of grapefruit juice; some guava jelly; a Key lime pie—and a hundred other things. A volunteer board runs the market. Pictured here, manager Eric Sebenick, board member Brenda Gibbons, former chairman Linda Hudson, and chairman Harley Cowles receive a certification of appreciation from Judy Cruz, chief executive officer of Treasure Coast Food Bank. The farmers market is the annual venue of the Treasure Coast Food Bank's Empty Bowls Initiative. (Above, photograph by the author; below, courtesy of Linda Hudson.)

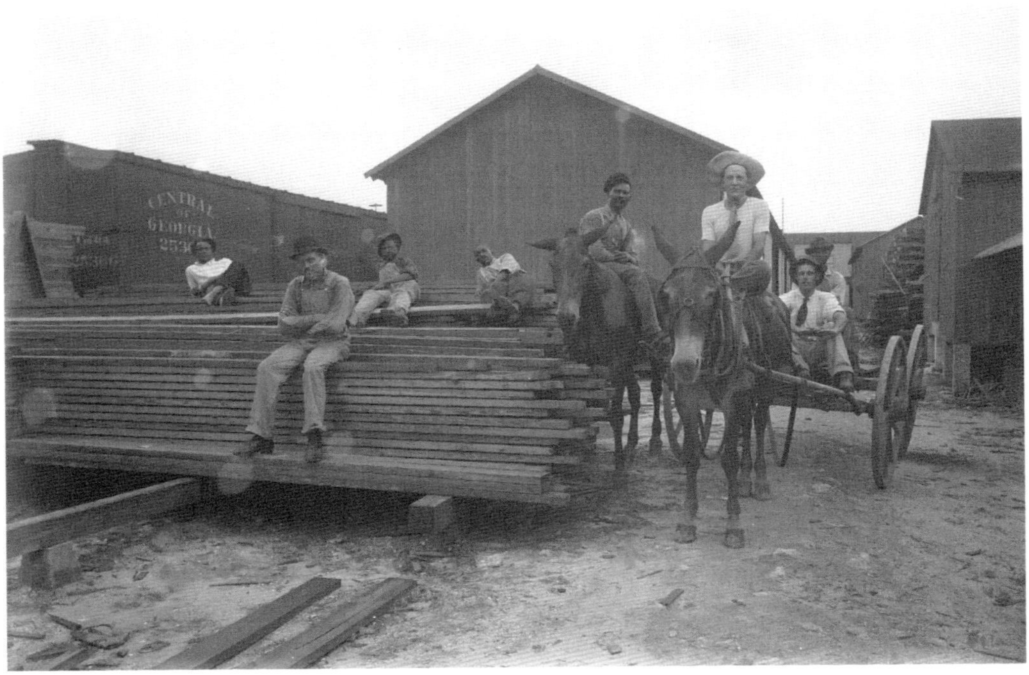

Supplying Builders to the Fourth Generation

Above, employees of East Coast Lumber Company yard are getting ready to deliver building materials to a customer before the age of the motor vehicle. Below, P. Allen Osteen, executive vice president of East Coast Lumber and Supply—the oldest family-owned business in Florida— stands in front of a portrait of (from left to right) company president William D. "Don" Osteen Sr., Paul Osteen, and P. Allen Osteen. The Osteens have seen the lumber business through depression, boom, bust, hurricanes, war, and recession by being conservative with their money and generous to their employees. In more than 110 years of existence, the company has expanded and contracted with the economic times, with operations as far south as Miami and as far north as Eau Gallie. (Above, SLCRHC; below, photograph by Tom Baumker.)

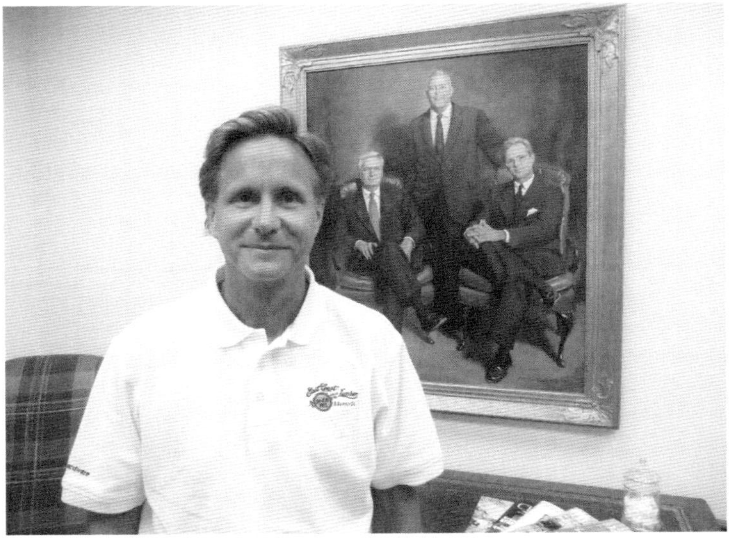

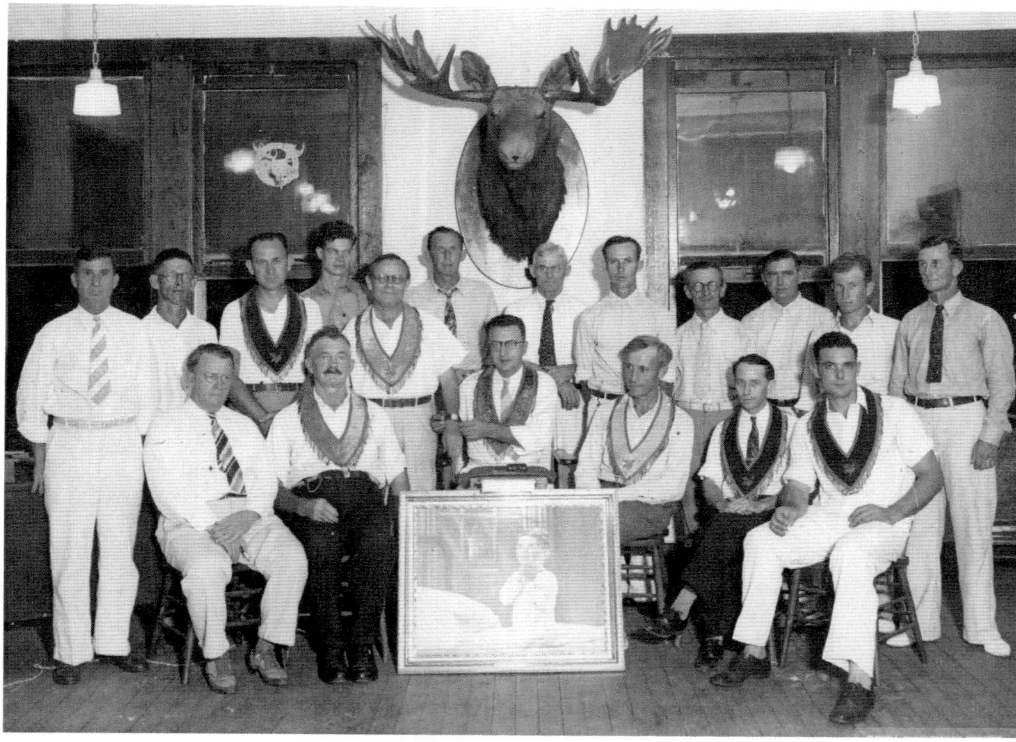

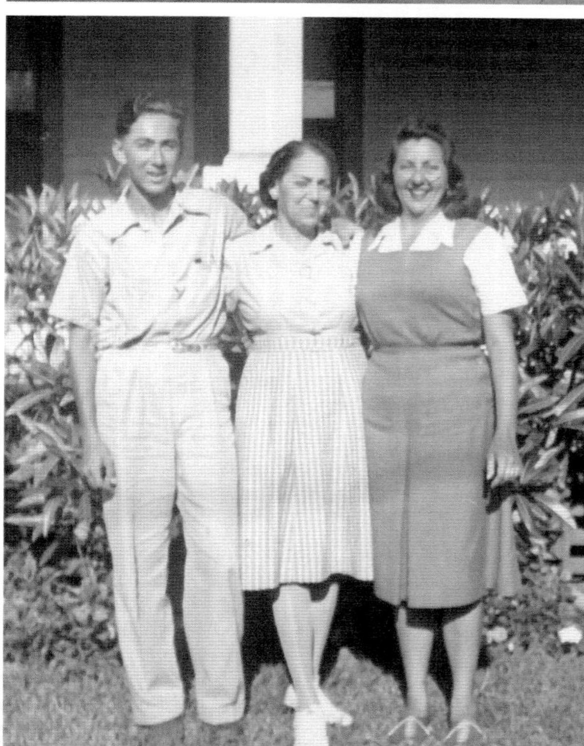

Where Statements Were Facts
The motto of Holtsberg's Department Store was "Where statements are facts." It was founded by Harold Holtsberg's grandfather Isadore in 1912 and sold to a Rubin kinsman in 1928. Most of old Fort Pierce remembers Rubin's Department Store as the premier downtown emporium when busy stores lined Second Street. The Holtsbergs and Rubins were founding members of Temple Beth El. Harold Holtsberg, his mother, Mattie, and his sister Lois Ann are pictured (left) at the old family home place, built by grandmother Sarah in 1924; it is still standing. Harold is a faithful supporter of the St. Lucie Historical Society. His father, Fred, was a town leader, and he and his cousin Arthur Rubin both served as mayors of Fort Pierce. Fred Holtsberg (above, center) is pictured as a leader of the Moose club in 1937. (Both photographs courtesy of Harold Holtsberg.)

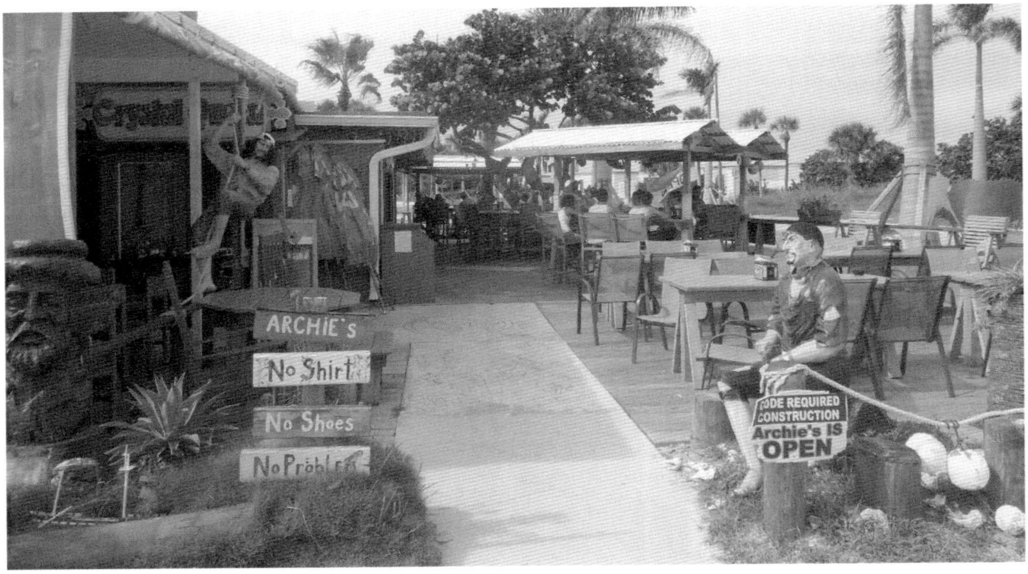

Iconic Beach Bar

In the 1940s, after the Navy left, Archie's Seabreeze was a small beer shack operated by Archie Summerlin, a descendant of the pioneer fishing family Summerlins. In 1994, Patty McGee acquired the establishment from his heirs retaining Archie's motto, "No shirt, no shoes, no problem."

Seasonal visitors find changes to Archie's Seabreeze every year: a new swinging table, umbrellas with ersatz palm fronds, or still another extension of the deck. Patty is constantly expanding and improving. A sign reads, "You are a stranger here but once," which expresses another facet of her philosophy of hospitality. The eclectic crowd is composed of elderly couples in Docksides, sleeveless body-builders, women in bikinis, and men in work uniforms. Patrons can play pool and can bring their dog or parrot.

Patty has a soft touch for any charity and many fundraisers take place at Archie's. Hog Wild is an event during which motorcyclists raise money for different causes. Archie's has afternoon Bingo for charity, and Reach Community Church holds services at Archie's every Sunday. The musical entertainment ranges from karaoke to hard rock to solo guitarists in order to suit the varying moods of Patty's eclectic clientele.

When twin hurricanes Jeanne and Francis hit in 2004, Patty was featured on the front page of the *New York Times*, standing amid the wreckage of Archie's. With the help of friends and patrons, Patty pulled herself together and rebuilt. Patty manages the wait staff—which consists of both transients and longtime residents—in such a way that one reviewer said, "the staff here really hustles to deliver the food and drinks with chaotic precision. They really earn their tips." (Both photographs by Tom Baumker.)

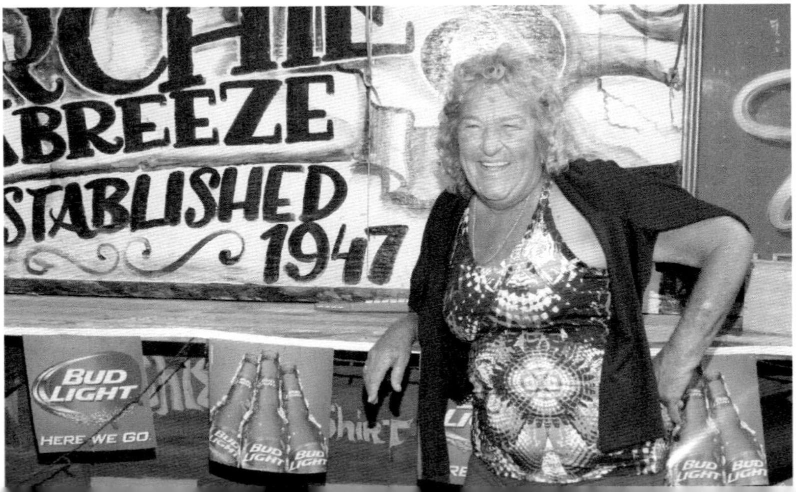

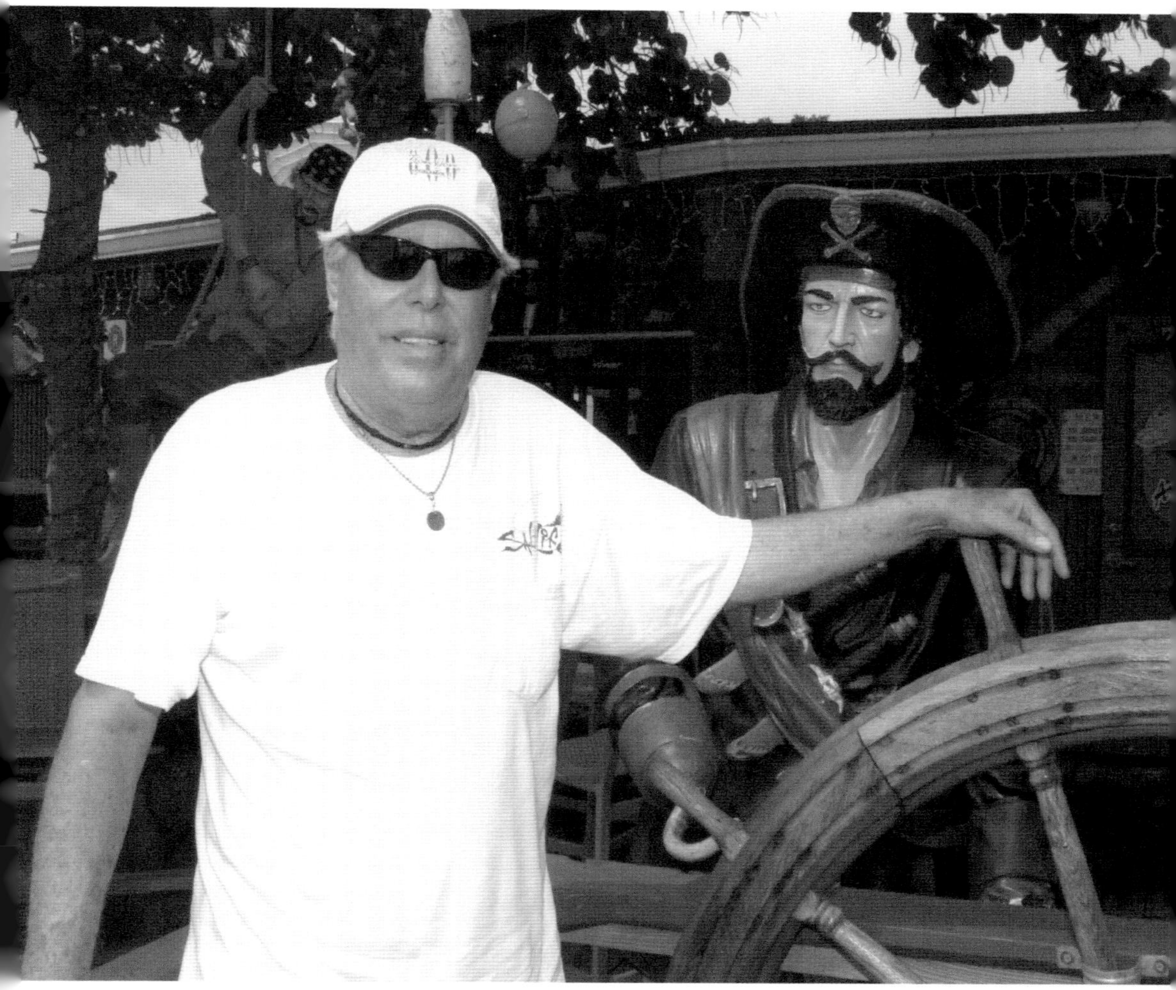

His Honor, the Mayor

Pete Austgen has been, to his modest wonder, chosen "Mayor of South Beach" by acclamation. South Hutchinson Island, in St. Lucie County, has not yet gone completely to the dark side of million-dollar condominiums and $300-a-night hotels like other ocean-side enclaves along Florida's southern coast. Folks of modest means can still live there. In 1952, Pete's father moved his wife and five sons to Fort Pierce Beach. Coming from Chicago, Pete thought he had found a child's heaven, with the ocean just across the dune and the river at his back, making it easy to live barefoot year round. His mayoral "office" is on a stool at Archie's Seabreeze, where he holds court. (Photograph by Tom Baumker.)

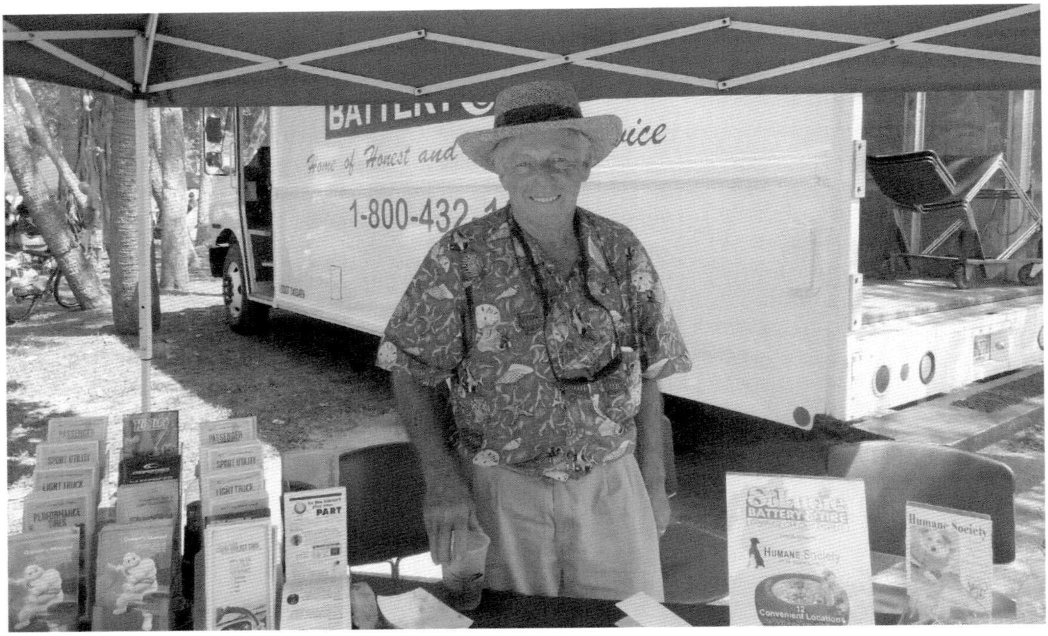

Joseph "Joey" Miller

In the photograph above, Joseph "Joey" Miller is participating in the annual Humane Society fundraiser of which his company is a major sponsor. The owner of St. Lucie Battery & Tire (pictured below), Joey started out as St. Lucie Battery in the mid-1960s, then grew the business into St. Lucie Battery & Tire in 1972. While leading his company into a dozen locations in the area, Joey has continuously sponsored a wide range of community events. Locals with a cause know that Joey will lend a sympathetic ear and help if he can. He has also been politically active, putting himself out there in the interests of good government, keeping up with what's going on at the local level, as all good citizens should. (Both photographs by the author.)

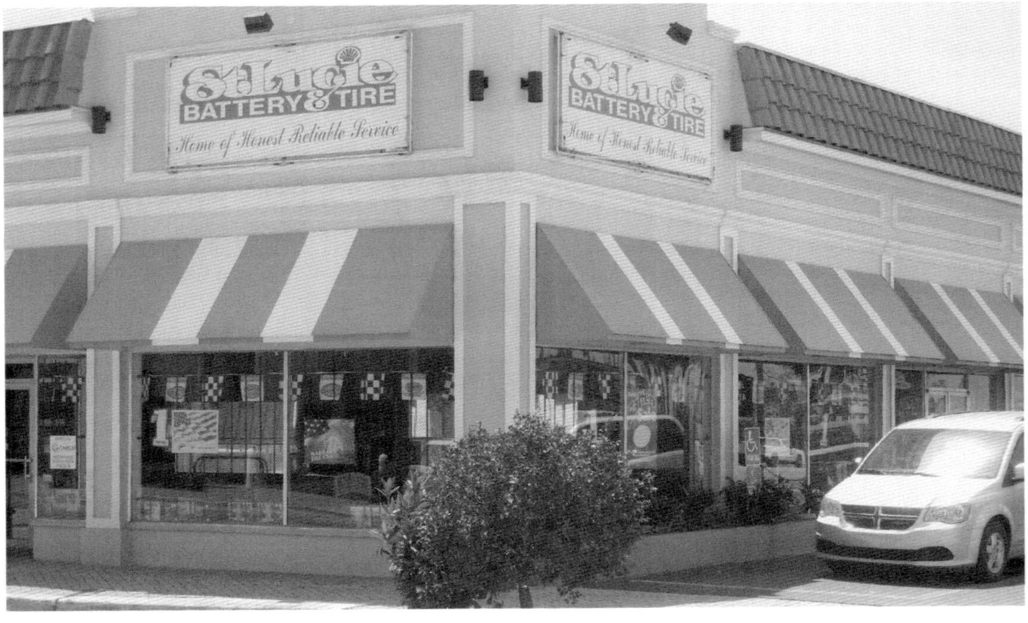

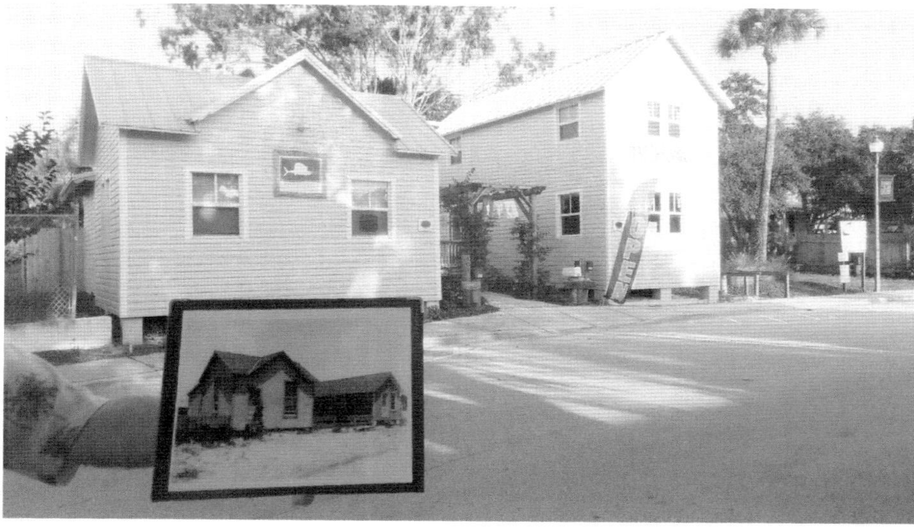

Florida Photographic Concern

Harry Hill came to Fort Pierce in 1897. He established an apiary on the St. Lucie River, and his first photographs were made to enliven the *American Beekeeper*, a publication printed and mailed from Fort Pierce. Fortunately, for posterity, Harry soon began to put all his energies toward photography and was later joined by his brother Fred in a burgeoning business. The Florida Photographic Concern, a vintage photograph of which is pictured above, has left a legacy of priceless photographs of early Fort Pierce and Flagler's Overseas Railway. Hundreds of glass negatives were saved and cleaned by Bob Gladwin, many of which are preserved in the St. Lucie County Regional History Center's archives. Harry Hill produced early color photographs and acquired patents on an early color movie process. After Harry died in 1937, the business continued under son Lowell Hill. The preserved building is now occupied by Sailfish Brewing Company, of which Dave BuShea and Nick Bischoff are the proprietors. (Above photograph by the author with historic photograph from SLCRHC; below, courtesy of SLCRHC.)

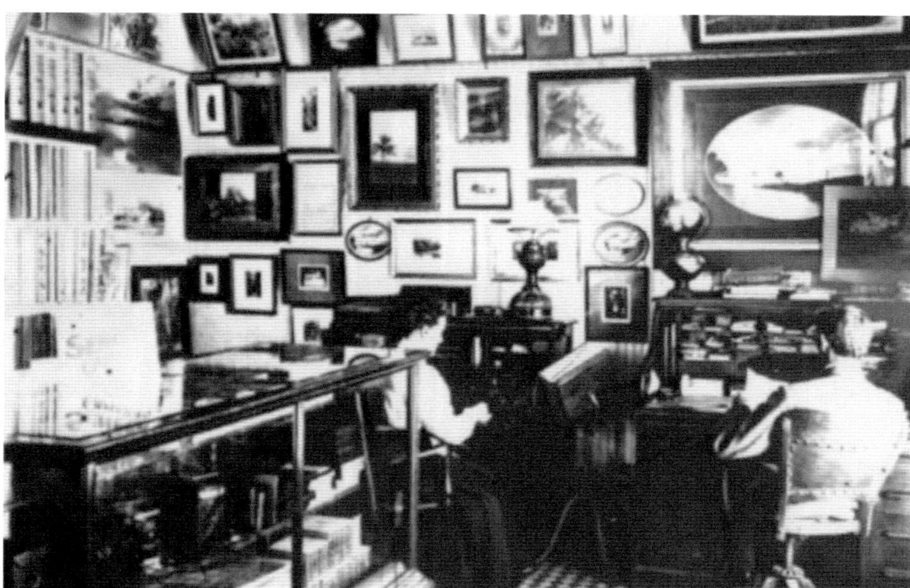

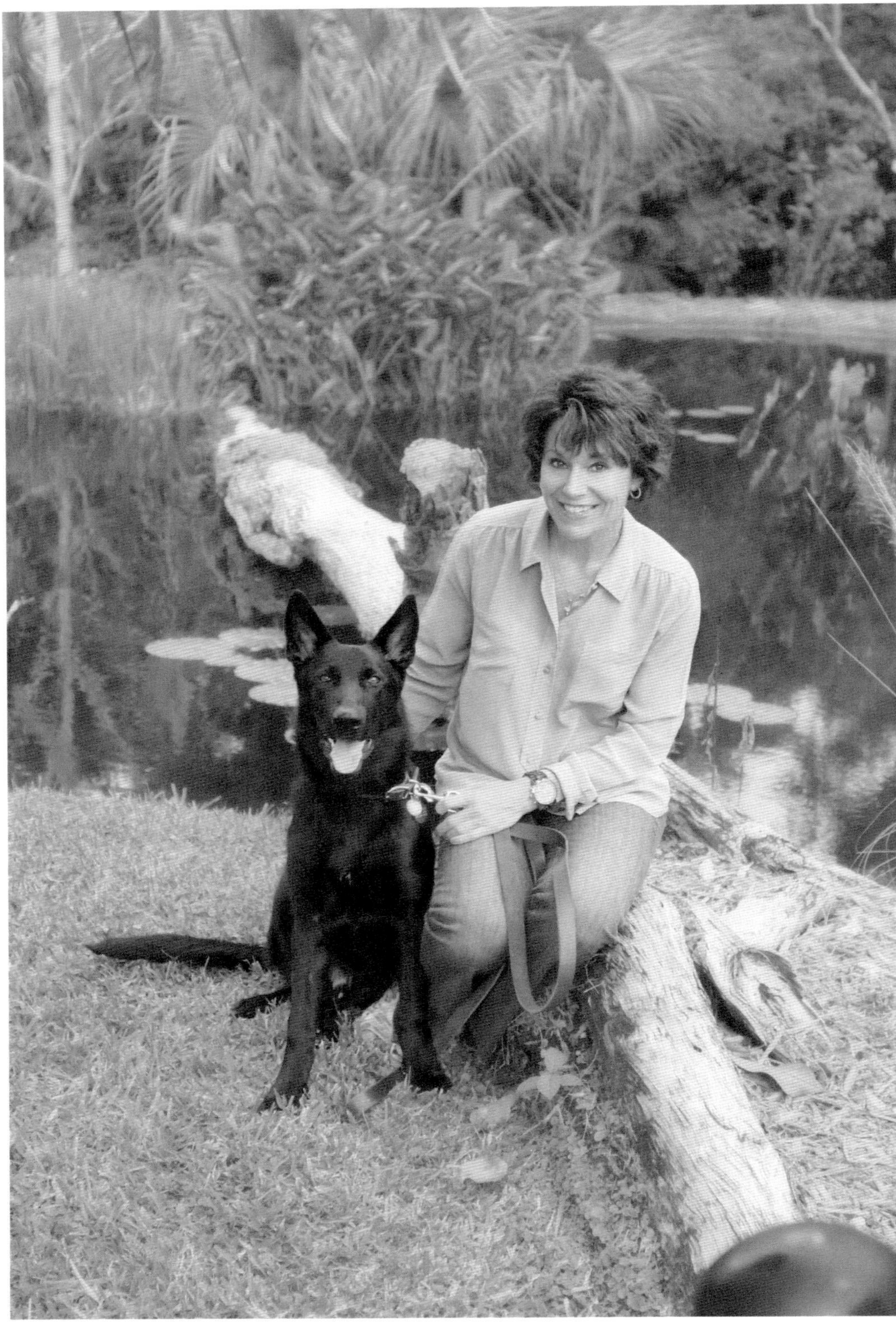

Taste Test Winner (BELOW AND OPPOSITE PAGE)
Pictured on the opposite page in a moment of relaxation is Marygrace Sexton, chief executive officer of Natalie's Orchid Island Juice Company, a family-owned Florida company. Marygrace and her husband, Robert Sexton, founded the business in 1989. Sexton, a fifth-generation citrus-grower and grandson of citrus pioneer Waldo Sexton, worked the land growing luscious Indian River citrus. Marygrace was a hard charging, no nonsense manager with untapped energy and a heart for quality and service. Together, they sought to produce high-quality, fresh juice from the citrus grown by Sexton in the heart of the Indian River growing region. Their dream was to introduce the world to the benefits of squeezed, fresh juice and the supremacy of Indian River citrus quality and flavor. Since its humble beginnings, Natalie's Orchid Island Juice Company has distinguished itself nationwide, consistently being voted number one for best taste and most nutrition by *Woman's Day, Good Housekeeping, Cook's Illustrated, Real Simple, Bon Appétit, The Today Show*, and *Serious Eats*. Natalie's Orchid Island Juice Company has won seven national taste tests in all, and is still counting. (Both, courtesy of Natalie's Orchid Island Juice Company.)

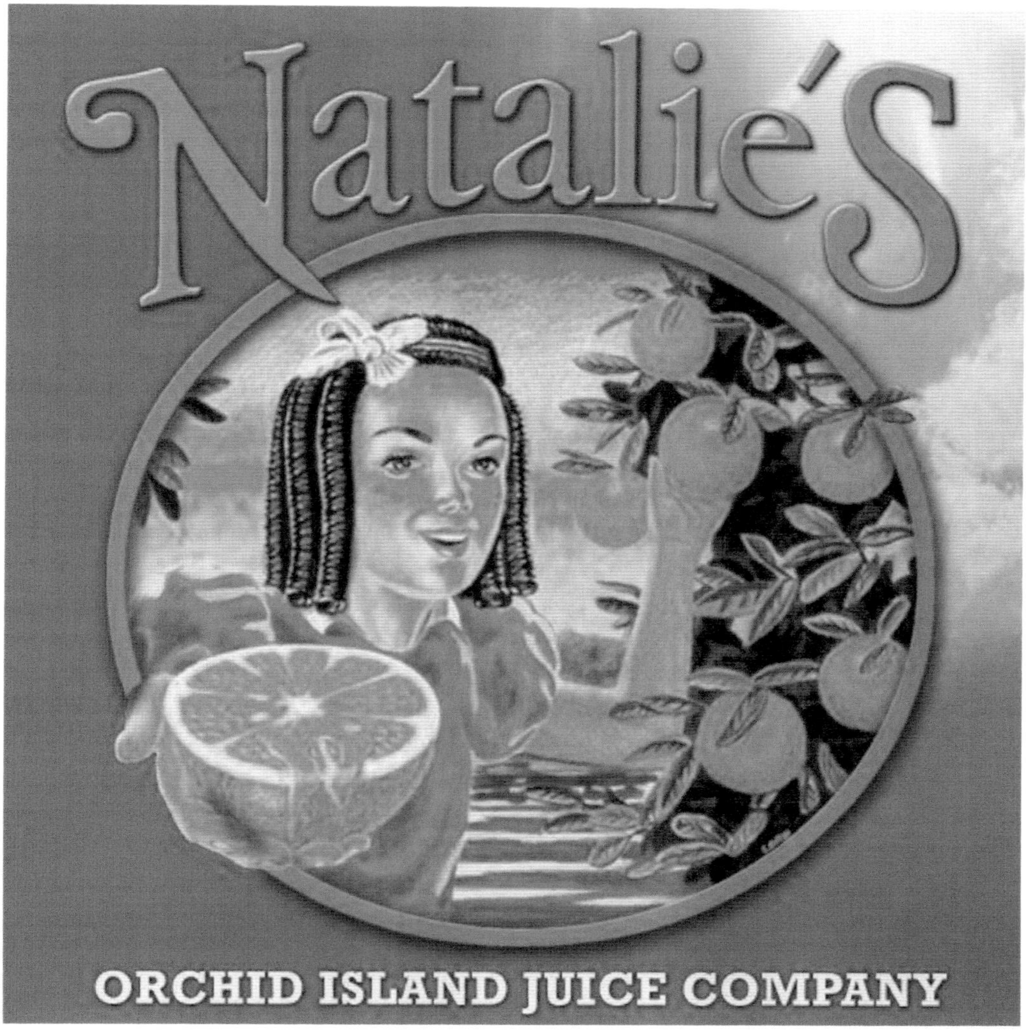

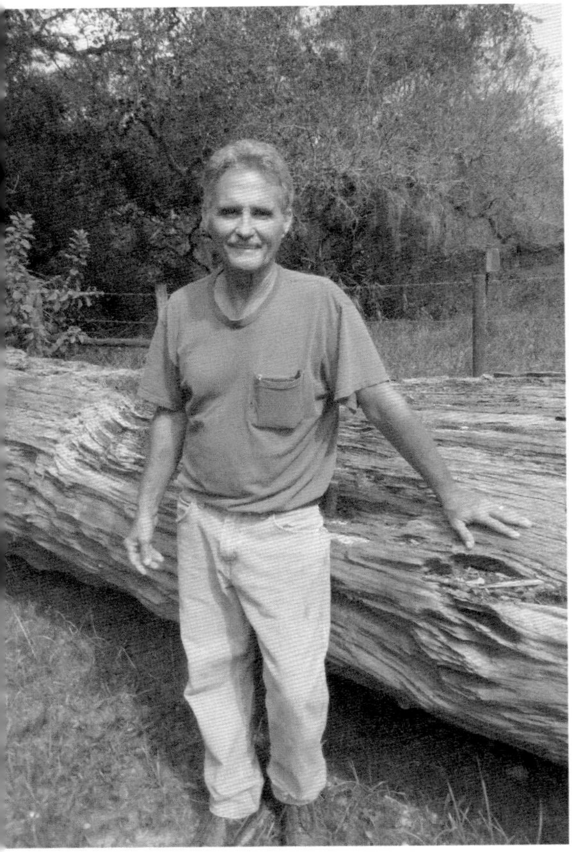

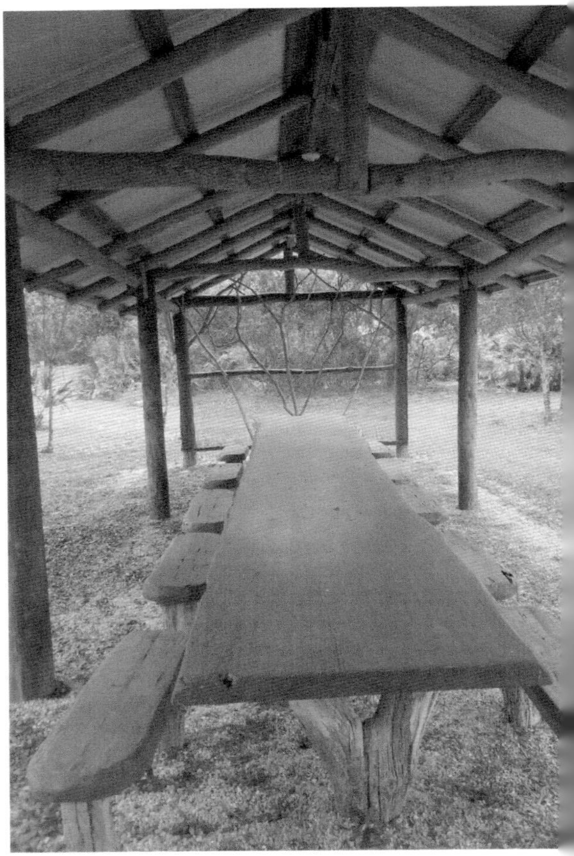

The Master's Apprentice (ABOVE AND OPPOSITE PAGE)

George Ivey III looks at a cypress log the way a sculptor looks at a piece of marble. Beginning as a conventional carpenter, he developed a zeal for "cracker" style design. "I love the way a selection of limbs, tops, snags, or a stump flow together for a special one-of-a-kind piece of furniture," he said. Ivey purchased his first sunken cypress log from John Clayton, a good friend and a diver with Dead Head Logging Inc., which has been in the Florida diving program since it began. Clayton is known for finding some of the biggest and best sunken cypress and longleaf pine logs in Florida. A lot of these "sinkers" were growing before Columbus discovered America. Since that first log, Ivey has acquired many more from Clayton. From these, Ivey makes tables and considers his best one to date to be the one he made using a single 33-foot cypress slab. Ivey incorporated in 2001 as Big Cypress Tableworks.

Limited to word-of-mouth advertising, people seem to find his isolated workplace and are welcome "if the gate is open." Through that gate have come buyers from all over the United States and beyond—London, Japan, and Canada. They can buy a chair, bench, or table that he has created or place an order.

George does not hesitate to tell the world the good news that he is saved. "The Lord, He is the one who put it all in me. I can be riding down the road and He'll show me something and I just go and do it," he says. George Ivey exudes an immutable integrity. His tree house (opposite) is a true sanctuary. (All photographs by the author.)

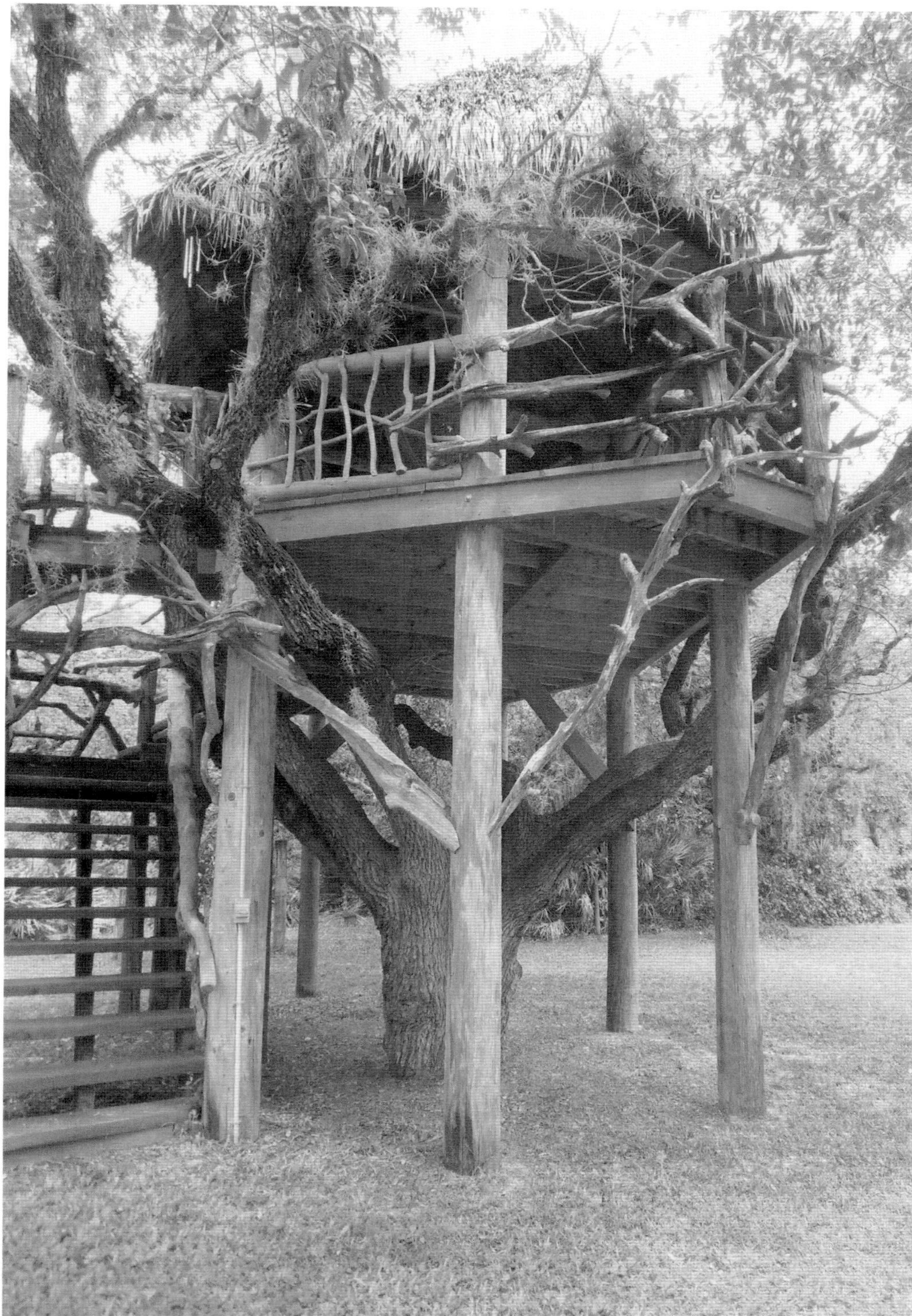

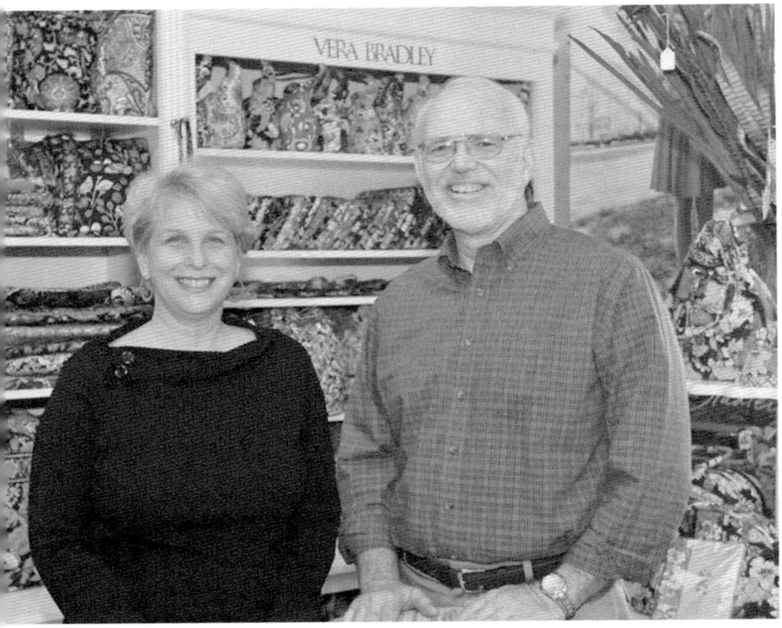

Uptown Fashion Downtown
Greg Rosslow and his wife, Cindy, are partners in every sense of the word. She does the buying and merchandising, he does the backroom duty and the numbers. Greg gradually took over the responsibility of the business from his parents, who opened Rosslow's after World War II. While so many businesses have left the once-crowded downtown shopping scene, Rosslow's stayed, and it now serves the granddaughters of the women who patronized the original store. (Courtesy of Greg Enns, *Indian River Magazine*.)

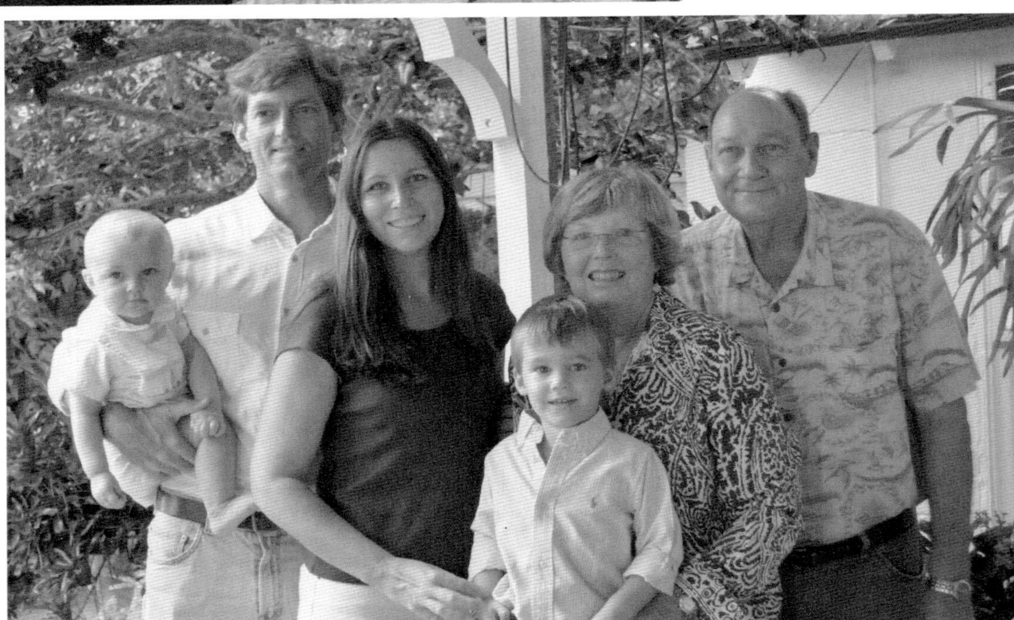

Deep Roots
Joseph Yates was a pillar of the community, active in a wide variety of fraternal and civic affairs for many years. He founded the funeral home that became Yates Funeral Home & Crematory in 1938, and bought out the old Fee Mortuary in the early 1940s. Son William "Bill" (far right) took over the funeral business from his father. He and Betsy (second from right) have been longtime supporters of many local institutions including the Backus Gallery and Restoration House. Their daughter Elizabeth "Beth" Jefferson serves on the Backus Gallery board, and husband, Tom, works with the Treasure Coast Food Bank and is a volunteer escort for the Honor Flight program. (Courtesy of Elizabeth Yates Jefferson.)

CHAPTER SEVEN

Scene of the Cause

People become community activists for a variety of reasons: good government, improvements in educational opportunities, upgrading quality of life for youngsters or seniors, civil rights, spiritual comfort, and public safety are just a sampling. Alexis de Tocqueville, observing American democracy in 1830, famously said, "Americans of all ages, all stations of life, and all types of disposition are forever forming associations. There are not only commercial and industrial associations in which all take part, but others of a thousand different types—religious, moral, serious, futile, very general and very limited, immensely large and very minor." Certainly, the people of Fort Pierce, when they see a problem, are likely to join an organization that is addressing it, or, if there is no such organization, a believer is liable to form one. Environmental concerns are probably the number one issue that motivates locals to unite, some of which can be found in chapter four, which concentrates on Fort Pierce's water assets. Included in this chapter are some very dynamic individuals who enrich the total experience of the community through their dedication to their causes.

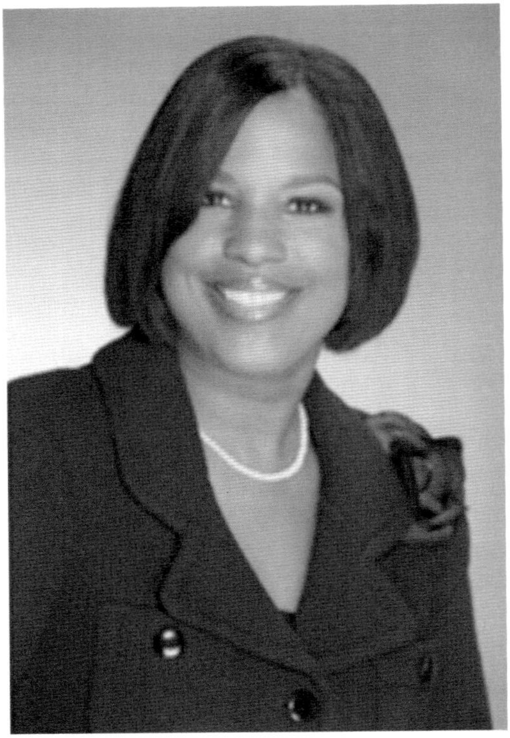

Voting Rights

With the country's first African American president seeking a second term on Election Day 2012, Roslyn Brock, the youngest person and fourth woman to lead the National Association for the Advancement of Colored People, came back to Fort Pierce, where she was born, to knock on doors for Obama. After meeting neighbors in the Get-Out-the-Vote canvass, Brock visited with family members who still reside in Fort Pierce. (Courtesy of Tiffany Adams.)

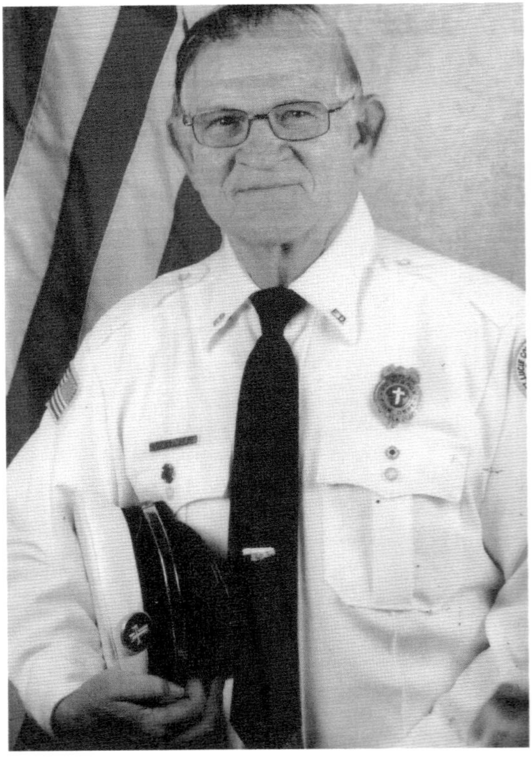

Chaplain Jack

Jack Favorite joined the fire department as soon as he was old enough, at age 18, in 1959. Over the years, his experience as a combat firefighter paralleled his search for meaning. Jack remembers, "I began to feel a very deep call within to serve God in some very positive way." In 1978, he was ordained as the department chaplain. After 28 years of service and 20 years of retirement, he continues to be on call as chaplain. (Courtesy of Jack Favorite.)

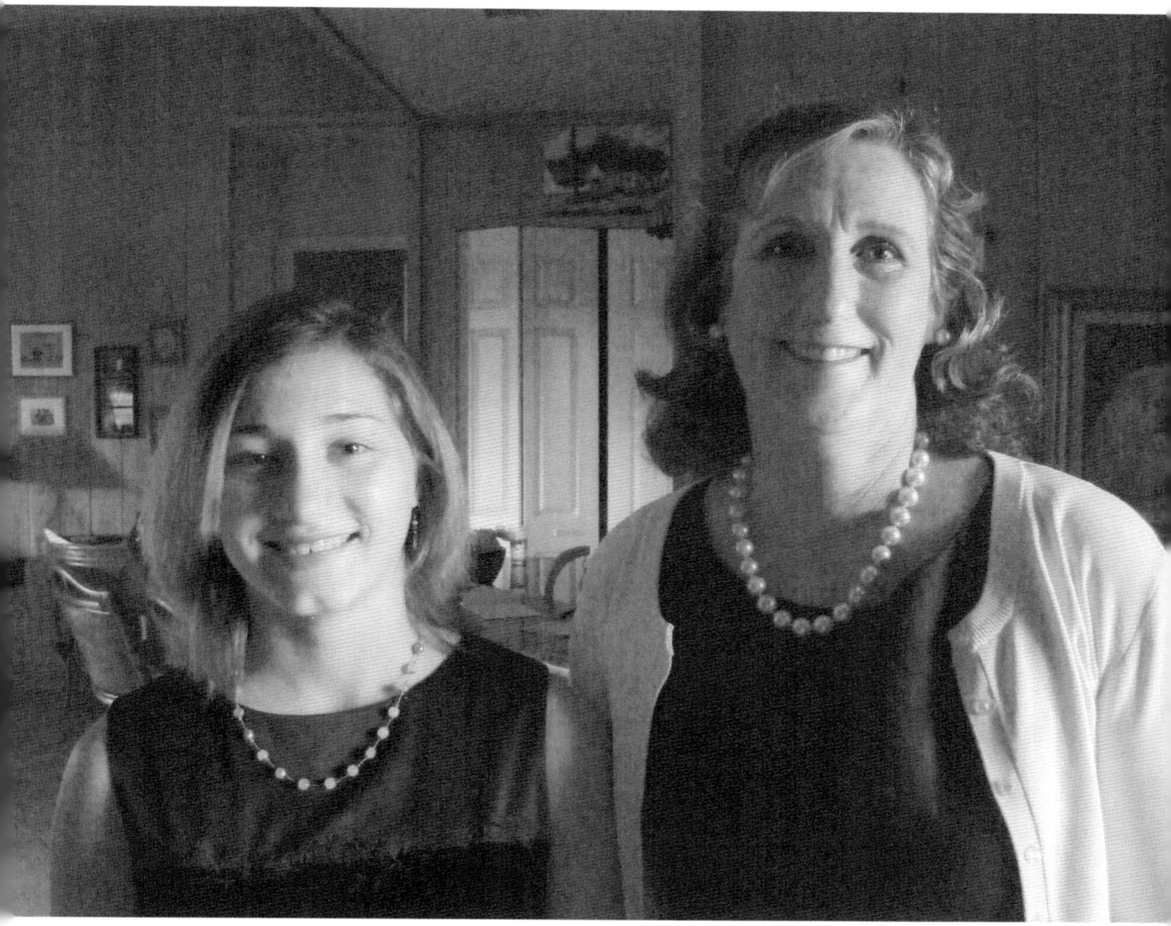

Glynda Cavalcanti
Glynda Cavalcanti is pictured with one of the girls she mentors, Alyssa Leal. Among other experiences the two have shared: they went horseback riding in Argentina. A swimmer, Spanish teacher, dedicated supporter of St. Anastasia's Church, certified public accountant, philanthropist, and advisor of her clients on charitable contributions, Cavalcanti has aided Cuban refugees and adopted a needy family living in a car, to whom she has provided assistance in times of crisis for a decade. She lent a major hand in the successful effort to save the old city hall from being razed and located her office in the building. (Courtesy of Linda Hudson.)

First Woman Mayor

Linda Gwyn Wilson Hudson was elected in 2012 to a four-year term as mayor of Fort Pierce. She is pictured here on a visit to a local school, one of her favorite privileges as mayor. Born in Fort Pierce, Linda attended Indian River Community College and the University of Florida. Her political education included a stint with the political arm of the American Medical Association in Chicago before she was lured away to serve as vice president of communication for the Illinois State Medical Society. Retiring after the untimely death of her husband, Mike, she returned to Fort Pierce and quickly became active in the community. She has served as chairman of the phenomenally successful Downtown Fort Pierce Farmers Market for several terms, president of the Treasure Coast Genealogy Society for two terms, and on the advisory board of the St. Lucie County Library. Linda is the daughter of the late Charles and Julia Wilson, the mother of Buell Hudson, the grandmother of Michael, and the wife of John Bailey. (Courtesy City of Fort Pierce.)

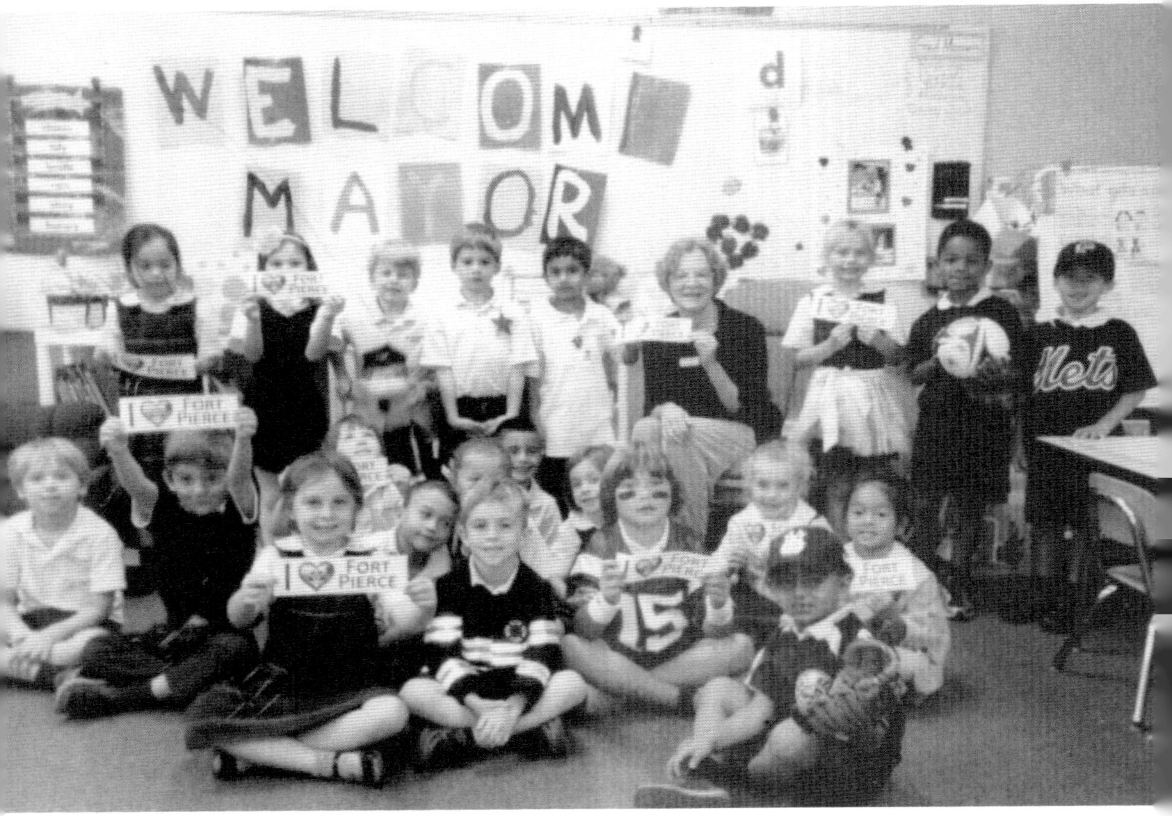

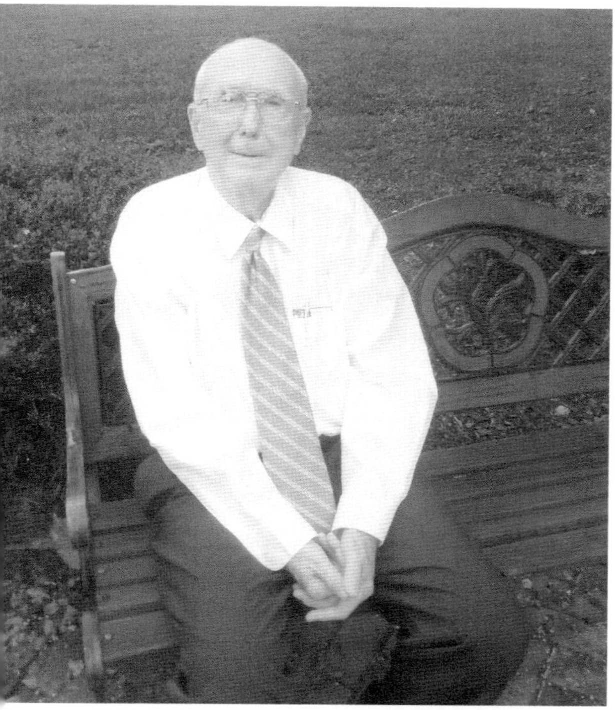

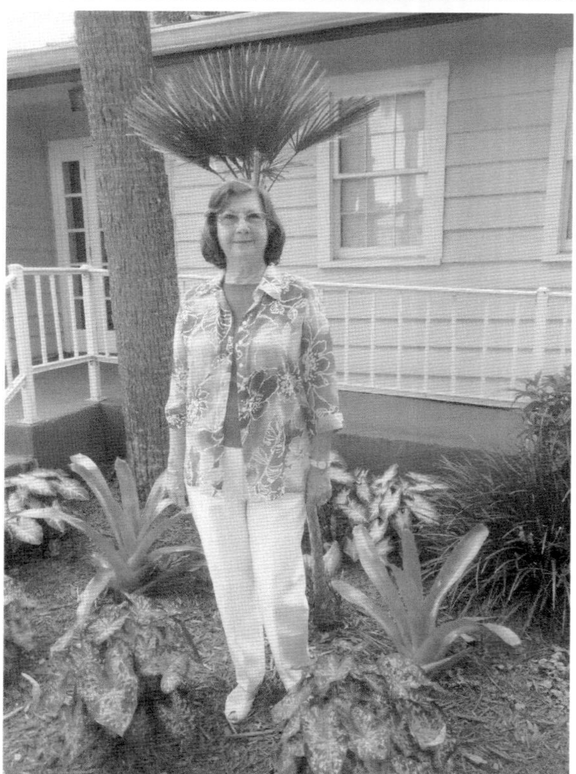

Town Solon
The definition of "solon," according to Merriam-Webster, is "a wise and skillful lawgiver," and that is what Dr. William Dannahower has been. His initial interest in politics was spurred by a local campaign to introduce water fluoridation. As a dentist, Bill knew the science of what the addition of fluoride to city water could do for the health of the next generation. Opposition was strong and included the charge of a "communist plot." Although a referendum was mounted and passed, city fathers were slow to move on implementing the flouride law. At the behest of supporters, Bill ran for mayor, won, and saw that the law was obeyed. In the 1980s, he reentered the political fray and was elected mayor for the second time. He also served for 12 years on the Florida Dental Board, which licenses Florida dentists and disciplines inadequate practitioners. In recognition of the doctor's efforts to bring a federal courthouse to Fort Pierce, the structure, which was dedicated in 2013, includes the Dannahower Atrium. Bill was raised on an orange grove west of downtown Fort Pierce, his parents having migrated to Florida from Kansas in the 1920s. He is legendary as Fort Pierce's revered senior statesman. (Photograph by the author.)

Astute Politico
Straight-talking Shirley Walker is proud of her friendship with former Florida governor and US senator Bob Graham and his wife, Adele. Through her work in campaigns, Walker met the Grahams and many other high officials. She was appointed a Senate coordinator in Washington, DC, by the Florida Association of Realtors. Walker's 40-year career in real estate began in 1973. Gardening is another of her passions and she is a member of the Garden Club of Fort Pierce, which is dedicated to helping residents improve the curb appeal of their houses. Walker works with the city to plan and assist in beautification projects. (Photograph by the author.)

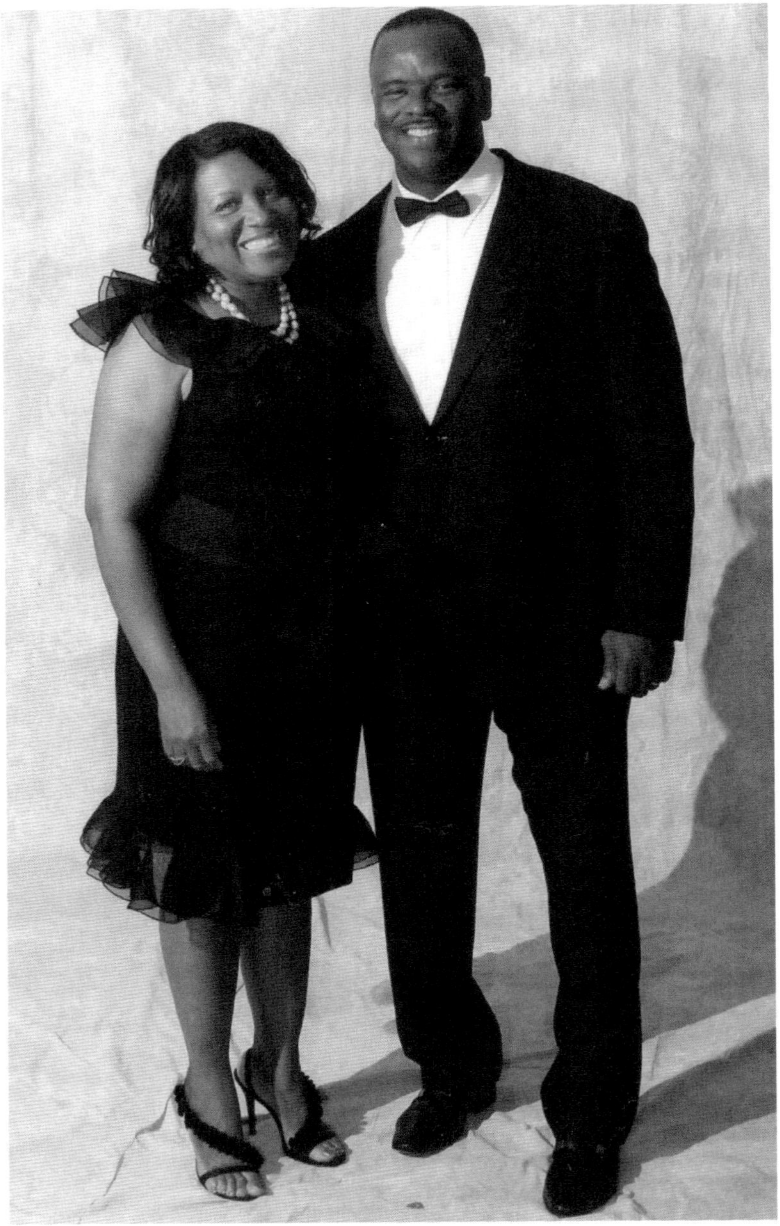

Power Couple

Larry and Alice Lee are a Fort Pierce power couple. Larry was elected to the Florida House of Representatives in 2012, the first African American to represent this area. He was a member of the legendary high school football team that won the state championship for Fort Pierce in 1971 and went on to be signed by the Denver Broncos. Larry founded "Pay It Forward" of Fort Pierce, cofounded the jazz society, and served as a director for the chamber of commerce. He has also worked with Big Brothers Big Sisters, United Way, and other organizations for community improvement. He owns a State Farm insurance agency. Alice Hoskins Lee owns and operates the local radio station, WFLM AM and WIRA 1400 FM. (Courtesy of Larry Lee.)

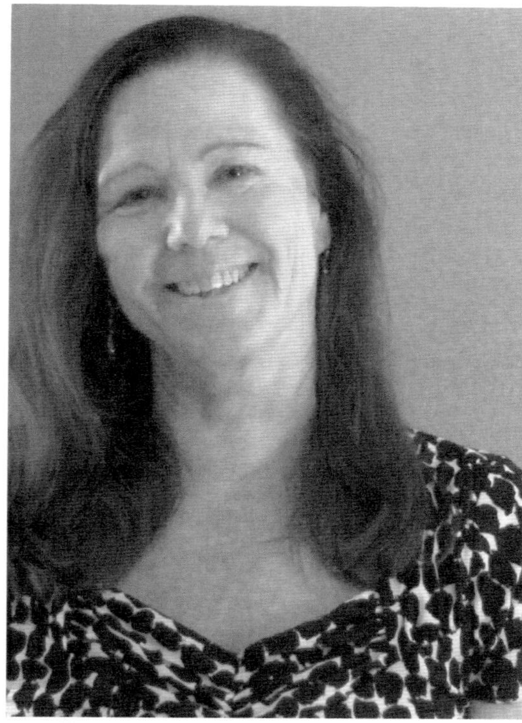

Blogging Fort Pierce
Robyn Hutchinson enjoys meeting people electronically on the "Growing Up in Fort Pierce" blog. Born and raised in Fort Pierce, her maternal grandparents came to Fort Pierce from St. Augustine in the early 1900s; her paternal grandparents met in Fort Pierce and were married in 1925. Robyn says, "I love my hometown of Fort Pierce and have a passion for its people and its history." She puts that passion to work in volunteering for Hope's Closet, Mustard Seed, and Fort Pierce Main Street. She volunteers with the St. Lucie Regional History Center, serves on the board of the St. Lucie Historical Society, and is a member of the Treasure Coast Genealogical Society. (Courtesy of Robyn Hutchinson.)

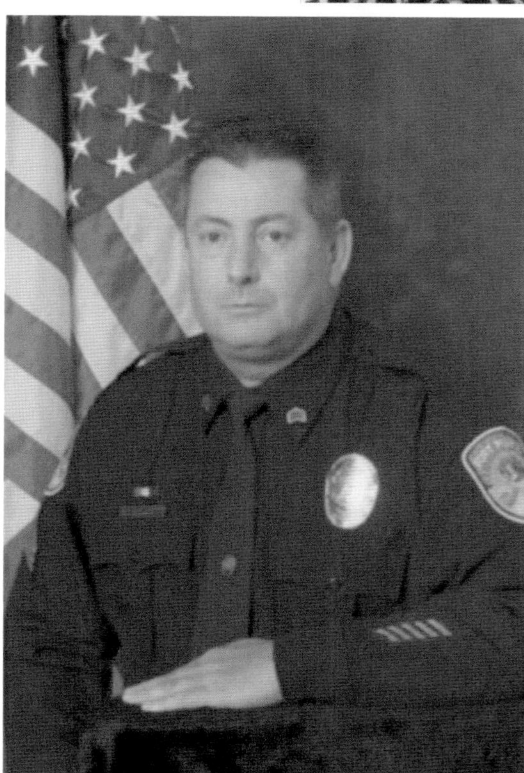

The Face of Law and Order
Sgt. Dennis McWilliams is the public information officer for the Fort Pierce Police Department. He never fails to respect the law-abiding citizen and enthusiastically cooperates with schools and churches in organizing programs to inform and educate. (Courtesy of the Fort Pierce Police Department.)

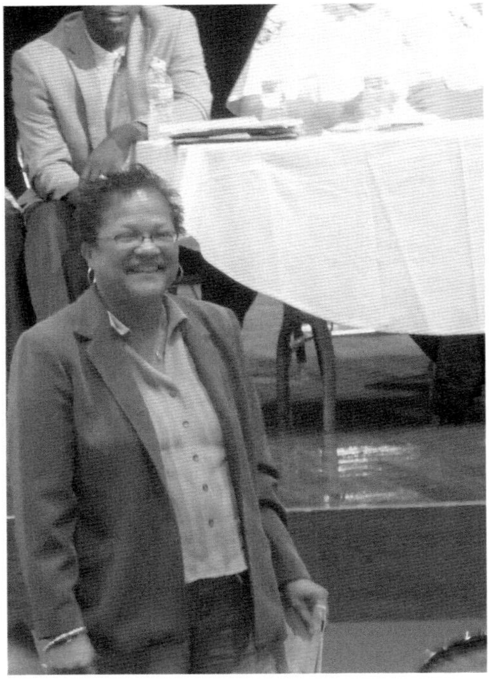

Tough Love

Fran O. Ross speaks to residents gathered at Lincoln Park Academy, urging parents to take responsibility for their children. A criminal defense attorney from 1988 to 2013, Ross is now the director of Criminal Court Operations for St. Lucie County. Ross has put herself out there by running for office. She has been vocal for a long time about what many consider to be unaffordable utility rates. Ross was the first daughter and the first granddaughter in her family. She has two sons, Noah and Israel. (Photograph by the author.)

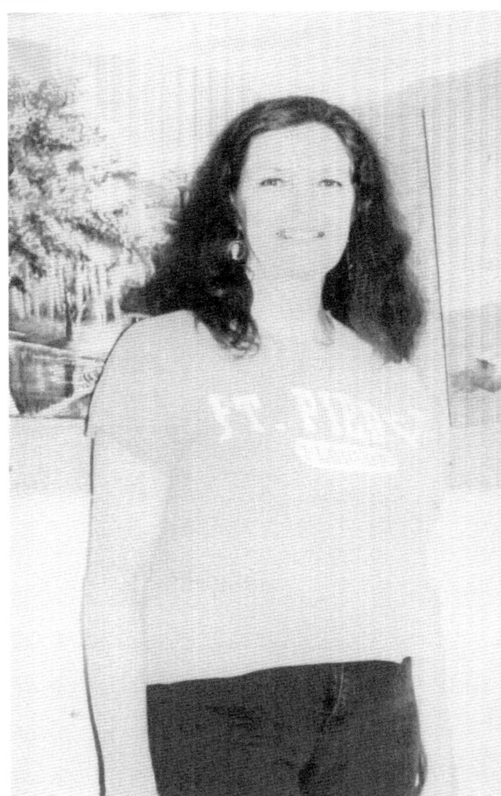

Tears of the Drug War

Ethel Rowland shows up everywhere and always adorns the crowd. Whether one agrees with her cause or not, she gently preaches it, and it is hard to not respect her determined advocacy of ending the new era of Prohibition—the outlawing of cannabis. She believes it results in the same kind of lawbreaking and violence as did the outlawing of alcoholic beverages in the 1920s and early 1930s. Exposed to the consequences of recreational drug use as a teenager, as an adult she began to preach decriminalization as a valid option. The murder of two toddlers and their parents in a violent drug dispute on the shoulder of I-95 at Fort Pierce sent her into a bout of personal grief and she set out to advocate for her cause in a new way—she began to paint her message. Since even talking about the merits of decriminalization borders on a taboo, "I show my art because it is important as a basis for discussion," Ethel says. Even her artwork has been barred from some venues because of the subject, such as her depiction of a fisherman landing a "square grouper." Ethel and her husband arrived in Fort Pierce on their sailboat *Velella* a decade ago and liked it enough to stay. (Photograph by Tom Baumker.)

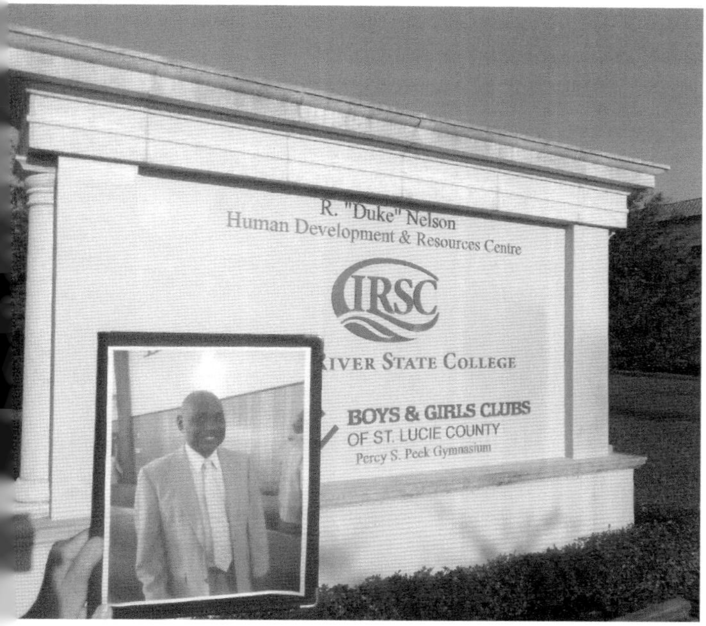

He Never Stops Serving
A retired Army colonel, Roosevelt "Duke" Nelson was ordered to Florida, his home state, during the Cuban missile crisis yet was refused a bed in a motel in Dade County while white officers under his command were permitted to register. A native of Fort Pierce, he played football for the Lincoln Park Greyhounds, graduating from Lincoln Park Academy in 1954. He has served on the Fort Pierce City Commission and is active in the AME church. He was instrumental in building a branch of Indian River College where practical skills like nursing, carpentry, and computer use are offered. (Photograph by the author.)

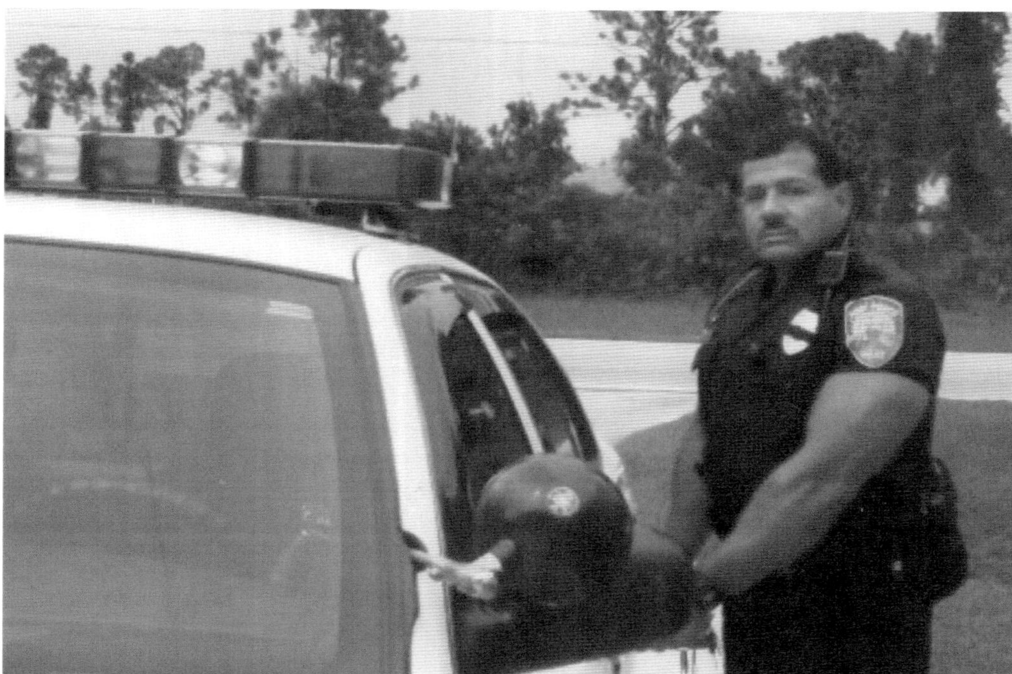

Friendly Neighborhood Policeman
Al Garcia is vigilant in protecting those who are least able to protect themselves—the young and the old. With young miscreants he is not heartless; he believes in second chances. Al moved from New Jersey in 1993 to work for the St. Lucie County Sheriff's Department, then in 1999, he started working for the Fort Pierce Police Department. (Courtesy of Al Garcia.)

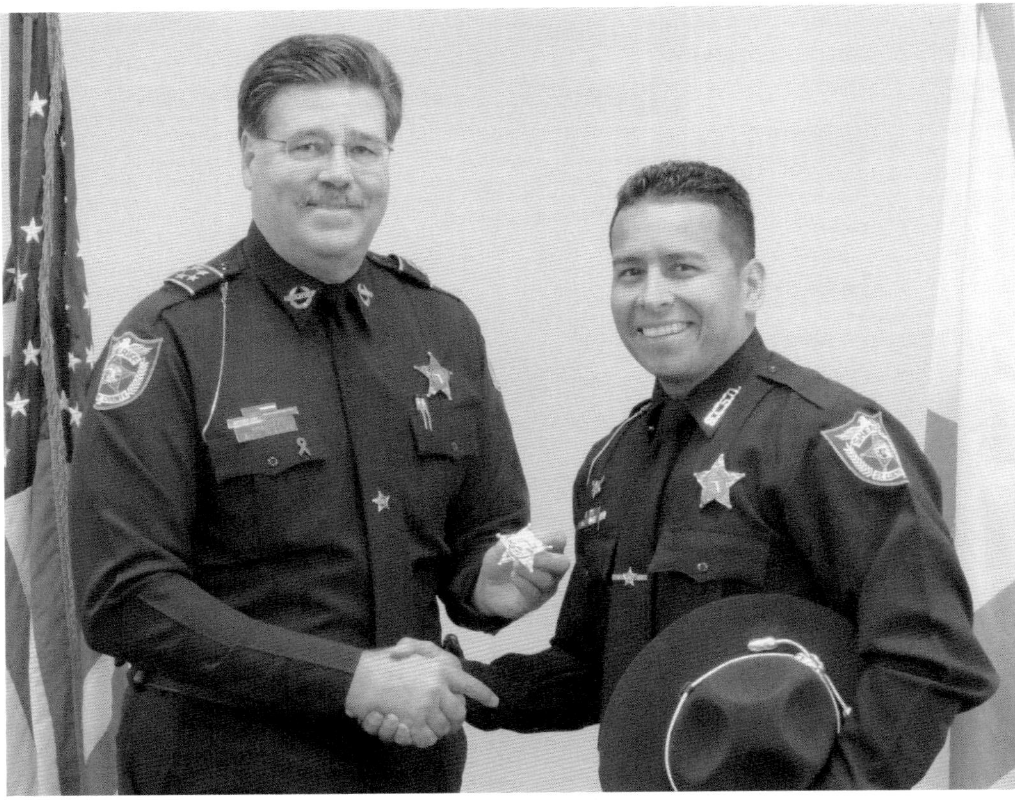

As Inexplicable as a Gunshot

Officer Gary Morales is pictured receiving his promotion to sergeant from Sheriff Ken Mascara on January 18, 2013. A few days later, on February 28, Sergeant Morales and other deputies were patrolling the Silver Lake neighborhood where a series of daylight burglaries had occurred. At 9:28 a.m., Sergeant Morales stopped a vehicle, but as he walked up to the window of the car, the driver sped away. Morales followed and pulled the car over a second time. The driver got out of his car and walked back to the deputy's car where Sergeant Morales sat behind the wheel using his computer, his gun in its holster. Backup officer Deputy Claude Bennett arrived in time to witness Eriese Tisdale shoot Morales three times through the window of his patrol car. Bennett and the shooter exchanged gunfire. The shooter ran, and two other officers joined Bennett in the chase. By 9:34 a.m., Tisdale was in handcuffs. (Above, courtesy St. Lucie County Sheriff's Department; below, photograph by the author.)

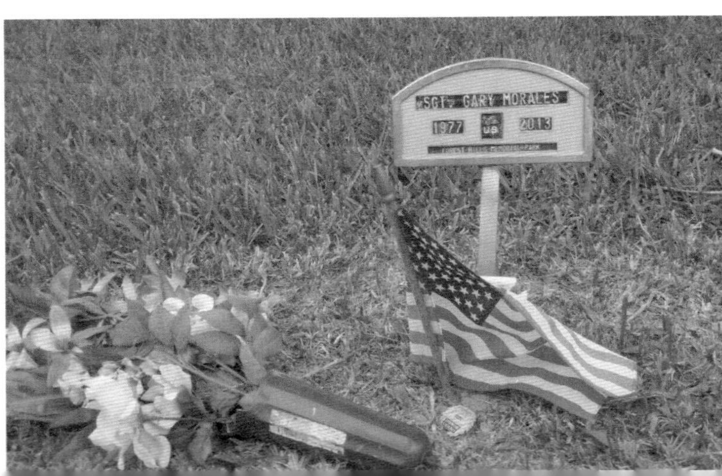

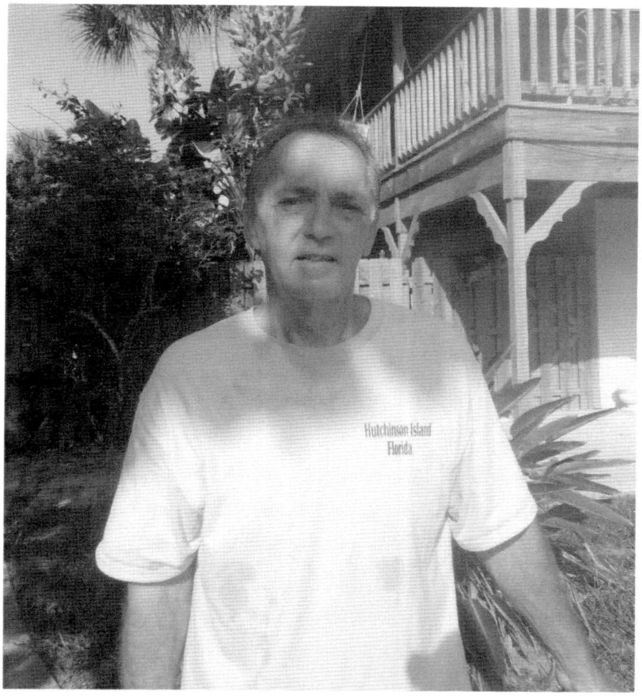

Sgt. William Springer

Humble and a good neighbor, William "Bill" Springer is pictured going on a walk with his dog on the quiet street where he lives with his wife, Lydie. Though he dislikes guns and does not come off as a macho type, he is indeed a hunter—searching for suspects. A cold case detective, Sergeant Springer has been featured on *On the Case with Paula Zahn, Sex, Lies, and Alibis,* and other similar programs. (Photograph by the author.)

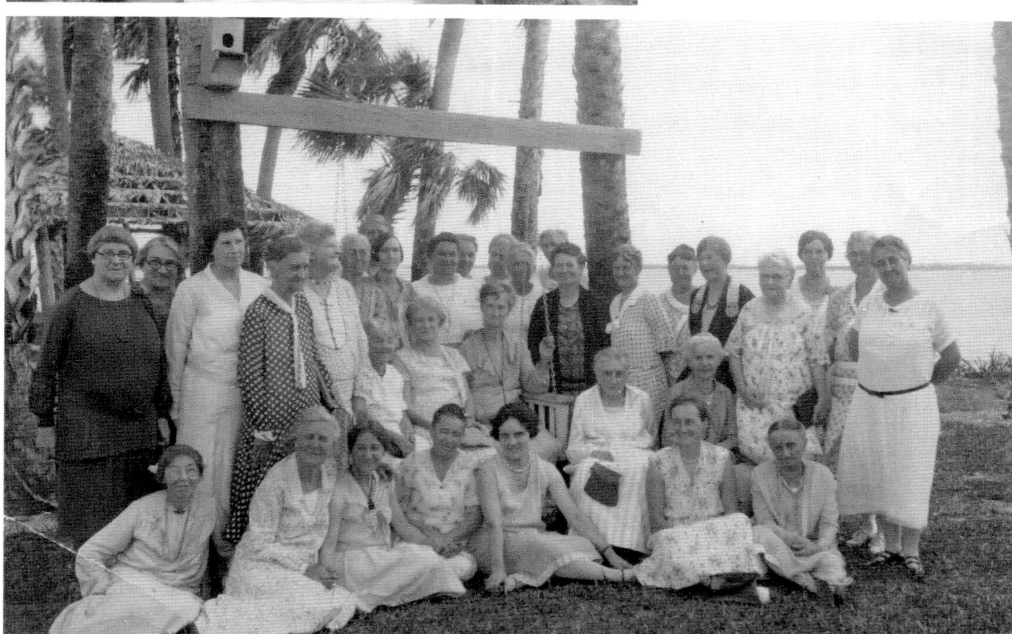

Ladies Circles

In the 1920s, the ladies circles of many Fort Pierce churches provided many good deeds. They worked closely with the local governments to care for the hungry. They provided clothes and sustenance to those in need. They opposed playing baseball on Sunday and the opening of saloons on any day of the week. (Courtesy of SLCRHC.)

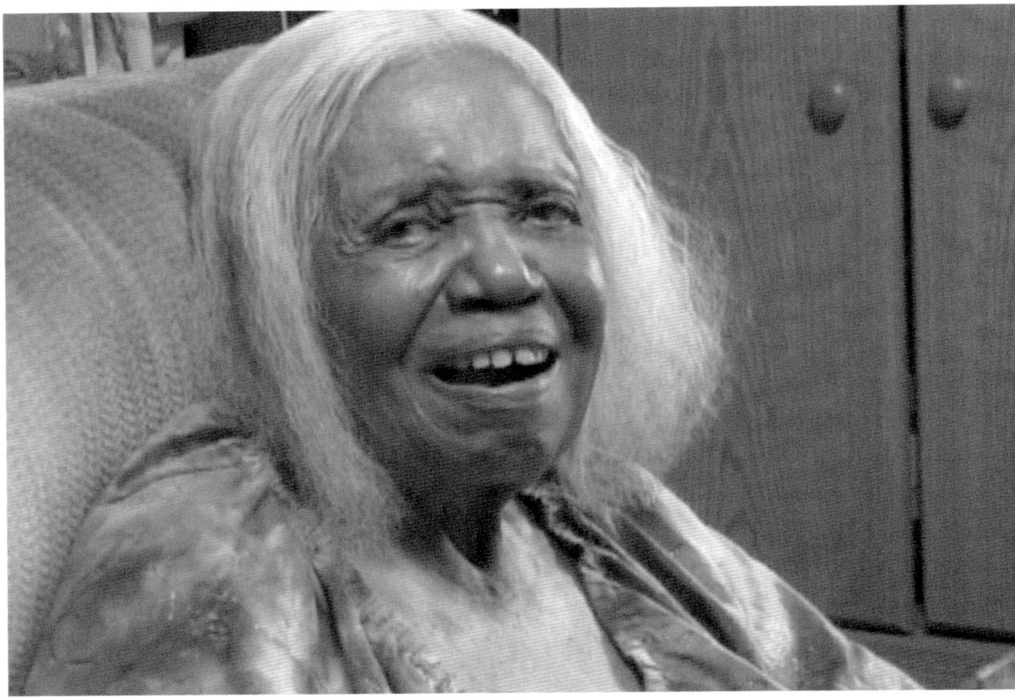

Mother Mary

Mary Brunson had 13 children, aided by a midwife, in her little house on Tenth Street. When she died just weeks before her 104th birthday, she had 78 grandchildren, 174 great-grandchildren, 91 great-great grandchildren, and 9 great-great-great grandchildren. Numerous Brunsons live and work in Fort Pierce. As a young mother, Mary worked in the fields west of Fort Pierce, picking tomatoes to help her husband, Ben, support the family. With a lavish love for all humanity, she worshipped at the Fresh Wind Fresh Fire Church, and no member was more fervent at praying. She explained how integration arrived in Fort Pierce: "Martin Luther King said you folks get all dressed up nice and go down to Woolworth's and sit down nice at the counter and behave like ladies and gentlemen and they did and we've been able to sit there ever since." As a child in South Carolina, she remembered following her mother to the cotton field; she had her own child-size bag for the cotton she picked. (Photograph by the author.)

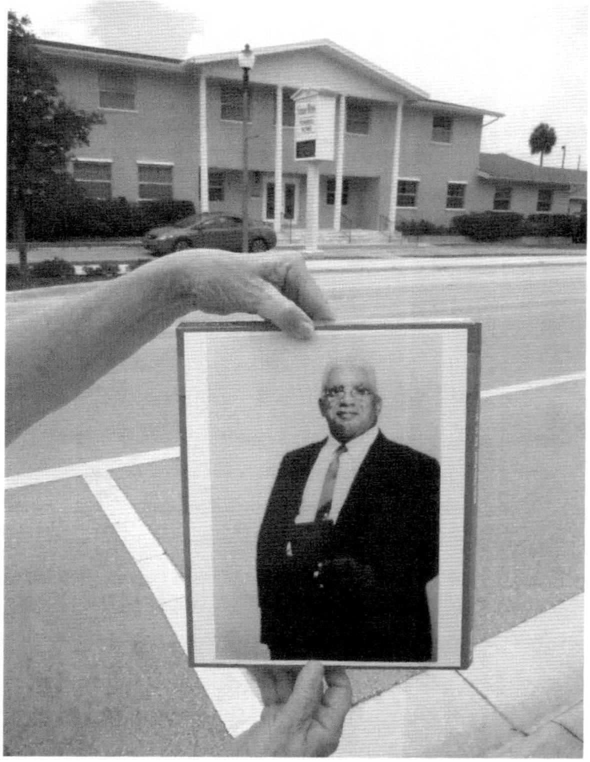

The Aboveground Railroad
The Rev. Albert T. Stone founded Stone Brothers Funeral Home in 1932. To help them reach safety, Stone would put a threatened African American, while very much alive, in a special aerated coffin and send it on a northbound train to a fellow Masonic undertaker who would then free the person inside. Reverend Stone established Pine Grove Cemetery west of the "white" cemetery. (Photograph by Tom Baumker; Reverend Stone photograph courtesy of Samuel Gaines.)

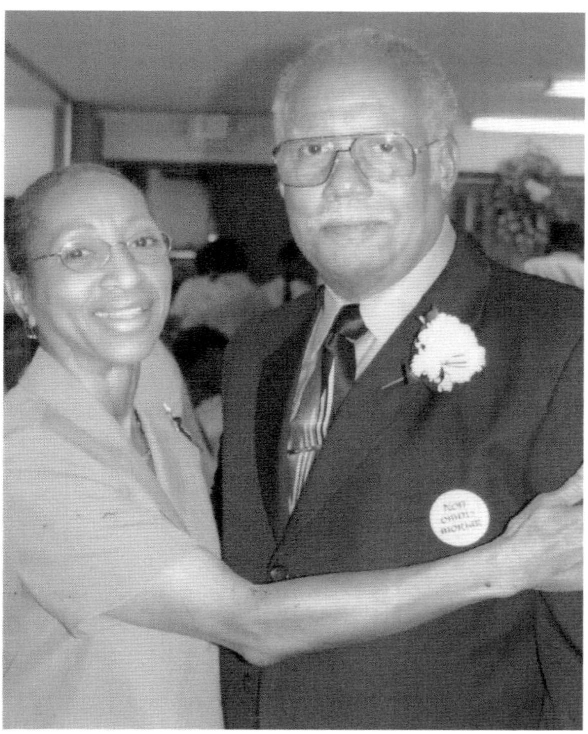

Samuel and Theresa Gaines
Samuel Gaines, the grandson of Reverend Stone, was the first black man to serve on the St. Lucie County school board. He served for 34 years. Gaines Academy, on Jenkins Road, is named for him. He has been honored by the national organization that represents African American undertakers. He is a 33rd-degree Mason. Samuel carries a wealth of Fort Pierce history in his head. His wife, Theresa Gaines, has taught, tutored, and nourished numerous young people to productive adulthood. She served as president of the ladies auxiliary of the Florida Morticians Association from 1981 to 1983 and is a contributing member of Delta Sigma Theta. (Courtesy of Samuel Gaines.)

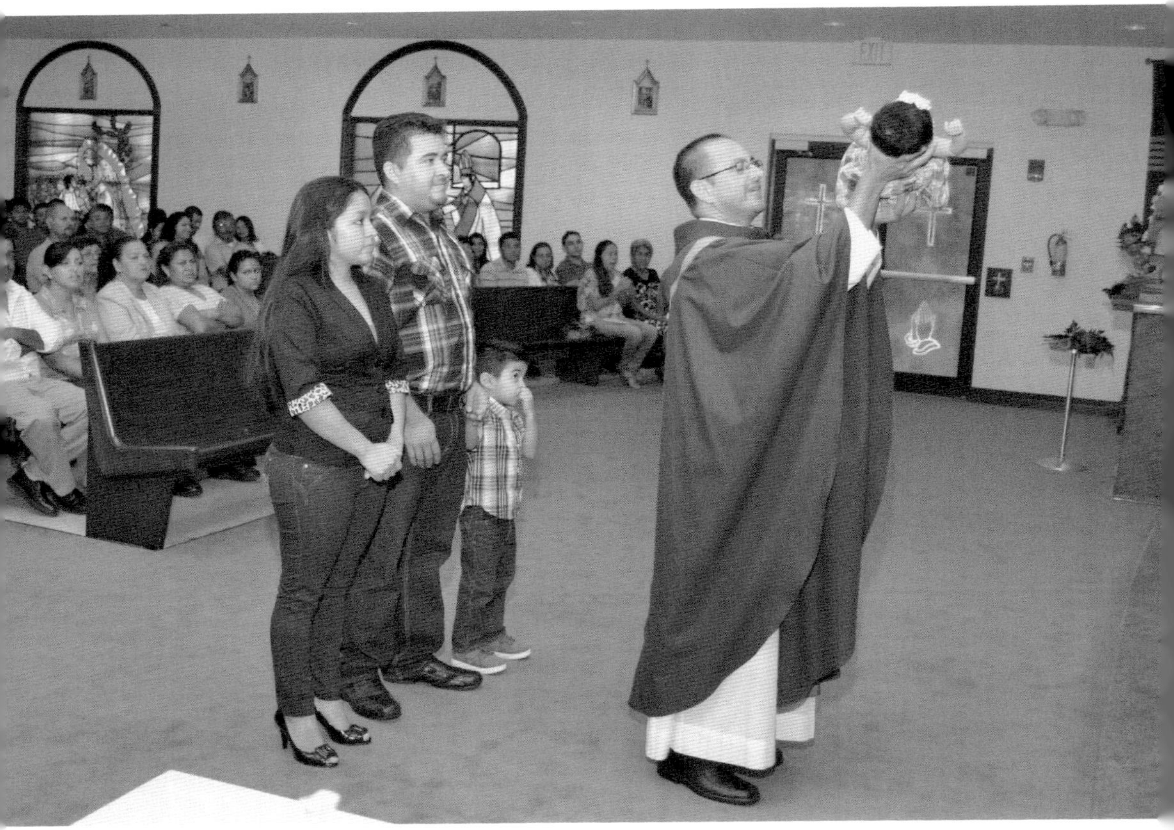

Misión Hispana San Juan Diego

Born in Colombia, Rev. Jaime Dorado joined the Diocese of Palm Beach in 2001, and after a decade of work with Hispanic immigrants in West Palm Beach, Stuart, and Indiantown, he was assigned to direct the San Juan Diego Mission church in Fort Pierce. Misión Hispana San Juan Diego was founded in 2001 by the late Rev. Gerard Don Bosco Redden to minister to both the religious and secular needs of area Hispanics. Since Father Dorado took over, the congregation has grown to 3,000-plus and catechism classes from 100 enrollees to 600. He has fostered the mission through annual religious celebrations and personal commitment to shepherding his flock and providing spiritual guidance. The church building has been remodeled with the help of the community and the support of Deacon Alberto Delgado, Rev. Richard George, Bishop Gerard Barberito, and the Diocese of Palm Beach. (Courtesy of Marcos Cazares.)

CHAPTER EIGHT

In Memoriam

Every year, Fort Pierce mourns the passing of one or more of her local legends. Many in this book have passed from life, with eulogies ranging from opulent to simple. Some have passed the torch to another and thus continue to contribute from beyond the grave. This chapter singles out two of our local losses because their passing was cause for national mourning. Fate cruelly selected these two innocent women to be victims of a national catastrophe.

They died tragically and they died courageously. Neither through lifestyle or carelessness put themselves in danger. Each simply did the right thing. Kimberly Bergalis went to the dentist, Ceecee Lyles went to work.

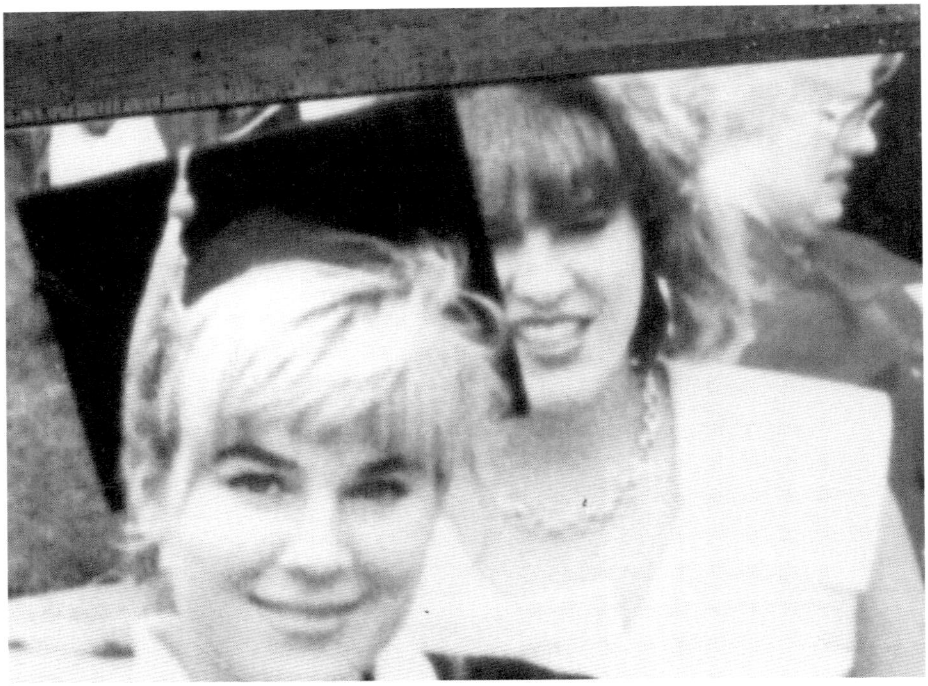

Kimberly Bergalis

"This was the happiest day of our lives," George Bergalis said of this photograph."Little did we know that great day that she had already been infected with the AIDS virus." Twenty-three-year-old Kimberly died in December 1991 in her home at Fort Pierce, having contracted the disease from her dentist. In the uneasiness surrounding the early years of the AIDS epidemic, a debate swirled about the risks lurking in the health-care setting. Driving past Kimberly Bergalis Park stirs memories of the tragic unfairness of young Kimberly's fate and her decision to use her waning energies to lobby for greater protection for patients who would be going to doctors long after she was dead, whispering her testimony before a Congressional committee. (Above, courtesy of Mr. and Mrs. George Bergalis; below, photograph by the author.)

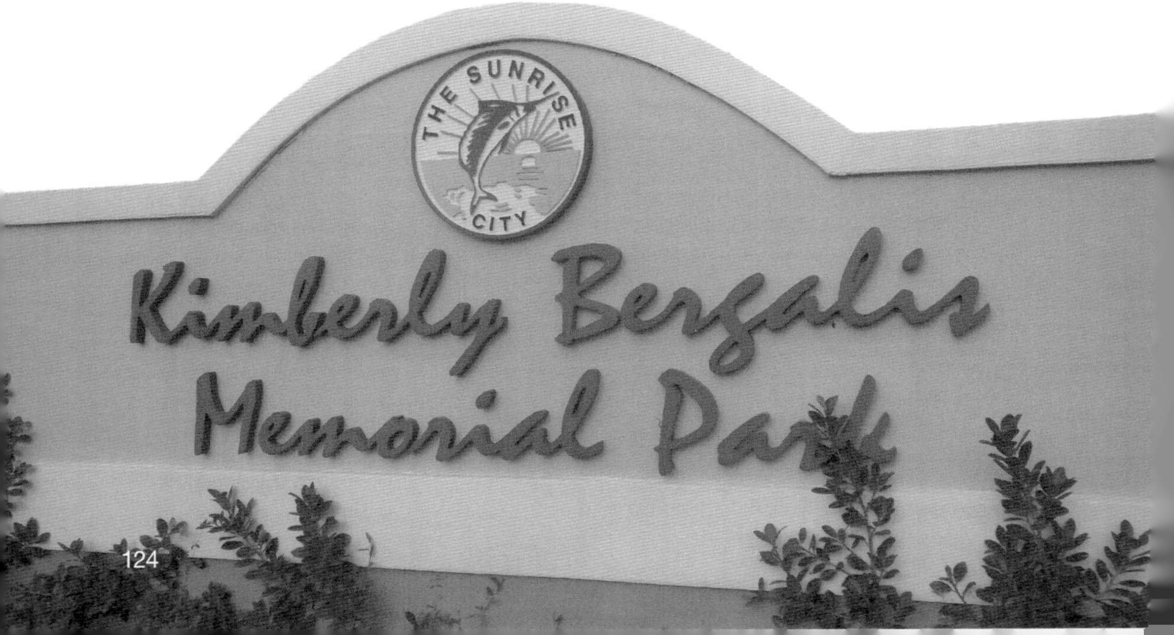

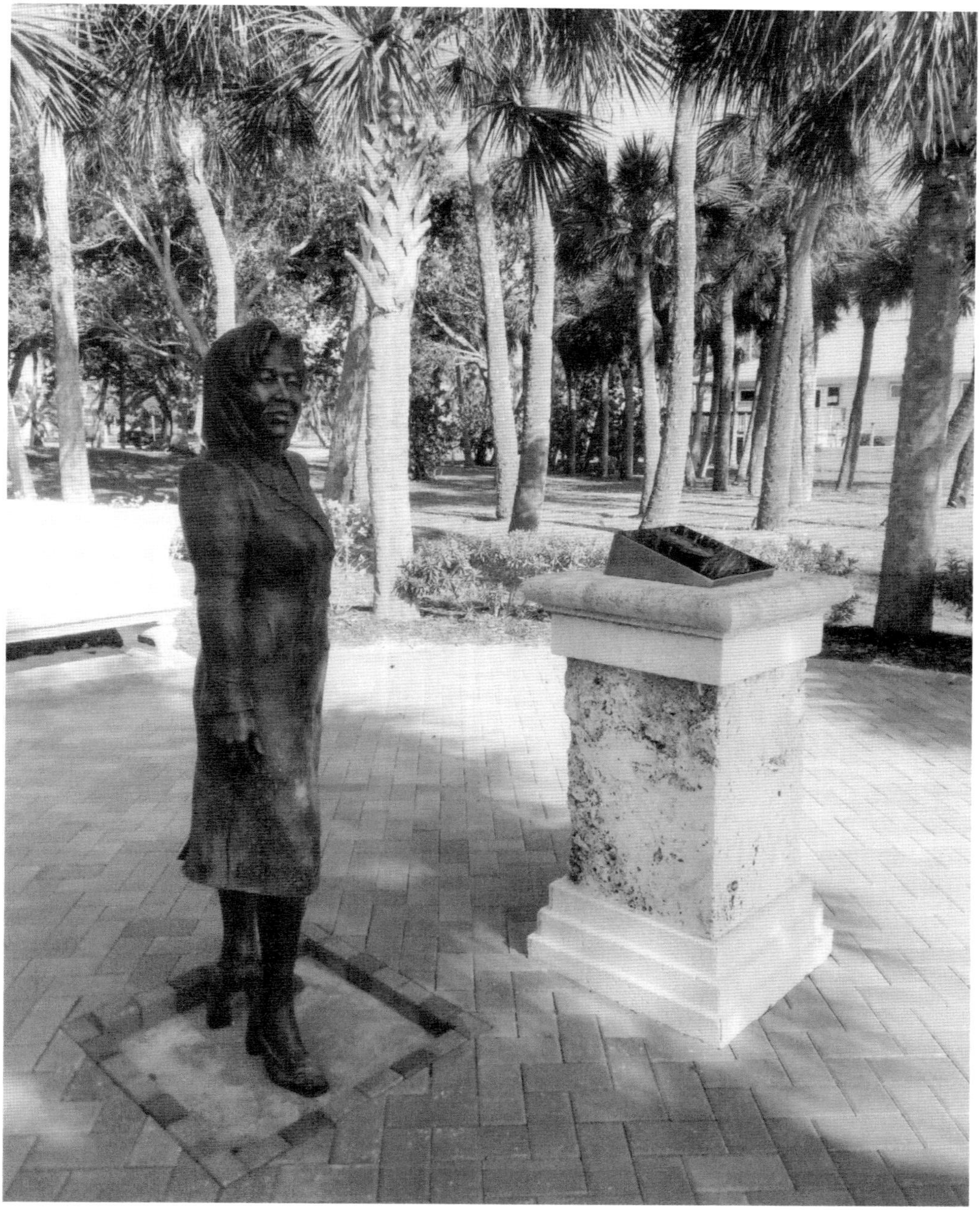

CeeCee Ross-Lyles
"I'm on a plane that's been hijacked . . . I want to tell you I love you, please tell my children that I love them very much . . . I don't know what to say, there are three guys that hijacked the plane . . . we're turned around . . . I hope to be able to see your face again. Bye." The voice cracked on the "Bye." This was the essence of the call made at 9:47 a.m. on September 11, 2001, by flight attendant CeeCee Ross-Lyles to her husband, Lorne, from United Airlines Flight 93 as it flew above Pennsylvania. Before taking to the skies as a stewardess, Lyles had been a Fort Pierce policewoman for six years. This statue of her stands in Fort Pierce Memorial Park. (Photograph by the author.)

INDEX